MURAOTR990

085#13

HISTORY OF WORLD ARCHITECTURE

Pier Luigi Nervi, General Editor

ARCHITECTURE OF THE RENAISSANCE

Peter Murray

Harry N. Abrams, Inc., Publishers, New York

Editor: Carlo Pirovano

Design: Diego Birelli

Photographs: Pepi Merisio

Drawings: Enzo Di Grazia

Standard Book Number: 8109-1000-4
Library of Congress Catalogue Card Number: 70-149850
Copyright 1971 in Italy by Electa Editrice, Milan

Printed in Italy by Fantonigrafica® - Industrie Grafiche Editoriali S.p.A. - Venice
Bound in Holland

Architectural criticism has nearly always been concerned with the visible aspect of individual buildings, taking this to be the decisive factor in the formulation of value judgments and in the classification of those "styles" which appear in textbooks, and which have thus become common knowledge. But once it is recognized that every building is, by definition, a work subject to the limitations imposed by the materials and building techniques at hand, and that every building must prove its stability, as well as its capacity to endure and serve the needs it was built for, it becomes clear that the aesthetic aspect alone is inadequate when we come to appraise a creative activity, difficult enough to judge in the past, rapidly becoming more complex in our own day, and destined to become more so in the foreseeable future.

Nevertheless, what has struck me most, on studying the architecture of the past and present, is the fact that the works which are generally regarded by the critics and the general public as examples of pure beauty are also the fruit of exemplary building techniques, once one has taken into account the quality of the materials and the technical knowledge available. And it is natural to suspect that such a coincidence is not entirely casual.

Building in the past was wholly a matter of following static intuitions, which were, in turn, the result of meditation, experience, and above all of an understanding of the capacity of certain structures and materials to resist external forces. Meditation upon structural patterns and the characteristics of various materials, together with the appraisal of one's own experiences and those of others is an act of love toward the process of construction for its own sake, both on the part of the architect and his collaborators and assistants. Indeed, we may wonder whether this is not the hidden bond which unites the appearance and substance of the finest buildings of the past, distant though that past may be, into a single "thing of beauty."

One might even think that the quality of the materials available not only determined architectural patterns but also the decorative detail with which the first simple construction was gradually enriched.

One might find a justification for the difference in refinement and elegance between Greek architecture, with its basic use of marble —a highly resistant material, upon which the most delicate carvings can be carried out—and the majestic concrete structures of Roman architecture, built out of a mixture of lime and pozzolana, and supported by massive walls, to compensate for their intrinsic weaknesses.

Would it be too rash to connect these objective architectural characteristics with the different artistic sensibilities of the two peoples?

One must recognize, therefore, the importance of completing the description of the examples illustrated with an interpretation of their constructional and aesthetic characteristics, so that the connection between the twin aspects of building emerges as a natural, logical consequence.

This consequence, if understood and accepted in good faith by certain avant-garde circles, could put an end to the disastrous haste with which our architecture is rushing toward an empty, costly, and at times impractical formalism. It might also recall architects and men of culture to a more serene appraisal of the objective elements of building and to the respect that is due to a morality of architecture. For this is just as important for the future of our cities as is morality, understood as a rule of life, for an orderly civil existence.

PIER LUIGI NERVI

TABLE OF CONTENTS

The problem in defining Renaissance architecture, or indeed the Renaissance in general, is that we look back on it as a complete historical phenomenon, and although we may argue about the years in which it began, flourished, and came to an end, we take it for granted that it had a beginning and an end. It is clear from the primary sources which have come down to us that the people most intimately concerned with the creation of the new style, later to be called Renaissance, were perfectly conscious that they were making innovations, and to this extent (in so far as they analysed their own motives) they must have realized that they were creating something which would develop and, presumably, come to an end. The very word *rinascita* — rebirth — implies death. In practice, they seem to have had a curiously ambivalent approach to what they were doing. On the one hand, they were acutely aware that they were creating something different, and something better by comparison with the traditional styles of building, or painting, or sculpture. To this extent they were creating a new style. On the other hand, they seem to have been equally confident that they were not creating *ex novo*, but were recreating a style which had once been practised but which, in the course of a millennium, had degenerated beyond recognition.

It is fairly certain that this antique style which they were painfully reviving was, to a considerable extent, a figment of their own historical imaginations. Much of what we now know of ancient Roman architecture was unknown to the men of the fifteenth century; and almost everything that we know of ancient painting was totally unknown to them. Antique sculpture seems to be the only art which was sufficiently well known, either in originals or copies, or even copies of copies, for the men of the Renaissance to have had roughly the same amount of information as we now have.

In the case of architecture, the balance was redressed by the existence, in the fourteenth, fifteenth, and sixteenth centuries, of many buildings which have since fallen into ruin or have even been completely destroyed. There is ample evidence for this, both in the written sources and in drawings and engravings: the most notorious examples of this vandalism on the part of men who professed to venerate the ancient world are the stripping of the bronze beams of the Pantheon to provide the metal for Bernini's Baldacchino — *quod non fecerunt barbari, fecerunt Barberini* — and the total destruction of the Septizonium. Fortunately, the drawings of the Dutch painter Maerten van Heemskerk preserve for us many of the great Roman ruins (including New St. Peter's) as they were in the 1530s, when he was in Rome (Plate 1). It is ironical that his drawings of the Septizonium are not only the most important documents for its appearance, but it was one of these very drawings that he chose to bear the mysterious epigram — perhaps invented by him — *Roma quanta fuit ipsa ruina docet*. Drawings and engravings of this kind, very rare in the Quattrocento, multiplied in the Cinquecento and are one of the most important of our sources of knowledge.

If we attempt to reconstruct the sources and materials available to a man like Brunelleschi, we find a surprising amount of evidence which can legitimately be regarded as firsthand. We can, for example, make stylistic deductions from the works of Brunelleschi himself and of his contemporaries, as well as use the writings and projects of other contemporaries such as Alberti. In addition, there are documents, literary sources, and the drawings and engravings already mentioned.

Sources are surprisingly numerous. The most important is, of course, Vasari, who wrote a *Life* of every major Italian architect from Arnolfo to his own day; but what is more important in the present context is his critical approach to architecture in general as well as his views on the works of individual artists. He was a competent professional, working in the middle of the sixteenth century, and his omissions and suppressions, no less than his inclusions, tell us a great deal about the development of architectural theory and practice between 1400 and 1550. Apart from Vasari, there are other *Lives*, such as the *Vita di Brunellesco* or the *XIV Uomini*, both of which have been ascribed to Antonio Manetti, and we also have guidebooks and similar writings, especially for Rome, where the tradition of the *Mirabilia* was strong.

We begin with the basic idea of the Renaissance, the rebirth or revival of the arts. The anonymous biographer of Brunelleschi, writing about 1480, says: 'And so he went to Rome, where in those days there were plenty of fine things still to be seen by the public, as there still are, though not many now, since Popes, cardinals, Romans and men of other nations have taken them away. And while he was studying the sculptures with a perceptive eye and an alert mind, he observed the ancient way of building and their laws of symmetry. It seemed to him that he could recognize a certain order in the disposition, like members and bones, and it was as though God had enlightened him... He was the more struck by it, since it seemed to him very different from the methods usual in those times.' Vasari was equally positive (in the Preface to Part II): 'First of all, through the studies and diligence of Filippo Brunelleschi, architecture rediscovered the proportions and measurements of the antique, applying them in round columns, flat pilasters, and plain or rusticated projections. Then it carefully distinguished the various orders, leaving no doubt about the difference between them; care was taken to follow the classical rules and orders and the correct architectural proportions...' That there was a change of attitude on the part of Florentine architects in the first half of the fifteenth

century is beyond dispute. Not only do we have the evidence of contemporary sources for this, but it is patent that the work of Brunelleschi differs from that of his immediate predecessors, and the difference is one of kind rather than degree.

If we compare the loggia of the hospital at Lastra a Signa, near Florence, with that of the hospital built only a few years later by Brunelleschi for the Innocenti (Plates 2, 5), it is evident that they are basically solutions to the same problem. Both consist of a covered passage with the vaulted roof supported on one side by a continuous wall, and on the other by columns forming an open arcade giving on to the street; yet there is a difference between the two buildings, and that difference is more precisely indicated in terms of likeness to (and difference from) classical Roman architecture. This poses the crucial question: what is really meant by phrases like 'the reviver of Roman architecture'? In this particular instance, it is clear that the Roman elements are by no means confined to Brunelleschi's work, and those which are — the size and shape of the columns, the decorative details of the capitals, the pattern of the vaulting — are superficial rather than essential. What is even stranger, it would be difficult to assert that the Spedale degli Innocenti bears a close resemblance to any known Roman building, although it probably derives from the classical *porticus* of the type used in villas, which were transformed during the Middle Ages into monastic cloisters, the immediate ancestors of both Lastra a Signa and the Spedale degli Innocenti.

Conversely, the difference between the two is clearly visible in the system of the vaulting, the placing of the columns in relation to each other and to the depth of the bays, all of which can be related to Roman building practice, either in extant monuments or in the mathematical rules laid down by Vitruvius. Nevertheless, no experienced eye would ever confuse Brunelleschi's forms with those current in ancient Rome. After his death, in the anonymous *Life*, the point is made that Brunelleschi was the hero of the revival of architecture, partly because of his study of Roman structural techniques and partly because of his rediscovery of the mathematical rules governing proportion and ornament. The first thesis, that he made a deeper study of Roman structure than anyone else, is demonstrated by the fact that he succeeded in covering Florence Cathedral where everyone else had failed. Indeed, this seems to be explicitly recognized by no less an authority than Alberti, when, in the dedication of his treatise on painting, written while the dome of the cathedral was still in progress, he says that Brunelleschi and others are the equals and in some ways the superiors of the ancient Romans, and he says of the dome: '...I must admit that the Ancients, having models to copy and people to teach them, found it less difficult to make a name for themselves in these supreme arts than it is for us nowadays, for whom it is difficult in the extreme; yet, for that very reason, how much greater will be our fame if we can discover arts and sciences never before known, and that without teachers or examples to imitate! There can be nobody so grudging and envious that he will not praise Pippo [Brunelleschi] when he sees that great structure, rearing up to heaven and large enough to cast its shadow over the whole population of Tuscany; a structure made without any centering and with no excess of wood. If I judge rightly, this feat of construction must seem incredible in our own days, and perhaps even the Ancients would not have known how to do it.'

There can be no reasonable doubt that Brunelleschi studied the structural science of the Romans and applied it to the circumstances of his own day, and his contemporaries recognized that he was doing so. The case is rather different when his anonymous biographer praises him in the following terms: '...He thought that, while studying the sculpture, he might also pay the same attention to the order and method of construction... and the ornaments. He saw many beauties and marvels in all these things, for they were built at different times, and mostly by good masters. These masters were not common men, but had had great experience and were enabled to study by the liberality of princes... He sketched almost every building in Rome and the surrounding countryside, with measurements of height, length, and width, as closely as he could estimate them. In many places, he and Donatello excavated parts of buildings... Thus, they could guess at the height, using bases, foundations, projections, and roofs of buildings, and this they noted on parchment with squares, and with numerical annotations understood by Filippo himself... He found many differences between the types of masonry, and of the columns; as well as in the bases and capitals, architraves, friezes and cornices, façades and building masses, many kinds of Temple, and the proportion of columns. His keen eye was able to distinguish all the different types — Ionic, Doric, Tuscan, Corinthian, and Attic — all of which he employed in his own buildings at the appropriate times and places...'

In fact, Brunelleschi was not really able to distinguish the Orders, and this reveals a curious weakness in the anonymous *Life*: clearly, its author was convinced that Brunelleschi, as the reviver, must have been able to do all that his successors could do, and, as Alberti was able to distinguish the Orders, it was necessary to prove Brunelleschi's Latinity by asserting — in the face of the evidence — that he, too, knew all the details of architectural syntax. Probably, this was due to the acceptance of the visual arts as Liberal in the technical sense. In the last years of Brunelleschi's life,

humanists like Alberti, Poggio, and Niccolò Niccoli began to agree that painting, sculpture, and architecture had demonstrably flourished among the Romans, and, therefore, they must be accepted as Liberal Arts. This was very important for the practitioners of those arts, and this is probably the reason why his biographer conferred posthumously upon Brunelleschi an interest which he does not seem to have felt.

It should be remembered that this early generation of humanists, whose knowledge of classical literature was not necessarily greater than that possessed by their predecessors, differed from them in one important respect. The great scholars of the later Middle Ages read extensively, but they read for theological or philosophical purposes because they were all clerics, and most of them were monks. It was only with the development of the city-state in Italy, and the need for a new, non-clerical class of professional administrators, that the humanist came into being. Humanists were simply men who read the classics for literary purposes. They earned their living as teachers of Latin or as Latin secretaries to a Prince or a commune: philology, grammar, and rhetoric were their interests and they were avid professionals in the subtleties of Latin usage. To them it seemed reasonable that a fellow-professional like Alberti should be interested in the niceties of the Orders, in what Summerson so aptly calls the Classical Language of Architecture. It is not difficult to understand the cast of mind that reasoned that, because Alberti was interested in such things and Alberti was a great architect, Brunelleschi, who was incontrovertibly a great architect, must also have been interested in them. It gives us a considerable insight into the mental processes of fifteenth-century architects when Brunelleschi's biographer singles out two of his churches — Santa Maria degli Angeli and Santo Spirito — as norms of a perfect architecture. For the small, centrally-planned church, Brunelleschi's design for the Angeli in Florence, though never realized, was nevertheless to be regarded as the modern version of a classical and, even more, an Early Christian type of *martyrium*. In the same way, Santo Spirito was the perfect type of the basilican parish church, because it was based on the ancient Roman secular basilica, on the Early Christian basilicas of Rome, and even on medieval versions such as Santa Croce in Florence, which, because they were evidently non-mathematical in their planning, could well be regarded as a rude, barbarous, and Gothic form which Brunelleschi had restored to its ancient perfection. There can be no doubt whatever that soon after the middle of the century this image of the new Florentine style was generally accepted in humanist circles throughout Italy. It was not the work of Brunelleschi alone, for, in the years following his death in 1446, the architecture of Alberti assumed an

even more strictly Roman and classical form.

Evidence for the belief that the new Florentine architecture had triumphed by this comparatively early date is contained in a fascinating document of 10 June 1468, issued by one of the most enlightened patrons of the age, in connection with what is one of the most beautiful buildings in Italy, the palace at Urbino. This document, a Brief appointing Laurana as the overseer of the palace, begins: 'We judge those men to be worthy of praise and honour who are manifestly endowed with genius and talents, and most especially with such talents, honoured by the ancients and moderns alike, as that of Architecture; based, as it is, on Arithmetic and Geometry, which are among the Seven Liberal Arts, and indeed among the major Arts, since they are *in primo gradu certitudinis*. Architecture is a matter of great skill and much talent, and held in great esteem by Us: indeed, We have searched everywhere, and especially in Tuscany, since it is the fountainhead of architects, yet We have not succeeded in finding anyone truly skilled in this art, or learned in the mystery of it. However, first by repute and then by actual experience, We have come to see and realize that the excellent Maestro Lutiano, the bearer of this document, is truly learned in this art, and, since We have decided to build, in Our city of Urbino, a beautiful palace worthy of Our station and of the honour of Our ancestors as well as Our own, We have accordingly elected and deputed the said Maestro Lutiano to be overseer of all those Masters who are concerned with the said building; whether master-masons or master-carpenters, smiths, and all others of whatever degree or skill in the said works, and thus We order the said masters and craftsmen, and also all Our officials and likewise Our subjects who have any concern whatsoever with this fabric, that they are to obey the said Maestro Lutiano and to follow his instructions as if they came from Us...' (P. Rotondi, *Il Palazzo Ducale di Urbino*, Urbino, 1951, I, 109-10).

It is of the first importance that this document can be connected with an existing building and also with many of the greatest names in the arts in the fifteenth century. The palace of Urbino was built by Federigo da Montefeltro, the most successful soldier of the age, who is perhaps better remembered as the friend and patron both of Piero della Francesca and of Alberti, as well as of Laurana and Francesco di Giorgio.

Laurana was working on the palace in the 1460s, at a time when Bramante was reaching manhood (he was born in the Duchy in 1444). A study of the palace in conjunction with works by Piero della Francesca such as the *Flagellation*, and with the architectural ideas expressed by Alberti in his writings and buildings, affords evidence for the mental attitude of architects and their patrons at one of the critical moments of the Early Renaissance.

Alberti's career as a practising architect did not begin until after the death of Brunelleschi in 1446, but he must have been interested in the theory of the art well before then, since we hear of an early version of his treatise *De re aedificatoria* being presented to Pope Nicholas V. His treatise on painting, *Della Pittura*, is even earlier, but his interest in the antiquities of Rome must date from about 1432, when he arrived in the city as secretary to Cardinal Molin. He wrote a short description of the ruins of Rome, the *Descriptio urbis Romae*, about 1432-34, the years when he was working among the ruins and beginning to formulate his ideas on ancient art — the very time when, in all probability, he accompanied both Donatello and Brunelleschi on their visits to the monuments. This makes it the more surprising that the *Descriptio* is unantiquarian and, indeed, rather uninteresting, since it consists very largely of a description of a surveying instrument and an account of its use in measuring buildings. Perhaps it was this interest in measurement that led to the anonymous biographer ascribing similar interests to Brunelleschi, but it is curious that the *Descriptio urbis Romae* does not describe buildings and so belies its title. As an archaeological handbook, it compares surprisingly poorly with its Trecento predecessors, such as Giovanni Dondi's *Iter Romanum* of about 1375. Dondi, who was a Paduan and a close friend of Petrarch, visited Rome as a pilgrim in that year and copied inscriptions and also measured some of the monuments. If nothing else, this proves that the ancient buildings were being studied intelligently two years before Brunelleschi was born. What is more immediately important, Alberti's *Descriptio* was not even in the main stream of development of topographical studies. The founders of modern archaeology were two of Alberti's fellow-humanists, although they did not share his professed interest in architecture — Flavio Biondo and Poggio Bracciolini.

Yet another *Descriptio urbis Romae* was written a year or two before Alberti's, by Niccolò Signorili. It has a dedication to Martin V (1417-31), with a long appeal to him to take over the government of Rome as the legitimate successor of the Emperors. Martin had returned to Rome, after the years of exile and schism, in 1420, and it was this fact that explains the sudden production of so many books of this type, with their nostalgic accounts of the glories of the past. With the return of the Popes there seemed, at last, a real prospect of a revival of Roman greatness. The humanists must have hoped for a literary revival as well when Nicholas V was elected in 1447, for he was Tommaso Parentucelli, the son of poor parents, whose career was entirely due to his humanistic learning — he was in fact the first humanist Pope. This was the intellectual climate in Rome in the 1430s and 40s which saw the production

5. *Filippo Brunelleschi, Florence, Spedale degli Innocenti, façade.*
6. *Filippo Brunelleschi, Florence, Spedale degli Innocenti, detail of a pilaster.*

7. *Filippo Brunelleschi, Florence, Spedale degli Innocenti, interior of Loggia.*

of several archaeological treatises, including Alberti's *Descriptio* as well as his far more important Vitruvian work, *De re aedificatoria*.

Probably soon after 1431, Poggio wrote a long treatise on the mutability of fortune, *De varietate fortunae*. The introduction to the first book contains an account of the ruins of Rome, as well as a noble lament for her past glories and present miseries. This has a parallel in the image of Rome as a widow mourning over the desolated city; but it is significant that this idea dates back to the fourteenth century — Fazio degli Uberti's *Dittamondo* was written about 1350 and belongs to the much older tradition of topographical writing summed up in the *Mirabilia*. What makes Poggio so important is the new, or 'modern', approach to the remains of ancient Rome, for his descriptions are based on the references in classical literature and on the inscriptions which could still be read on the buildings themselves. Many of the buildings mentioned by Signorili are also recorded by Poggio, but his descriptions are so much fuller that it is fair to call his work the first real attempt at topographical and archaeological description. Several of his buildings are, of course, wrongly identified and he frequently misidentifies an ancient temple in order to identify it with a modern church — thus, he claims that the Temple of Apollo is now a church, saying: 'The Temple of Apollo on the Vatican hill, near the basilica of St. Peter, was turned over to the divine worship and made to serve our religion', in spite of the mention by Propertius of the temple as on the Palatine, not the Vatican, hill.

Poggio also records facts of archaeological interest, such as the marble column which was still standing in his time in what he called the temple of Peace. This was the Basilica of Constantine, and the column was still standing in the sixteenth century, as we know from engravings (Plate 11). Poggio also says that the temple of Concord existed in his own day, but had been destroyed to make lime since he first came to Rome. Again, he says that the statue of Marcus Aurelius — which he calls Septimius Severus — was undoubtedly gilded. After this we come to the long meditation on the mutability of Fortune, in connection with the Capitol and Nero's Palace: 'Here Antonio Loschi, after looking around him, sighed and said, "Oh, Poggio, how remote are these ruins from that Capitol which our Virgil described as being *Aurea nunc, olim silvestribus horrida dumis*, and how easily we might reverse his lines and say that they were once golden, but now are squalid and overgrown with thorns". .' [Poggio continues] 'It is a terrible thing, and hardly to be related without amazement that this Capitoline Hill, once the centre of the Roman Empire, and the citadel of the whole world, feared by all Kings and Princes, climbed in triumph by so many Emperors and adorned with the gifts or the spoils of so many peoples, which, in

its great days, was the centre of the world's attention, is now so desolated and ruinous, so changed from its former golden age that vines now grow in the Senate and it has become a rubbish-heap and a tip for dung...'

Ten or fifteen years later, about 1445-46, Flavio Biondo wrote his *Roma instaurata* and dedicated it to Eugenius IV. This book was brought into being by the same impulses from the courts of Martin V and Eugenius IV which had inspired Poggio, and Biondo tells us that the Papacy of Eugenius came just in time to restore many of the monuments, both pagan and Christian, before their final collapse. Biondo says that Eugenius did this, and it is evident that he had a strong feeling for the quality of *romanitas*, the sentiment of unbroken continuity between ancient and Christian Rome, and the benefits conferred by the older upon the newer civilisation. For Biondo, and for others who felt like him, the reconstitution of the ancient monuments was a moral duty. Like Poggio, he had a scientific, archaeological outlook, and he exploited all the classical sources known to him, including coins and inscriptions. This, of course, was the professionalism of the humanist, and we know that he worked as a Papal Scriptor from 1436, so that he knew Poggio and was a friend of Alberti. Almost immediately after returning to Rome with Eugenius IV in 1443, he began to write his *Roma instaurata*, completing it in the autumn of 1446 — in architectural terms, the year in which Brunelleschi died, after beginning the lantern of Florence Cathedral, and Alberti began his architectural career with the Palazzo Rucellai. A great deal of the *Roma instaurata* is concerned with detailed accounts of Roman life and institutions, so that there are actually fewer descriptions of the buildings than in Poggio. There is, however, one splendid passage in Book III, in which he contrasts the present sway of Rome over all civilised people with that of the Empire, pointing out that the New Rome was not maintained by force of arms — it is Christ who is *imperator* and the city is the seat, the citadel, and the home of an eternal religion, so that what was once a rule of fear is now a sweet subjection.

It is essential to understand this feeling of continuity to appreciate its effects on writers and artists in the Renaissance: Giovanni Marliani summed it up in 1534, in his *Antiquae Romae topographia*, when he observed that 'what was written by Biondo about the Palace of the Emperors we can nowadays say about the Vatican Palace'. There was a similar feeling among writers, who believed that the Early Christian authors were an inseparable part of the classical heritage. Lactantius, the greatest writer of the fourth century, was known as 'the Christian Cicero': he firmly believed that Christianity needed the pagan past, and particularly the literature

of the ancients, for its own enrichment as well as a means of mental training to assist in the formulation of doctrine. These views would have been welcome to men like Alberti — or even Nicholas V — and it is significant that Lactantius was one of the first authors to be printed in Italy.

From all this, it is evident that Alberti's concern with ancient Rome was by no means unique and, indeed, it had perhaps been better studied by others. He was, however, determined to recreate the sole surviving classical author on architecture, rather than to describe ancient Rome from its extant remains. By doing this, he initiated the idea, so potent in the later fifteenth century and all through the sixteenth, that the true model of architecture was to be sought in a reconciliation between the text of Vitruvius and the monuments. Alberti's great theoretical treatise is planned on the same lines as Vitruvius, and even has almost identical chapter headings in a number of cases. Nevertheless, there are passages which indicate that Alberti was well versed in the study of the monuments as well as in the text of Vitruvius. At the very beginning he gives a definition of Design in Platonic terms: 'The whole art of building consists in the Design and in the Structure. The whole force and rule of the design consists in a right and exact adapting and joining together of the lines and angles which compose the face of the building... It is the property of Design to appoint to the edifice and all its parts their proper places, determinate number, just proportion and beautiful order... We can in our thought and imagination contrive perfect forms of buildings entirely separate from matter, by settling and regulating in a certain order the disposition of the lines and angles...'

Later, in Book VI, he describes how the remains of ancient Rome were visibly mouldering: 'There remained many examples of the ancient works, Temples and Theatres, from which as from the most skilful of masters, a great deal was to be learned; but I saw with tears that they were decaying from day to day.' On the other hand, in the famous letter to Matteo de' Pasti, recently rediscovered by Grayson, he writes of his Tempio Malatestiano at Rimini: 'You can see where the sizes and proportions of the pilasters come from: if you alter anything you will spoil all that harmony.'

From this it is clear that Alberti thought of the art of architecture as essentially governed by mathematical laws and proportions, and this would have been confirmed by the statements made by Vitruvius himself about harmony and proportion. Accepting Vitruvius as a guide to the arcane theory, he, and others like him, would tend to follow Vitruvius in his descriptions of the details of ancient buildings. Finally, he would check Vitruvius against the monuments, partly because they constituted a separate tradition in their own right and partly because, as he complains, the text of Vitruvius is extremely obscure. There is, however, one interesting exception to his following of Vitruvius — the Composite Order. Alberti's description must be based on his own observation, since Vitruvius never mentions this enriched version of Corinthian: indeed, the earliest recorded use of Composite dates from A.D. 82, on the Arch of Titus, which is presumably after Vitruvius's death. Alberti himself used a rather curious variant of the Order in his Rucellai Palace (cf. p. 67), but the earliest correct usage in the Renaissance is probably connected with him as it occurs in the palace at Urbino, and earlier examples in painting occur in the *Annunciation* (Arezzo) and the *Flagellation* (Urbino), both by Piero della Francesca (Plates 99, 113). Once more, Urbino is at the centre of architectural innovation and it was said of Federigo da Montefeltro that: 'Though he had his architects about him, he always first realized the design and then explained the proportions and all else; indeed, to hear him, it would seem that his chief talent lay in this art.'

By comparison with the descriptions of a Poggio or a Biondo, with their skilful handling of ancient sources, the drawings of fifteenth-century architects seem very unsophisticated, even when they were working from actual monuments. What is more, no drawings of this type have come down to us from the period — the 1440s — and it is not until the end of the century that we can point to surviving drawings of the monuments of ancient Rome made for the purpose of study or record. There are two main categories, which may be described in Wölfflinian terms as painterly and architectonic. The painterly type consists of landscapes which happen to have buildings in them, and, since occasional glimpses of Roman buildings such as the Colosseum can be found in the backgrounds of pictures dating from quite early in the fifteenth century (and still earlier in manuscripts), such drawings must have been made quite early in the century. This type is well represented by the sketchbook known as the *Codex Escurialensis*, made by a member of Ghirlandaio's studio about 1491. Some of these are landscapes with ruins (Plate 10), but others are archaeologically useful and valid — for example, the view of the interior of the Pantheon (Plate 9) showing it before the alterations to the attic storey.

The second, 'architectonic', category is more relevant to the present enquiry, in that it consists of drawings of the monuments, as architecture, made by or for architects. Measured drawings in the modern sense are, of course, still a long way in the future, although a quotation from the anonymous *Life* of Brunelleschi seems to claim this great discovery for him as well: 'and this they [Brunelleschi and Donatello] noted on parchment with squares, and with numerical annotations understood by Filippo himself'.

The *Codex Barberini* may represent this class. It is a sketchbook which belonged to Giuliano da Sangallo and is said to have been begun in the 1460s, although some of the drawings in it are certainly datable in the 1490s. Giuliano was a major architect of the period, yet his drawings are less factual and informative than those in the *Codex Escurialensis*, which were made for pictorial rather than architectural purposes. Many of the *Codex Barberini* drawings have a fairytale charm, as though the whole book (a very beautiful vellum codex) were intended as a thesaurus of magical architectural formulae rather than a working collection of record drawings. How little some of the romantic drawings of the antiquities are actually related to the monuments may be seen by comparing Giuliano's drawing of the Theatre of Marcellus — a major prototype for sixteenth-century architects such as Giuliano's nephew Antonio — with a sixteenth-century engraving of it, or his drawing of Trajan's Forum with its present appearance. In fact, although Giuliano records a large number of plans and details, it is only rarely that he attempts to give a complete description of a building by means of a plan, section, elevation, perspective, and one or more details. Significantly, one case where he does attempt such a complete description is Santa Sophia in Constantinople. It had fallen to the Turks in 1453, and Giuliano could never have seen the building itself, so he must have relied on drawings by Ciriaco d'Ancona. The development of such a technique of descriptive drawing is of fundamental importance to the way in which an architect visualizes buildings — to the very processes of his thought — and the technique of architectural (as distinct from pictorial) drawing was in a critical stage of development at the end of the fifteenth century. For this reason, we must take into account the way in which an architect thought about ancient Rome, Vitruvius, the technique of drawing, and the traditional usages of the building trades, with their independently-minded craftsmen.

It is unfortunate that no drawings by Brunelleschi or Alberti have survived, but we do know that both men made frequent use of models as well as drawings. The elevation drawing was certainly known — as witness, for example, the famous drawing of the façade of Orvieto Cathedral — and it is known that models of wood or even stone were frequently employed. The payments in the Opera del Duomo accounts for Brunelleschi's dome of Florence Cathedral prove this beyond all doubt, but the Italian word *modello* is very ambiguous and can mean 'model' or merely 'drawing'. Nevertheless, there are cases where we can be sure that a three-dimensional model is meant, and Alberti specifically recommends the use of wooden models, going so far as to suggest — what seems to have been the general practice — that such models should be

kept as simple as possible, distinguishing them from a type of painter's architecture which is perhaps represented by the famous panel by Piero in the Galleria Nazionale at Urbino.

The wooden model made by Giuliano da Sangallo for the Strozzi Palace in Florence still exists and is a documented example of what must have been a fairly elaborate specimen made for a very important commission. On the other hand, we know that Francesco di Giorgio was paid 75 lire in July 1484, for a drawing and a model of his church at Cortona. In the following June, it is recorded that he made a wooden model after visiting the site, and that the church was being constructed according to the model.

Francesco di Giorgio's treatise is broadly modelled on Alberti's, and in it he goes to a good deal of trouble to equate human and architectural proportion, as Vitruvius had done. Both Francesco and his older contemporary, Filarete, were transitional figures, struggling to combine Vitruvian proportion, antique detailing, and the traditional building methods in which they were brought up. Filarete's drawings, like those in the *Codex Barberini*, possess almost no architectonic quality, and it is evident that the draughtsmanship of all three men, though adequate for their own purposes and adequate for the illustration of their treatises, was not advancing the art of architecture. At the end of the century there was an apparent standstill. By then, it seemed that there was a real possibility of reviving something of Roman grandeur: the vast ruins were seen as signs and symbols of ancient Roman glory, with Imperial Rome merging into Early Christian and Early Christian into modern, so that the continuity was emotionally apprehended in spite of the fact that the men of the Renaissance were the first to realize they were no longer ancient Romans, but were separated from them by the vast chasm of the Middle Ages, which had to be bridged by a conscious act of will. Good architecture — architecture *in primo gradu certitudinis* — was based on mathematical proportion, and here again Vitruvius and the ancients had shown the way, so that good modern architecture had to consist of a concordance, a *concinnitas*, between Vitruvian proportional theory, the ancient monuments, and the traditional skills of the building crafts. The details of the Orders were still, in the fifteenth century, of minor importance, because the architect thought in terms of three-dimensional models, using drawing for his own instruction and, especially, for the accumulation of antique *exempla*. The actual cutting of a capital was still largely the province of the master-mason, and the impetus to architectural thought was to come from a further development of the art of draughtsmanship. This change, fundamental to the architecture of the sixteenth century, was wrought by Leonardo and Bramante in Milan in the last years of the fifteenth century.

It is a paradox that Brunelleschi's fame and the idea of his reviving the ancient methods of construction are both due to his success in finding a solution to the apparently insoluble problem of the dome of Florence Cathedral. This is not really a 'Renaissance' work at all, since its essential principle could not have been put into practice without the Gothic tradition which Brunelleschi, in common with his masons, had inherited from the previous century.

The problem arose because the Florentines, in attempting to assert their dominion over the whole of Tuscany, had decided as far back as 1294 to rebuild their ancient cathedral. The first design for the new building was made by Arnolfo in the years preceding 1300, but it was greatly enlarged by Francesco Talenti half a century later, partly in order to exceed the cathedrals of Pisa, Lucca, and Siena by a comfortable margin. There seems no doubt that Arnolfo's original plan consisted of a long nave with a great octagonal crossing, with apsidal choir and transepts opening off three sides of the octagon. The idea of an octagon, rather than a square, is almost certainly due to the presence nearby of the Baptistery (Plate 13), which was then believed to be an ancient Roman temple dedicated to Mars and rededicated to the Baptist, Patron of Florence. The Baptistery has a domed roof some 90 feet in diameter over the octagon, but it would hardly have been possible to cover the cathedral in this way, since the opening had now been enlarged to 138 feet 6 inches. The intention to vault the cathedral is implicit in the earliest designs, although we do not know exactly how Arnolfo intended to accomplish this. The fresco by Andrea da Firenze in the Spanish Chapel of Santa Maria Novella (c. 1367) is proof that in the late Trecento a dome without a drum was regarded as a possible solution, even after Talenti's enlargement of the plan.

Brunelleschi was first consulted about the cathedral as early as 1404, but it seems certain that it was not until several years later that he really began to think about the problem which had been becoming more and more pressing since the last years of the fourteenth century. The new octagon had been so much enlarged that it was now impossible to find timber long enough or strong enough to use as centering on which to build a dome. From the point of view of a traditional mason it was, therefore, impossible to cover the cathedral, and the Florentines found themselves faced by the prospect of having to abandon their grandiose undertaking (backed, as it was, by the state itself) and becoming the laughing-stock of their neighbours. Some idea of the dilemma in which the *operai* found themselves can be gained from the stories in the anonymous *Life* of Brunelleschi and in Vasari. What made matters worse was the extraordinary decision, taken as late as 1410, to build a drum

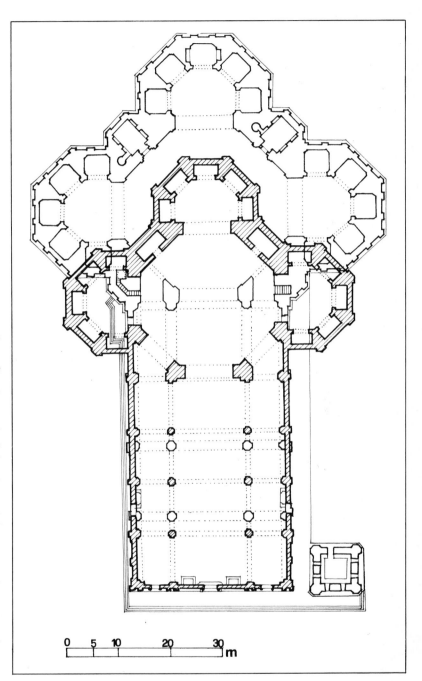

12. Arnolfo di Cambio and Francesco Talenti, Florence, Cathedral, plans.

13. *Florence, Baptistery.*
14. *Florence, Cathedral.*

15. *Filippo Brunelleschi, Florence, Cathedral, drum and dome.*
16. *Filippo Brunelleschi, Florence, Cathedral, dome.* ▷

17. *Francesco Piranesi, Rome, Temple of Minerva Medica, engraving.*
18. *Andrea Palladio, Rome, Pantheon, drawing of section.*

19. *Rome, Pantheon, detail of oculus and coffering.*

above the opening of the octagon, so that the total height from the ground to the top of the drum, when it was completed in 1413, was about 180 feet. The almost inexplicable decision to increase their own difficulties by building this drum must perhaps be explained by a desire to temporize while waiting for a solution to the dome problem to evolve itself. In fact, the drum had to be relatively thin-walled, since there was nowhere to put any buttresses to take the side thrusts; which meant that any dome built on top of it would have to exert even less side thrust than one built directly on top of the octagonal opening, of the type shown in the Spanish Chapel fresco and, probably, the type planned by Arnolfo from the beginning.

It was probably after this decision that Brunelleschi first began to think seriously about the problem. He must have realized that immortal fame would be assured to anyone who could solve it. The documents of the *Opera* contain numerous references to Brunelleschi and others, in connection with drawings and models, and, by 1417, they show that he was devoting much time and knowledge to the problem. His biographer seems to imply that he had already been to Rome at least once; this is the more likely since it can only have been by combining his knowledge of Gothic construction with firsthand experience of Roman vaulting methods that Brunelleschi was able to divine the principles of Roman vaulting and to apply them to his own problem. He must have studied the Baptistery itself and then gone on to various smaller buildings in Rome in a state of partial ruin — for example, the so-called Temple of Minerva Medica (Plate 17) — as well as making an intensive study of the only complete building to survive from classical times, the Pantheon. This, which had been preserved as the church of Santa Maria ad Martyres, has a perfectly preserved hemispherical dome 142 feet across, with a great central oculus 27 feet across (Plates 18, 19). It provided incontrovertible proof that it was possible to cover a space as big as Florence Cathedral, but Brunelleschi must soon have realized that he could not copy the Pantheon dome directly, since it was supported on cylindrical walls of immense thickness, and the whole construction of mass-concrete was so obviously heavy that even in the most attenuated form it could not have been erected on the substructure of Florence Cathedral. Brunelleschi's inspiration came from realizing that the Pantheon must have been built without centering, since, like himself, the Roman architects would have been unable to find big enough trees: therefore, it was possible to build a huge dome without centering. At the same time, he must have realized that one of the essentials of their solution was the absorption of side thrusts into the immense walls — the very thing that the building of the drum prevented him from doing. The

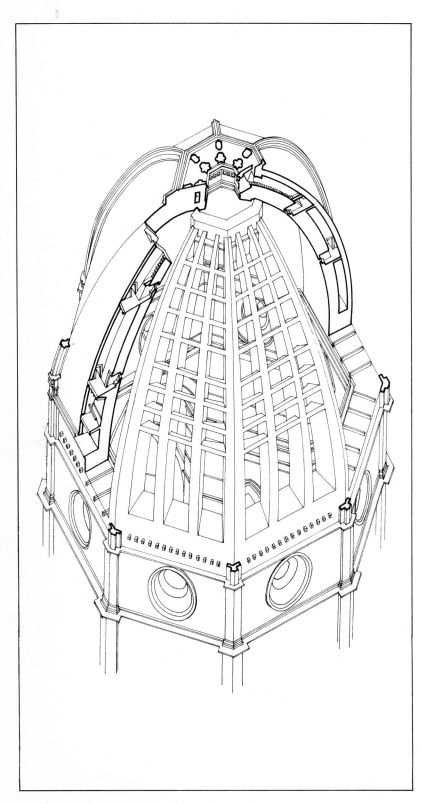

study of ruined domes must have helped him to recognize that the Pantheon was built without centering by casting rings of concrete in horizontal, concentric layers, each of which was allowed to harden before the next, smaller ring was set on it. This explains the huge open eye at the top, which, to a contemporary mason thinking in terms of vertical ribs meeting at a keystone, must have seemed absolutely inexplicable.

It was Brunelleschi's own experience of Gothic rib-construction that enabled him to combine vertical ribs as weight-bearing elements with a horizontal method of construction, the concentric rings of which are no more than Gothic ribs laid in the horizontal plane (Plates 20, 22). In 1420, he presented a Memorandum to the *operai* (preserved in slightly differing versions). It is not very lucid, because he was struggling to find words to express an idea which he himself could only imagine, and which was beyond the grasp of most of his audience. Nevertheless, he makes the essential point that it was necessary to build one major rib at each corner of the existing octagon, with a pair of smaller ribs between them. There would be twenty-four ribs, rising in self-supporting courses, and they would form a skeleton on which the skin of the dome would be stretched: '...I have decided to turn the inner part and also the exterior faces of this vault in gores, using the proportions and curves of a pointed arch; this is because the curve of this kind of arch always thrusts upwards, and so when the lantern is loaded, both will unite to make the fabric durable. At the base the vaulting must be $7\frac{1}{2}$ feet thick and it must rise like a pyramid, narrowing towards where it closes at the junction to support the lantern. At this point it must be $2\frac{1}{2}$ feet thick. Over this vaulting, there must be another vault, 5 feet thick at the base, to protect the inner one from the weather. This must also diminish proportionately, like a pyramid, so that it meets the lantern like the other; and at this point it should be $1\frac{1}{2}$ feet thick. There must be a rib at each of the angles, making eight in all; there must be two ribs for the middle of each face, making sixteen; two ribs must be built between the angles, for the inside and the outside, each being 8 feet thick at the base... As well as the twenty-four ribs with the vaults built round them, there must be six cross-arches of *macigno* stone... The two vaults of the cupola must be built as I have described, without centering, up to a height of 60 feet, and from there on as the builders decide, since experience shows what has to be done.'

Originally, Brunelleschi undoubtedly wished to imitate the form of the Pantheon by making his dome a perfect hemisphere, since it is likely that by this time he was so enthusiastic over the structural qualities of Roman architecture that he wished also to imitate its external forms. In this he was opposed to almost every other architect of the fifteenth century, particularly Alberti, since they all started from the assumption that one must imitate Roman architecture for the beauty of its forms — the hemisphere being of its very nature more beautiful than the pointed arch — and that the constructional principles employed by the ancients were not necessarily the concern of a modern architect. In this, of course, they were merely following the example given by the humanists in their choice of Cicero as a model of style.

Brunelleschi's dome is in fact pointed, being just over 100 feet high, against a radius of less than 70 feet. It is evident from the Memorandum that he had been forced to use the pointed form, since the whole experience of Gothic engineering indicated that a pointed arch exerts much less side thrust than a round one. His second innovation, the use of a double shell, was intended to save as much weight as possible, and again he must have realized that the Pantheon, with its beautiful pattern of deep coffering, was so designed in order to reduce the weight of concrete in the actual dome.

In this unique combination of ancient and modern engineering and aesthetic principles, Brunelleschi was feeling his way over a period of some twenty years. The stories about his refusal to explain to the *operai* exactly how he proposed to do the impossible all confirm that he evolved the solution over a lengthy period, and that he had had to make small-scale experiments, such as the two little hemispherical domes he built in Florence, as a demonstration that his basic principle was correct. The cathedral documents, particularly those recording payment to Donatello in 1419 for a large stone model, show that the solution was not attempted without careful consideration; but it is evident that from 1420 onwards, when the dome was actually being built, there was still an element of mystery about it, which is alone sufficient to account for the fame enjoyed by Brunelleschi ever since. Nevertheless, the dome of Florence Cathedral by itself would not justify us in regarding him as a stylistic innovator or as the 'reviver of ancient architecture', and it is only in his other works, where the constructional problems were straightforward, that one can see him in this role.

Brunelleschi's work on the dome occupied him from the beginning of construction in August 1420, until the completion in August 1436 of the dome proper and the preparation of the base of the lantern which he designed but did not live to build. During those sixteen years, most of his attention must have been given to the dome, but at the same time he undertook a number of other works, which show the development of his style in a way which proves that his aesthetic ideas could develop independently of the

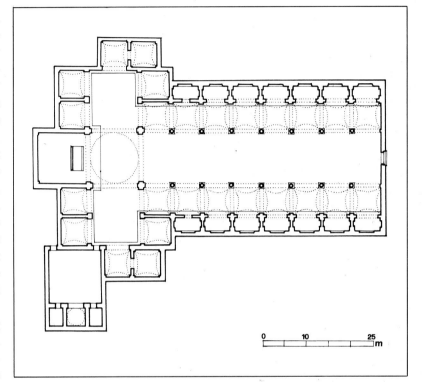

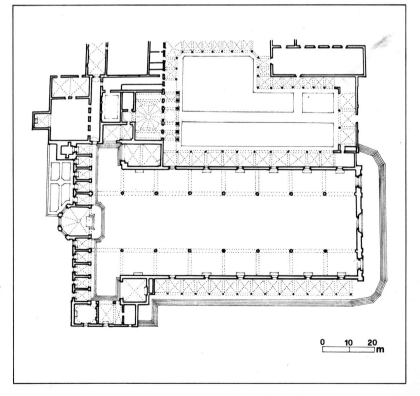

25. *Florence, Santo Spirito, plan.*
26, 27. *Filippo Brunelleschi, Florence, Santo Spirito, interior, view of nave.*

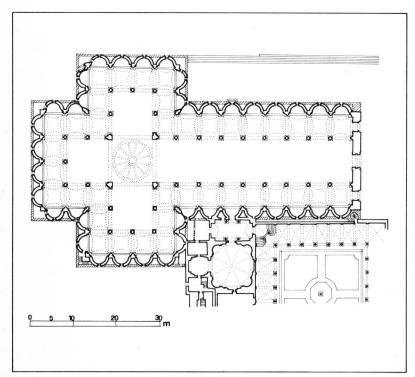

28

constructional work which was his preoccupation at the cathedral. His profound study of Roman constructional methods had made him so familiar with ancient architectural forms and ideals that it is not surprising that his own architecture took on an ever more Roman form. In this sense, it is possible to say that the initial impetus to Renaissance architecture in Florence arose directly from Brunelleschi's constructional studies, and was, therefore, different from the impetus to painting and sculpture which Masaccio or Donatello derived from a study of the purely formal qualities of classical sculpture. Nevertheless, as the anonymous *Life* clearly shows, by about 1480 Brunelleschi's forms were accepted as a criterion of classical style, and his churches became models for both the Latin cross type of plan and for the centrally-planned church, which was to be such a preoccupation of later Quattrocento and early Cinquecento architects.

The Spedale degli Innocenti was his earliest work, but much of it seems to have been executed by others, since Brunelleschi himself was too busy with the cathedral. This was the anonymous biographer's explanation of the apparent solecisms in the building, such as the treatment of the main entablature with its frieze ending in a moulding, and the architrave bent downwards parallel with its supporting pilaster (Plate 7). This feature occurs in the Baptistery, and it is likely that Brunelleschi was still unable to distinguish between it and genuine Roman work, in the sense that the decorative features of the Baptistery must have seemed perfectly compatible with what he knew of Roman decoration in general.

The first of his two Latin cross churches was San Lorenzo, where he began with the rebuilding of the Old Sacristy under the direct patronage of the Medici. The lantern is said to bear the date 1428, so the construction (if not the decoration) of the Sacristy was the earliest part of the building to be completed. The church itself, however, together with its successor, Santo Spirito, provided later generations with a norm of a basilican chuch. Essentially, the Latin cross plan of San Lorenzo (Plate 23) derives from the type established in the Middle Ages and represented in Florence by Santa Croce (Plate 24) with a long, wide nave and two aisles, relatively small transepts joining the nave to form a square crossing, and completed by a large chapel forming the choir, with several smaller chapels on either side of it. This type of plan was a direct descendant of the Early Christian basilicas in Rome, but had been modified by the influence of French Cistercian churches during the twelfth and thirteenth centuries. Brunelleschi, who must have been well acquainted with the great Roman basilicas, returned to the more traditional type of plan with modifications designed to make the church more convenient for modern usage. Santa Croce has

31-33. *Filippo Brunelleschi, Florence, San Lorenzo, interior.*

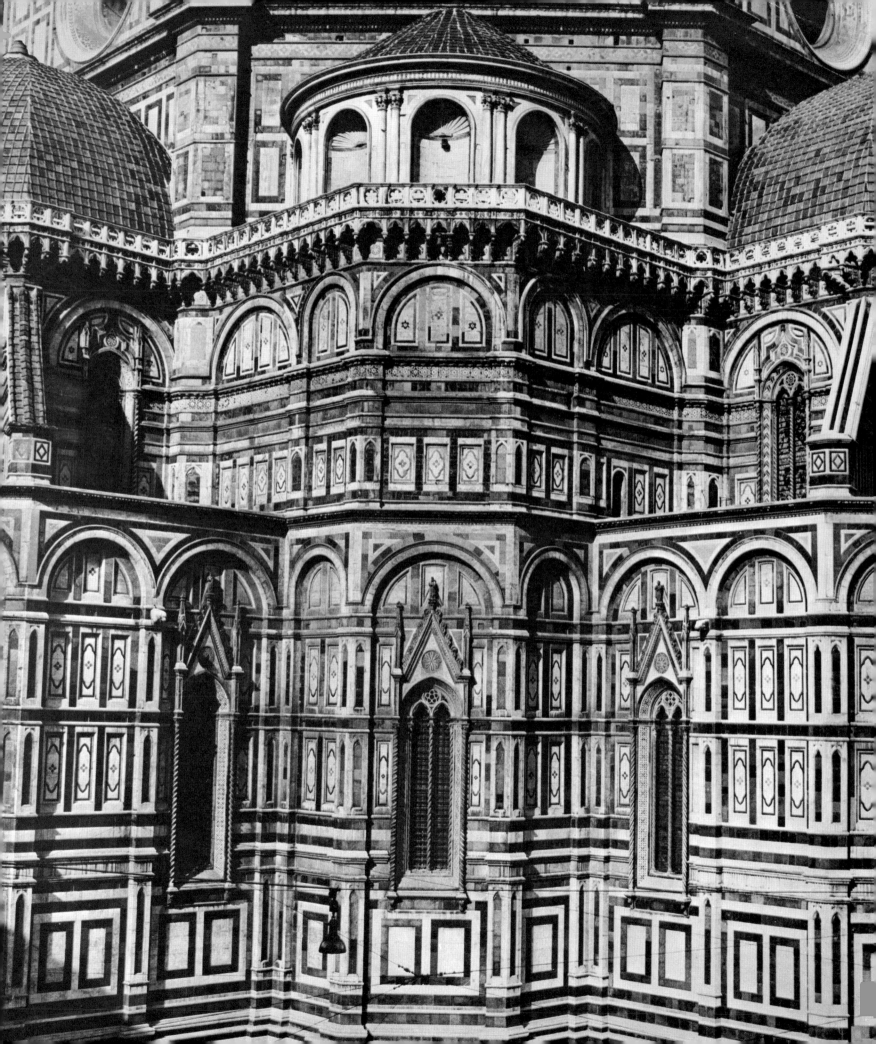

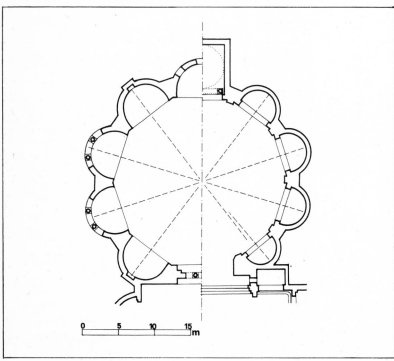

ten subsidiary chapels at the east end, and the practice of providing small chapels under the patronage of individual families had taken root during the Trecento. In the Early Christian period this custom was unknown, nor did all priests celebrate Mass daily, and the Roman basilicas were therefore designed with only one major altar-space. In the plan of San Lorenzo, Brunelleschi provided the same number of chapels as in Santa Croce, but he modified the rest of the church in such a way that it resembles the spatial sequences of a building like the fifth-century Santa Sabina. The plan shows that he began with a square crossing-unit, and created choir and transepts by simple repetition of this square. The nave is made up of four squares, and the aisles of squares each of which is one quarter the area of the main unit. In order to preserve the essential symmetry, the chapels on either side of the choir must be the same size as one of the aisle bays, and, in order to provide a sufficient number — five on each side — he had to continue them round the transept, allowing space at one angle for the Old Sacristy. The original plan of San Lorenzo, drawn up in 1419, was modified in the 1440s by the addition of twelve extra chapels beyond the aisles, obtained by opening the aisle wall and creating a small rectangular space half the area of one of the aisle bays. From this it follows that the plan of San Lorenzo is subject to simple mathematical relationships of the 1:2 or 1:4 type, which must be what his biographer meant by saying: 'he saw... the symmetry of the ancients... and their musical proportions.'

Precisely this harmonic simplicity was lacking in churches like Santa Croce or Santa Maria Novella, and Brunelleschi's return to a classical prototype was successful, primarily because of its mathematical discipline, which was in tune with the mood of the arts in Florence in the 1420s, and, to some extent, the 1430s. What was more obvious was his 'classicism' in details, such as Corinthian columns with reasonably accurate capitals carrying semicircular arches, and the traditional flat nave roof, painted to look like coffering (in fact, neither San Lorenzo nor Santo Spirito was roofed in Brunelleschi's lifetime). The tentative nature of his classicism in the design for San Lorenzo is best seen by direct comparison with Santo Spirito (Plates 25-30). In San Lorenzo, the mathematical proportions are evident on plan, but less so in elevation since the height of the aisles bears no simple relationship to the height of the nave. Brunelleschi certainly exploited his perspective studies in the treatment of the receding arches of nave and chapels (Plates 31-33), just as he exploited the contrast between the smooth Corinthian columns of the nave and the shallow, channelled pilasters at the entrances of the chapels. In Santo Spirito, classicism was carried a stage further by subjecting the whole of the interior space to the same math-

40. *Filippo Brunelleschi, Florence, San Lorenzo, Old Sacristy, interior.*
41. *Filippo Brunelleschi, Florence, San Lorenzo, Old Sacristy, dome.*

42. *Filippo Brunelleschi, Florence, San Lorenzo, Old Sacristy, detail of a pilaster.*
43. *Filippo Brunelleschi, Florence, San Lorenzo, Old Sacristy, the two domes.* ▷

44. *Filippo Brunelleschi, Florence, Santa Croce, Pazzi Chapel, exterior.*
45. *Florence, Santa Croce, Pazzi Chapel, plan.*

46. *Filippo Brunelleschi, Florence, Santa Croce, Pazzi Chapel, Loggia, exterior.*
47. *Filippo Brunelleschi, Florence, Santa Croce, Pazzi Chapel, detail of interior of Loggia.* ▷

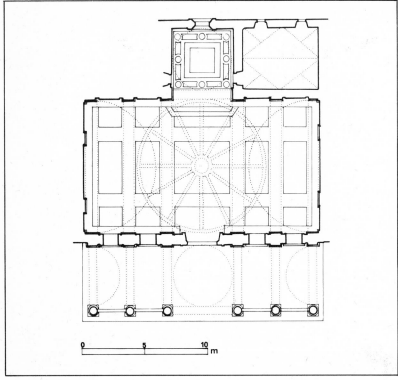

BELVEDER CON PITTI

ematical principles as governed the plan, and, at the same time, the detailing was made heavier and more sculptural — closer, in a word, to Imperial Roman prototypes. The treatment of the view from the nave into the aisles is identical, except that in Santo Spirito the aisles are half the height of the nave elevation, thus establishing a proportional relationship lacking in San Lorenzo. More obviously, the elements of the arcade, the vaulting, and especially the half-columns at the entrances of the chapels, impart a heavier and grave rhythm to the interior. It has been suggested that Brunelleschi intended, in his final revision of Santo Spirito, to have a semicircular barrel-vaulted roof instead of a flat ceiling, and this would certainly add another dimension to the complex interlocking curves of the design, but there seems little evidence to support this, and, in any case, a flat ceiling is more typical of the Early Christian prototypes such as San Paolo Fuori le Mura. This Roman *gravitas* is particularly noticeable in the forest of columns surrounding the choir and transepts (Plates 26-29), and it is very probable that the original design continued this arcade right across the west end. The numerous chapels differ from those in San Lorenzo by being semicircular in plan, though still proportioned to the aisle bays. The repetition of deep concave curves against the convex half-columns at the entrances gives a massively sculptural feeling to the whole interior of Santo Spirito and makes San Lorenzo by contrast seem rather flimsy (Plates 31-33).

There seems no doubt that Brunelleschi's original plan also provided for the curved walls of the chapels to be visible externally which, at first glance, would have given an unusual serrated outline to the church. This feature was probably copied from a building (now destroyed) at the Lateran, but its importance lies in the fact that it is characteristic of Imperial Roman architecture to mould the internal spaces of a building into complex shapes, regardless of the exterior effect. If, as seems likely, Brunelleschi was drawing increasingly closer in spirit to Roman architects of the fourth and fifth centuries, it is possible that this advance in his appreciation of the formal qualities of Roman architecture was due to renewed contact with it. There is no mention of Brunelleschi in any Florentine document between December 1432 and July 1434, although his name occurs regularly before and after those dates: from this it has been inferred that he made another, extended, visit to Rome. This would coincide with the period Donatello is known to have spent there, and may well be the time, recorded in the lives of both men, when they worked together in Rome in search of classical antiquities.

Stylistically, the increased heaviness and *romanitas* of Brunelleschi's

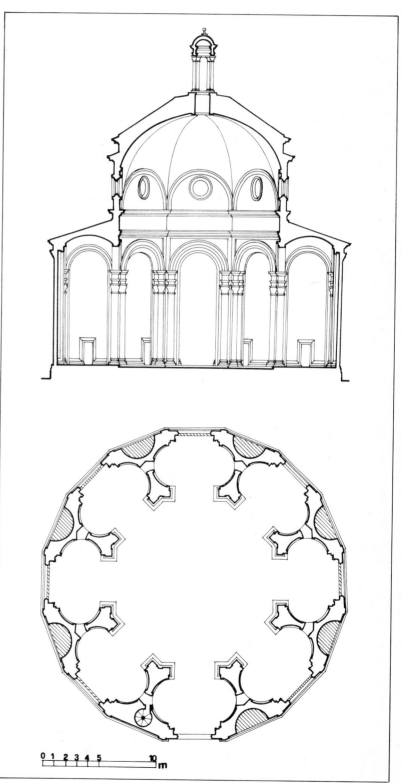

50. *Filippo Brunelleschi, Florence, Santa Croce, Pazzi Chapel, section.*
51. *Fiesole, Badia Fiesolana, interior.*

52. *Florence, Santa Maria degli Angeli, Marchini's reconstruction and plan.*

0   5   10
m

0 1 2 3 4 5   10
m

43

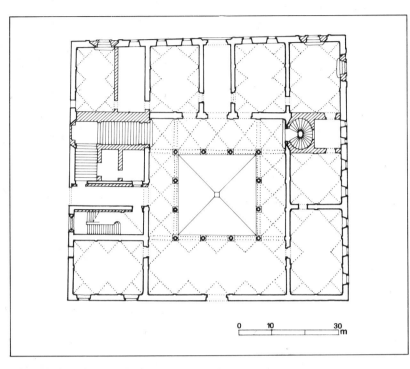

works can be dated in the last decade of his life. The huge task of the dome was completed by the addition of the lantern, designed about 1436, and also by the decorative exedrae below the level of the drum (Plates 34-36). Two significant facts emerge from a study of the exedrae; firstly, that they were begun in 1438, and, secondly, that the design was modified by the substitution of half-columns for the pilasters mentioned in a document. The plan shows that they resemble halves of a centrally-planned church, with an alternation of concave and convex curves precisely the same as the chapels in Santo Spirito. The central-plan type of the exedrae has parallels in the plan of the lantern and both derive from Roman prototypes such as the Temple of Minerva Medica (Plates 17, 38). Comparison between the exedrae and the pulpit designed after 1428 by Donatello and Michelozzo for Prato Cathedral (Plate 39) shows that the pulpit derives directly from Roman sarcophagi — Donatello was actually summoned back to Prato from Rome to continue work on it — but the greater sophistication of the exedrae shows how much Brunelleschi had absorbed of the essential quality of ancient architecture.

Even more than in the exedrae and lantern, the fully developed classicism of Brunelleschi's late style can be seen in his centrally-planned buildings. Vasari says that, if it had been completed according to Brunelleschi's intentions, Santo Spirito would have been 'the most perfect church in Christendom' — not the 'most beautiful', but 'perfect', implying that it was an *exemplum*. The series of central plans left by Brunelleschi were to be regarded as *exempla* for such buildings, in the same way as his basilican churches were norms of a perfect architecture, and the progress of his style can be traced from the Old Sacristy, begun in 1419, through the Pazzi Chapel, up to the unfinished Santa Maria degli Angeli, begun in 1434, immediately after the hypothetical Roman period.

The Old Sacristy of San Lorenzo consists of a cubical main space, with a dome over it that appears from inside to be a hemisphere, although it is externally a drum and conical roof (Plates 37, 40, 41). Opening from the main space is a smaller 'choir' or altar-space, also with a square plan. This subsidiary space has its own hemispherical dome (Plate 37), which, like the larger one, is carried on pendentives. The walls are divided into a grid pattern by pilasters and entablatures, but the overall impression is one of uncertainty — the tiny strips representing pilasters in the angles (Plate 40), and the brackets carrying lengths of entablature that would otherwise be unsupported. Like the church of San Lorenzo itself, the impression is one of planes and angles, linear rather than plastic.

The Sacristy was finished by 1428, and two years later Brunel-

leschi began to work on the first designs for the Pazzi Chapel in the cloister of Santa Croce. Recent restorations have revealed the dates 1459 and 1461 on the outer surfaces of two of the domes, so the chapel must have been in progress during the whole of Brunelleschi's later years. Internal evidence makes it seem that the design was modified in the light of his own stylistic evolution. The plan (Plate 45) shows an advance over the Old Sacristy in that it is more symmetrical, with minor domical spaces (the altar- and entrance-bays) on the E-W axis, and transeptal forms with barrel vaults as balancing shapes on the N-S axis. Above all, the difference between the entrance loggia — which should be compared with the Innocenti (Plates 4, 7) — with its pilaster responds, its straight entablature, its barrel vault, and its Pantheon-like entrance dome, and the upper part of the façade is immediately striking (Plates 44, 46). The Roman heaviness of the loggia makes it seem likely that it was designed after 1434, while the upper façade was probably executed by an assistant after Brunelleschi's death. The meagre forms and insensitive proportioning are reminiscent of another work of the Brunelleschi school — the Badia Fiesolana (Plate 51). There is a close parallel with the Pazzi loggia in the forms Brunelleschi projected, but never executed, for the sixteen-sided church of Santa Maria degli Angeli. As reconstructed by Marchini (Plate 52) from engravings and drawings, this building, with its sculptural moulding of the spaces in and between the chapels, its majestic order of pilasters, and above all its Pantheon dome, show it to have been in keeping with Santo Spirito, and Brunelleschi's final word on the problem of centrally-planned domed churches expressed in purely Roman terms. It was to be one of the most important links in the long chain of central plans leading to Bramante's New St. Peter's.

Brunelleschi as a domestic architect is hardly known to us. He designed a palace for Cosimo de' Medici, who rejected it ('Envy is a plant one should never water'), and Brunelleschi destroyed the model. In recent years attempts have been made to ascribe the original Palazzo Pitti to him (Plate 48), but in fact this was not begun until after his death, and, in any case, the heavy rustication and non-Roman treatment render the attribution implausible.

The Palazzo di Parte Guelfa (Plate 53), though damaged, shows that Brunelleschi was the first to apply pilasters to the façade of a palace, but it was Alberti who developed this idea. Brunelleschi's most important contribution to the development of the Florentine palace was made at second hand, through his great influence on Michelozzo.

The Palazzo Medici, begun in 1444, explains how the Pitti may

be ascribed to Brunelleschi. It is very large (and was always so, even before the seventeenth-century additions), with the sense of scale much increased by the simplicity of the three-storey façade with graduated rustication (Plates 55, 57) culminating in a huge over-hanging modillion cornice. The plan, based on the traditional Florentine internal court, is symmetrical and the court elevation is no more than the façade of Brunelleschi's Innocenti bent round to form a square. This means that the angles meet over a single column, and the windows above, centred over the arches, come too close together at the corners. The high frieze, unsupported by an order of its own, and the small cornice acting as a sill for the windows, are proof of Michelozzo's lack of architectural subtlety compared with Brunelleschi: he was, however, a competent builder and planner, and his Library at San Marco (another Medici commission), or his Cappella del Crocefisso in San Miniato al Monte, with its varied columns (Plates 61-63), show him to better advantage. His work in Venice, Dalmatia, Pistoia, Montepulciano (Plate 64), and Milan (Plate 160) is indicative of the part he played in spreading ideas derived from Brunelleschi outside Tuscany.

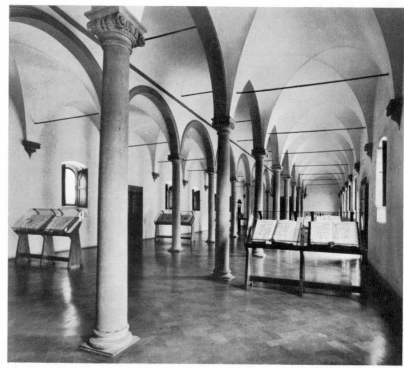

Not only was Leon Battista Alberti some twenty-seven years younger than Brunelleschi, but his whole background and training was entirely different. The Alberti family, though Florentine, were in exile at the time of his birth, and he was born and educated in the north of Italy, not visiting Florence until about 1428, when he was in his twenty-fifth year. By this time he had already established the beginnings of his reputation as a humanist, and had demonstrated his mastery of Latin. In Florence he became friendly with Brunelleschi, Donatello, and Masaccio (or at least he knew them well enough to dedicate his treatise on painting to them). His career as a Papal Civil Servant began in the 1430s, and it does not seem that he ever intended to become an artist, although he is supposed to have practised all three arts. His mind was fundamentally literary and it was natural that, as soon as he became interested in the arts, he should consider them from the point of view of theoretical principles and from the scholarly and historical point of view as well.

The writings of the ancients on the arts must have been much more extensive than the material which has survived, but the major treatise on architecture by Vitruvius would naturally have attracted Alberti's attention. It is an established myth that Vitruvius was unknown throughout the Middle Ages and was dramatically rediscovered by Poggio about 1415, thus determining the whole course of Renaissance architecture. In fact, the earliest, and best, surviving manuscript of Vitruvius was written, probably in the eighth century, in the north of England, and Vitruvius was sufficiently well known to have been quoted by Boccaccio and Benvenuto da Imola in the fourteenth century. There can be no question of a dramatic rediscovery. The element of truth in the myth is that Poggio certainly recovered many manuscripts of classical authors. In the first quarter of the fifteenth century ancient authors were being studied with great zeal, and, as a result, new manuscripts were being recovered all the time. When Alberti went to Rome, about 1432, he would naturally have turned to Vitruvius, although at the time when he wrote his own *Descriptio* he had not made a very close study of the text. In all probability, reading Vitruvius and studying the ruins influenced him to begin his own treatise on architecture about 1443, and it is characteristic that he began to write a treatise before erecting a building. His earliest works, the Palazzo Rucellai in Florence and the Tempio Malatestiano in Rimini, are not earlier than 1446. It seems that all his buildings are practical demonstrations intended to reconcile the principles of ancient architecture, as he had deduced them from Vitruvius, with the ruins he had studied at first hand in Rome, and which he, re- alized, did not correspond with Vitruvius. By combining these two

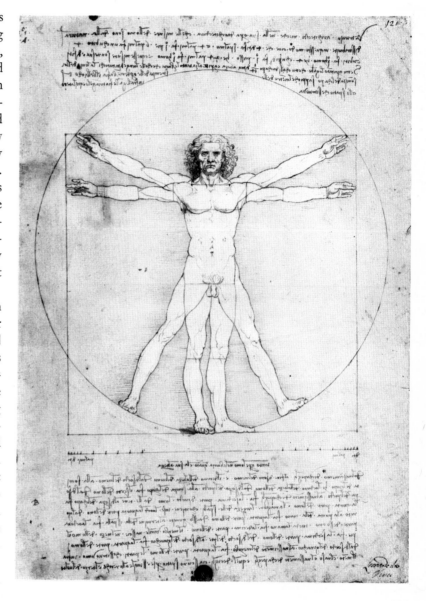

65. *Leonardo, drawing of Vitruvian Man (Venice, Gallerie dell' Accademia).*

sources of information, he set out to provide new forms for new purposes: for example, the façade of the church of Santa Maria Novella in Florence and the two churches in Mantua.

When he came to write *De re aedificatoria*, he divided it into ten books and dealt with the material in a manner virtually similar to Vitruvius's *De architectura libri decem*. One of Alberti's principal reasons for thus rewriting Vitruvius was that the text was extremely obscure. Vitruvius's Latinity was a constant source of complaint by Alberti, and he also used a number of Greek technical terms which can hardly have been understood in the fifteenth century. Vitruvius himself quotes many earlier writers (all of them now lost), and the state of the text in Alberti's time must have driven him to despair. In addition to the near-impossibility of understanding whole passages in Vitruvius, Alberti must soon have realized the other great drawback, which is that Vitruvius lived in the time of Augustus (perhaps before 27 B.C.), and Alberti, like Poggio and his fellow-humanists in the fifteenth century, had already realized that most of the finest buildings in Rome are much later in date. Vitruvius, therefore, was no guide to the best period of Roman Imperial architecture. From him, however, Alberti derived general information about building types, and, above all, Vitruvius's description of the Orders and his theory of proportion.

In his treatise Alberti gives the first satisfactory modern account of the classical Orders, and he was the first architect to attempt to characterize them and to distinguish between them. Brunelleschi, who was not interested in this kind of archaeology, was content to use a rough-and-ready Corinthian Order for almost all purposes.

The most important part of Vitruvius, from Alberti's point of view, was undoubtedly his theory of proportion, particularly the passage in Book III in which Vitruvius equates human and architectural proportions: 'The planning of temples depends upon symmetry... It arises from proportion... Proportion consists in taking a fixed module, in each case, both for the parts of a building and for the whole, by which the method of symmetry is put into practice. For without symmetry and proportion no temple can have a regular plan; that is, it must have an exact proportion worked out after the fashion of the members of a finely-shaped human body. For Nature has so planned the human body that the face from the chin to the top of the forehead and the roots of the hair is a tenth part of the whole height... The other limbs also have their own proportionate measurements. And by using these, ancient painters and famous sculptors have attained great and infinite praises. Similarly, the parts of temples ought to have their dimensions closely related to the magnitude of the whole. In the human body, the natural centre is the navel. If a man lies on his back with hands and

feet outstretched and a pair of compasses is centred on his navel, then his fingers and toes will touch the circumference of the circle: in the same way, it is possible to fit the human figure into a square, since the height from the top of the head to the sole of the foot is the same as the width of the outstretched arms... (Plate 65). Therefore, if Nature designed the human body so that its members are pro-portioned to the figure as a whole, the ancients had good reason to lay down the rule that in perfect buildings the different parts must bear an exact symmetrical relation to the whole..." (Vitruvius, *De Arch.*, III, i, 1-4).

This idea of the fundamental importance of the human form as a measure of all proportions is basic to Renaissance architecture, distinguishing it sharply from Gothic, and, with its overtones of the harmony of the spheres of the universe, led ultimately to those elaborate musical harmonies underlying the proportional systems used by Palladio and others. Brunelleschi's anonymous biographer was probably telling the truth when he said that Brunelleschi per-ceived relationships in the ancient ruins, but it seems unlikely that the theory of proportion advanced by Vitruvius and elaborated by Alberti (in *De re...*, IX, 5-6) would have found favour with Brunel-leschi.

De re aedificatoria was probably begun about 1443, only three years before the death of Brunelleschi. Although one version was complete by 1452, Alberti seems to have gone on working on it until his death in 1472; it was widely circulated in manuscript, and printed in Florence in 1485.

Alberti's buildings can be seen as three-dimensional demonstrations of his theories. The Palazzo Rucellai in Florence (Plates 66-68), begun about 1446, although later than Brunelleschi's Palazzo di Parte Guelfa, was the first full-scale attempt to use the Orders to articulate the fa-çade of a palace. The purpose was partly to emphasize the grandeur of the building, since Alberti believed that the size and grandeur of houses should reflect the status of the owners; and, secondly, to use the Orders to distinguish between the storeys. He took the idea of pilasters applied vertically to a wall-surface from the Colosseum, with its arrangement of Doric, Ionic, and Corinthian three-quarter columns followed, on the top storey, by Corinthian pilasters. In detail (Plates 67, 68) it is not easy to recognize the traditional Doric-Ionic-Corinthian upward progression in Alberti's façade, since he uses something which is neither Doric nor Ionic (nor even Tuscan) on the ground floor, followed by a fairly correct, rather rich Corinthian on the *piano nobile*, perhaps with the intention of emphasizing it as the important floor. The top storey has what seems a simpler form of Corinthian, so he may have followed the Colosseum in using two Corinthians, but it is possible that he intended it as a different Order.

He speaks of what he calls the Italic Order, but this is probably the Composite, and, in fact, he knew the correct form of the Composite Order, to judge from the capitals of the consoles in the Palazzo Rucellai (Plate 67).

At about the same time, he began work on the church of San Francesco, Rimini, recasing it as a monument to the glory of the tyrant of Rimini, Sigismondo Malatesta. Wittkower has shown that this was achieved by applying the Roman triumphal arch to the façade, using both the Arch of Constantine in Rome and the Arch of Augustus in Rimini itself, so that the tombs originally projected for the west front would lie in a triumphal arch and would be seen as a triumph over death — a sort of *Trionfo della Fama*, in contemporary terms — while at the same time serving as a classical version of the church façade. The medal by Matteo de' Pasti, the acting architect, shows that the original project also included a huge Pantheon-like dome, probably intended to add to the air of glory (Plate 74). A letter from Alberti to Matteo, dated 18 November 1454, contains interesting details: 'As for what you tell me Manetto says about cupolas having to be twice as high as they are wide, I, for my part, have more faith in those who built the Baths and the Pantheon and all those noble edifices, than in him, and a great deal more in reason than in any man... Remember and bear well in mind that in the model, on the right and left sides along the edge of the roof, there is a thing like this, and I told you, I am putting this here to conceal that part of the roof... and the object must be to improve what is already built, and not to spoil what is yet to be done. You can see where the sizes and proportions of the pilasters come from: if you alter something, all that harmony is destroyed... As to the matter of the round windows, I do wish the man in the trade knew his job... Many arguments could be adduced on this account, but one must suffice — namely, that you will never, never find in any building praised by those who once understood what nobody understands today, any round window at all except like a tonsure in the summit of cupolas: and this happens in certain temples dedicated to Jove and Phoebus, who are patrons of light, and they have special justification in their great size. I have told you this to show where the true explanation lies...'

Between 1460 and his death, Alberti built two churches in Mantua, both of which can be seen as exercises in adapting the classical temple front to the needs of the traditional Christian church. In San Sebastiano, designed about 1460, Alberti avoided the problem by designing the church as a Greek instead of a Latin cross, applying the temple front to one of the arms. The central-plan form was new in that the earlier experiments by Brunelleschi were not Greek cross in shape, and Alberti certainly derived the idea from

76. *Leon Battista Alberti, Mantua, San Sebastiano, façade.*
77. *Mantua, San Sebastiano, Wittkower's reconstruction.*
78. *Mantua, San Sebastiano, plan.*

79. *Rome, Temple of Fortuna Virilis.*
80. *Mantua, Sant' Andrea, plan.*

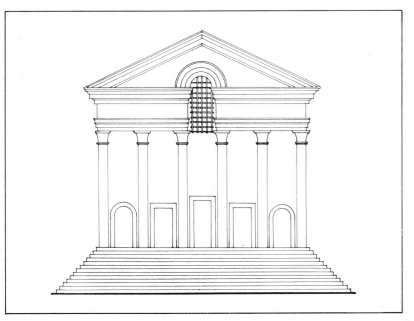

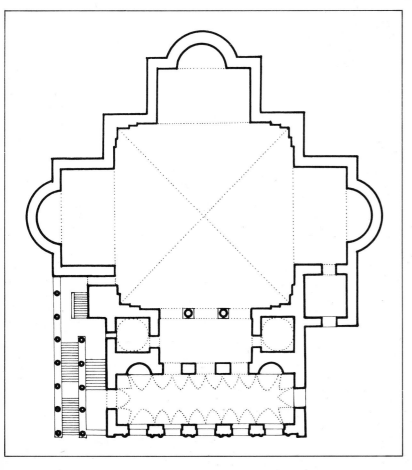

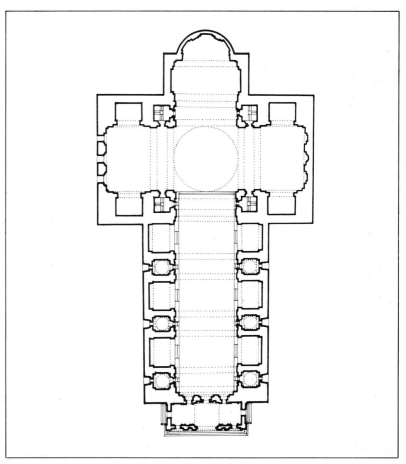

81. *Mantua, Sant' Andrea, axonometric drawing.*

82. *Leon Battista Alberti, Mantua, Sant' Andrea, façade.*
83. *Leon Battista Alberti, Mantua, Sant' Andrea, entrance.*
84. *Leon Battista Alberti, Mantua, Sant' Andrea, detail of portico.* ▷

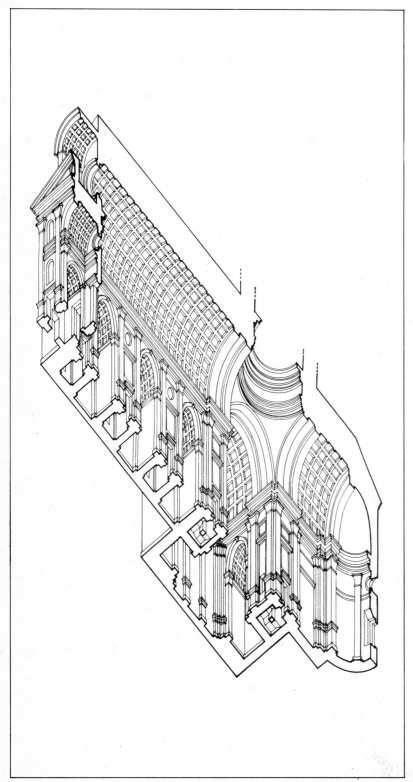

Roman tombs and Early Christian *martyria*: the mausoleum of Galla Placidia at Ravenna provides an obvious prototype. At San Sebastiano, the classical type of temple front (such as the Temple of Fortuna Virilis in Rome, which Alberti had already used in the façade of San Pancrazio in Florence) is adapted to facing the arm of the cross by applying the Orders directly to the wall-surface. The present façade of the church does not show this, but it has been demonstrated by Wittkower that there should be six pilasters on the façade, and that the building should, in accordance with Alberti's theories, be set upon a high podium (Plates 76-78).

More important, and certainly more influential, was Sant'Andrea, designed about 1470, where he turned his attention to the traditional Latin cross plan and applied a combination of a temple front and a triumphal arch to the façade. In Santa Maria Novella in Florence, he had produced a solution to the problem of a west end with a high nave and lower flanking aisles by giving the nave a pediment and masking the aisles by scrolls (Plate 86). At Sant'Andrea he not only produced a new façade design, but abandoned the nave-and-aisles type of basilica church which Brunelleschi had used, turning instead to a Latin cross form with a barrel-vaulted nave and a series of alternating chapels and supports on either side (Plate 85). The direction of the main axes is thus different from that in the Brunelleschian type, since the main east-west axis of the nave is countered by the cross axis of the alternating bays at the sides. The intention behind this was to build a great barrel vault much higher and more imposing than any previously erected, and to do this Alberti realized that the great barrel vaults of the Roman baths could not possibly be supported on columns like those used by Brunelleschi. He therefore adapted his system of support and based it on those used by Roman builders in, for example, the Basilica of Constantine, thus introducing an even more 'antique' form than Brunelleschi had been able to do. The nave elevation is repeated as part of the entrance portico, and the effect is closer to Roman prototypes than anything previously built, as a comparison between the interior of Brunelleschi's Santo Spirito and Sant'Andrea makes clear (Plates 26-30, 85).

Alberti's influence is difficult to trace, in that comparatively few of his buildings were copied directly, yet the influence of his treatise was enormous and his personal influence seems to have been equally great. We know, for example, that he was a welcome guest at Urbino, and the combination of the Duke himself, his architect Laurana, and his painter Piero della Francesca owes much to the influence of Alberti even though it is not easy to pinpoint it. Alberti's direct influence is more easily seen in the buildings of Pienza, where the work was done by Bernardo Rossellino, Alberti's

86. *Leon Battista Alberti, Florence, Santa Maria Novella, façade.*
87. *Ideal City, in a painting attributed to Piero della Francesca (Urbino, Galleria Nazionale delle Marche).*
88. *Ideal City, in a painting attributed to Piero della Francesca, detail (Baltimore, Walters Art Gallery).*
89. *Pienza, town plan.*

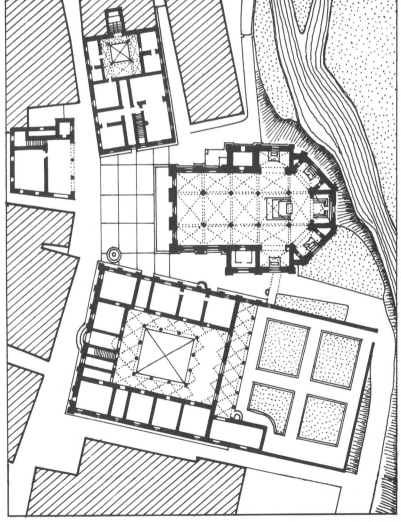

90. *Pienza, Palazzo Piccolomini, elevation and plan.*
91. *Bernardo Rossellino, Pienza, Palazzo Piccolomini, façade.* ▷

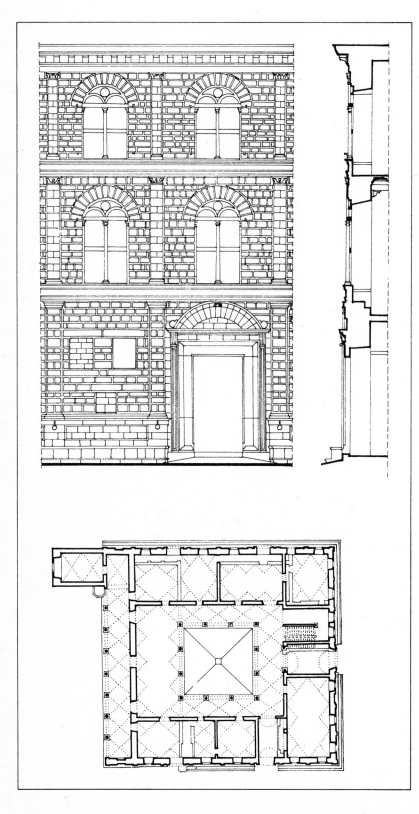

92. *Bernardo Rossellino, Pienza, Palazzo Piccolomini, well-head.*
93. *Bernardo Rossellino, Pienza, Palazzo Piccolomini, court.*

94. *Bernardo Rossellino, Pienza, piazzetta.* ▷

assistant at the Palazzo Rucellai. Even there, however, the directing mind was that of Pius II, and the result is therefore less Albertian than it might otherwise have been.

Aeneas Sylvius Piccolomini was a professional humanist whose career was similar to Alberti's, except that in 1458 Aeneas was elected Pope and typically chose to recall Virgil's *pius Aeneas* by taking the name Pius II. In the spring of 1459, according to the autobiographical *Commentarii* — themselves reminiscent of Julius Caesar — he decided to rebuild his native Corsignano, a village in the hills about thirty miles south of Siena, and to make it into a city-memorial. It is not only one of the first examples of Renaissance town-planning, but also probably the first time since Pliny the Younger that anyone had taken the view into account. There is a splendid panorama from the top of the hill towards Monte Amiata, and the *Commentarii* make it clear that Pius deliberately exploited this, and, indeed, spent large sums to build up the substructures of the Piccolomini Palace and the cathedral. The layout of Pienza, as it was re-named, shows (Plate 89) that the piazza at the heart of the town is a trapezoid, widening towards the south, with the cathedral occupying the greater part of this side, the Palazzo Piccolomini to the right, and the Bishop's Palace to the left, while the town hall, a much smaller building, occupies the north side. This is not a rigidly symmetrical layout, and one is immediately reminded of the replanning of the Borgo by Alberti and Pius's predecessor Nicholas V, which was almost certainly conditioned by existing buildings. There is also the haunting and mysterious picture, now in the Galleria Nazionale at Urbino (Plate 87), which many people believe, with reason, to be the work of Piero della Francesca, perhaps collaborating with Alberti in an interpretation of Vitruvius. This also represents a piazza flanked by noble palaces and with a temple as the focal point of the main side, although in this case the style is more consistently classical. It is, indeed, the most puzzling feature of the whole Pienza project that the Pope did not call upon Alberti to design it, seeing that he had more experience of town-planning problems than any other architect and was, in any case, already an employee of the Curia. Perhaps Pius wanted to design his own monument, but he certainly employed an assistant of Alberti as his executant (and he also speaks with respect of Alberti as an archaeologist). At any rate, Alberti's influence is plainly evident in the façade of the Palazzo Piccolomini. Bernardo Rossellino had been the contractor for the Palazzo Rucellai in Florence a few years earlier, and it is clear that he took it as a model of a palace *all'antica*, a model accepted by Pius as suitable for his own family palace. Nevertheless, there are considerable differences between Rossellino's building and its prototype, in the façade and, more importantly, in the rear elevation. The façade of

95, 96. Bernardo Rossellino, Pienza, Cathedral, façade.

the Palazzo Piccolomini is based on the Colosseum motive used by Alberti in Florence (Plate 91) even to the doubled Corinthian Orders of the *piano nobile* and the top storey, although the Tuscan pilasters of the ground floor are more correct than Alberti's and are one of the earliest examples of this Order in the Renaissance. In other respects, the palace is less satisfactory than its prototype, especially in the change of proportion in the bays, so that the window-arches now come to the top of the bay, whereas in the Palazzo Rucellai there is space all around them: the bays of the *piano nobile* of the Piccolomini Palace are square, whereas those of the Rucellai are twice as high as they are wide.

The really original feature of the Piccolomini Palace is the treatment of the garden front. This consists of a triple loggia, uninteresting in itself since the forms are those normal for a double cloister in any monastic foundation. It was Pius, not Rossellino, who sited the palace and designed the loggia, and he describes it thus: 'On the fourth side [of the palace], which has a most delightful view of Monte Amiata to the south, were three porticoes raised above one another on stone columns. The first with its high and splendid vaulting provided a most delightful promenade near the garden: the second, which had an elaborately painted wooden ceiling, made a very pleasant place to sit in the winter. It had a balustrade which with its cornice was as high as a man's waist. The third was similar to the second but less elaborate in its coffering.' Pius then goes on to describe the view in terms which show that, although he was consciously linking himself in thought to Pliny the Younger, describing his beloved villas, or with the Virgil of the *Georgics*, praising the immemorial beauty and fertility of the Italian countryside, yet he also genuinely loved his native place: 'The view from the upper floor extends to the west beyond Montalcino and Siena to the Pistoian Alps. As you look to the north, diverse hills and the lovely green of forests are spread before you for a distance of five miles. If you strain your eyes you can see as far as the Apennines and make out the town of Cortona on a high hill not far from Lake Trasimene, but the valley of the Chiana, which lies in between, cannot be seen because of its great depth. The view to the east is less extended, reaching only as far as Poliziano [Montepulciano]... and the mountains which separate the valley of the Chiana from that of the Orcia. The view from the three porticoes to the south is bounded, as we have said, by towering and wooded Monte Amiata. You look down on the valley of the Orcia and green meadows and hills covered with grass in season and fruited fields and vineyards, towns and citadels and precipitous cliffs, and Bagni di Vignoni and Montepescali, which is higher than Radicofani, and is the portal of the winter sun.'

In purely architectural matters Pius was less classically minded,

and, by Alberti's standards, must have seemed easily satisfied with anything that might pass as *all'antica*. This is evident in the description he gives of the building of the cathedral, which, as he explains, is really two churches, an upper and a lower, because of the steep slope of the hill (he had visited the double church at Assisi in 1459). 'The upper church is 140 feet long, 60 feet high and as many wide, not counting the space taken by the chapels which add to both the length and the width. Of necessity its greatest length, contrary to custom, is from north to south... The façade itself is 72 feet high, made of stone resembling the Tiburtine, white and shining as marble. It was modelled on those of ancient temples and richly decorated with columns and arches and semicircular niches designed to hold statues. It has three beautifully proportioned doors the centre one larger than the others, and a great eye like that of the Cyclops. It displays the arms of the Piccolomini, above them the Papal fillet wreathed about the triple crown, and the keys of the Church between. The façade is of the same breadth all the way from the foundation to the roof. From there to its top it has the form of a pyramid decorated with charming cornices. The other walls are of less precious material...

'As you enter the middle door, the entire church with its chapels and altars is visible and is remarkable for the clarity of the light and the brilliance of the whole edifice. There are three naves, as they are called. The middle one is wider. All are the same height. This was according to the directions of Pius, who had seen the plan among the Germans in Austria. It makes the church more graceful and lighter. Eight columns, all of the same height and thickness, support the entire weight of the vaulting. After the bases were in place and the columns with four semicircular faces had been set upon them and crowned with capitals, the architect saw that they were not going to be high enough. He therefore placed above the capitals square columns seven feet high with a second set of capitals to support the arches of the vaulting. It was a happy mistake, which added charm by its novelty.'

The most striking thing in this passage is the cheerful acceptance of an error of seven feet as a charming novelty, but this is probably explained by the rather Gothic tastes of the Pope, with his adoption — almost unique in Italy — of the hall-church type of plan which he had seen in Austria, perhaps in Vienna Cathedral. In the same way, his obsession with light — 'It makes the church more graceful and lighter... windows which, when the sun shines, admit so much light that worshippers in the church think they are not in a house of stone but of glass' — reads more like a description of the Sainte Chapelle than an Italian church, and is flatly contradicted by Alberti: 'The windows in the Temple ought to be small

and high, so that nothing but the sky may be seen through them; to the intent that both the priests that are employed in the performance of divine offices, and those that assist upon account of devotion, may not have their minds anyways diverted by foreign objects. That horror with which a solemn gloom is apt to fill the mind naturally raises our veneration, and there is always somewhat of an austerity in majesty...' (*De re aed.*, VII, 12).

More interesting, however, is the description of the façade as 'modelled on those of ancient temples'. This is one of the best examples of the way in which a fifteenth-century humanist could see classical parallels that elude us, as it would hardly have occurred to anyone that the Pienza Cathedral façade was modelled on an ancient building except in the most general sense — it has a triangular pediment and there are some ill-proportioned columns, though Pius's phrase 'richly decorated with columns and arches' suggests that they were not structural. What he must have meant is surely that the façade is divided vertically by buttress-like strips at each end and between each pair of columns. If we regard these strips as having the function of columns — i.e. carrying the triangular pediment — then we have a tetrastyle temple front, since the height is equal to the width and four 'columns' support a pediment. This can be compared with contemporary works by Alberti — the Tempio Malatestiano or San Sebastiano — as well as with a genuine Roman temple such as Fortuna Virilis. This general air of antiquity can be seen in such contemporary buildings as the Triumphal Arch of Alfonso of Aragon at Naples (Plate 98), but it must not be confused with the true knowledge and understanding of basic principles displayed by men like Alberti, or Luciano Laurana, who was about to take over the design of the palace of Federigo da Montefeltro in Urbino.

This building demonstrates the complexity of the architectural situation in the years around the middle of the century in those circles which were open to the influence of Alberti's ideas. Urbino is a small city, high up in the mountains of the Marches, which was totally transformed by its greatest ruler, Federigo da Montefeltro, the most famous and successful *condottiere* of the age, Captain-General of the Papal forces, and, unlike most of his fellow-*condottieri*, devout, learned, and a model ruler. It is arguable that Urbino, between the birth of Bramante in 1444 and the birth of Raphael in 1483, was one of the most civilised places on earth.

The small principality was ruled by Federigo, first Count, and then, from 1474, Duke, and his wife, Battista Sforza. For nearly thirty years he was occupied with the building of a palace 'worthy of Us and of Our ancestors' as well as with the creation of the great Urbino Library (now in the Vatican), with its beautifully written

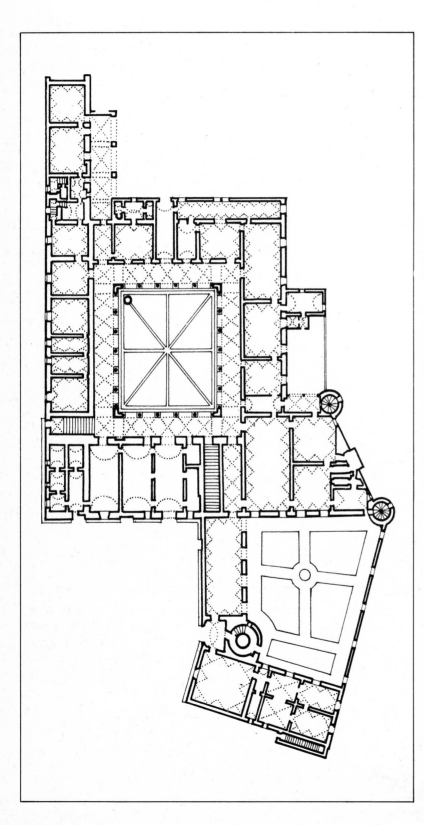

101. *Urbino, Palazzo Ducale, plan.*
102. *Luciano Laurana, Urbino, Palazzo Ducale, general view.*

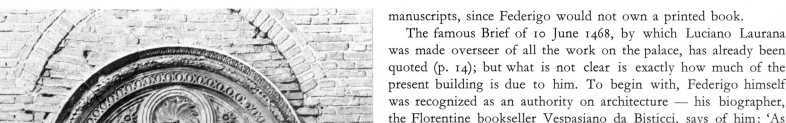

103. *Luciano Laurana, Urbino, Palazzo Ducale, window.*
104. *Luciano Laurana, Urbino, Palazzo Ducale, main entrance façade.*

105. *Luciano Laurana, Urbino, Palazzo Ducale, west ('Torricini') façade.* ▷

manuscripts, since Federigo would not own a printed book.

The famous Brief of 10 June 1468, by which Luciano Laurana was made overseer of all the work on the palace, has already been quoted (p. 14); but what is not clear is exactly how much of the present building is due to him. To begin with, Federigo himself was recognized as an authority on architecture — his biographer, the Florentine bookseller Vespasiano da Bisticci, says of him: 'As to architecture, it may be said that no one of his age, high or low, knew it so thoroughly. We may see in the buildings he constructed, the grand style and the due measurement and proportion, especially in his palace, which has no superior among the buildings of the time, none so well considered, or so full of fine things. Though he had his architects about him, he always first realized the design and then explained the proportions and all else; indeed, to hear him discourse it would seem that his chief talent lay in this art, so well he knew how to expound and carry out its principles.' In addition to this we know from Landino and others that he was friendly with Alberti as well as Piero della Francesca. Piero's *Flagellation* (Plate 99), originally in Urbino Cathedral, was almost certainly commissioned by Federigo, who also commissioned the double portrait of himself and his Duchess, Battista Sforza, as well as the great *Brera Madonna* (Plate 100), one of the most significant pictures of the fifteenth century.

The earliest parts of the palace were probably begun by Federigo before 1460, and the surviving parts — mainly the east façade — are in a style deriving from Florentine work of a few years earlier. Laurana was in Mantua in 1465, where he must have seen Alberti's San Sebastiano in building, and probably arrived in Urbino in 1465-66. He was appointed *Capomaestro* in 1468 and left for Naples in 1472. After this date, Francesco di Giorgio, the Sienese painter, architect, and military engineer, seems to have taken charge. In August 1474, Federigo was made Duke and those inscriptions in the palace which read FE. DUX are presumed to date from after 1474: nevertheless, there are some (e.g. in the loggie of the tower façade) which have been altered from F. C. (*Fredericus Comes*), so this method of dating must be treated with caution (Plates 105, 111).

Francesco di Giorgio's is the style which ought to be associated with the post-1474 work, but as there are at least three styles discernible in the palace, it is not easy to identify Laurana's, especially since so little is known of his career outside Urbino. He was a Dalmatian, perhaps from Lovrana or La Vrana, and he may have been related to the sculptor Francesco Laurana, who worked on the triumphal arch in Naples (Plate 98), which bears a marked resemblance to the west façade at Urbino, with its triple loggie between two towers (*I Torricini*). As this was begun before 1474, it is probably Laurana's work. Just before going to Urbino, in 1465, Laurana was

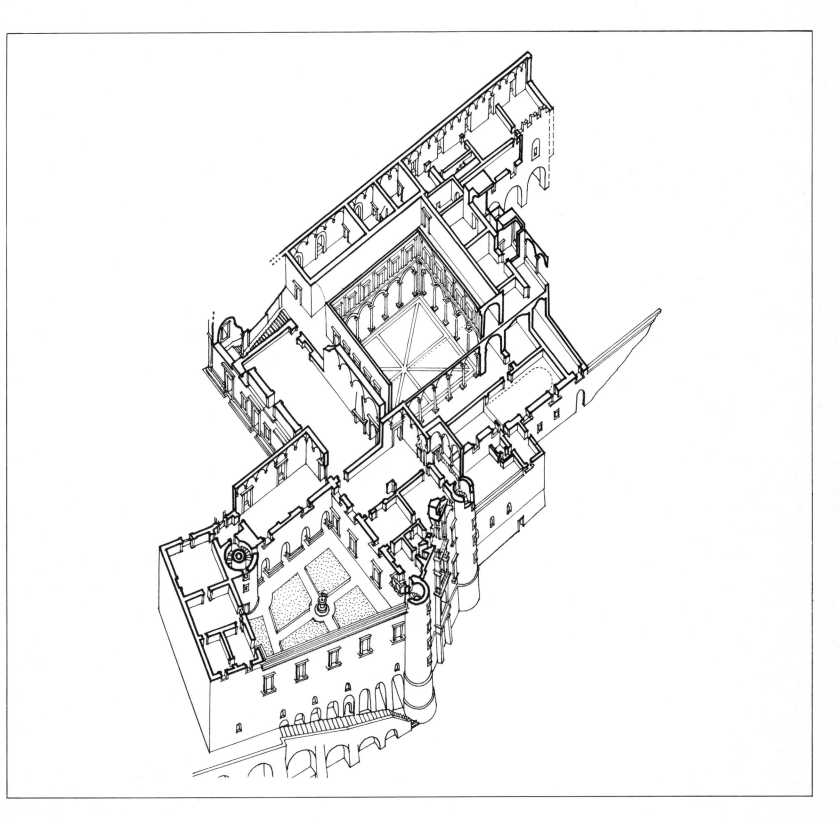

114. Cortona, Santa Maria del Calcinaio, plan.
115. Francesco di Giorgio, Cortona, Santa Maria del Calcinaio, interior of dome.
116. Francesco di Giorgio, Cortona, Santa Maria del Calcinaio, exterior. ▷

in Pesaro, and the windows of the Palazzo Ducale there (Plate 112) are so like those in parts of the palace at Urbino that they have been attributed to him.

If the arch at Naples is compared with the west front at Urbino, evident similarities emerge; for example, the tower and arch composition, and, more specifically, the scroll motif which crowns the topmost loggia. Similar stylistic characteristics can be found, more developed, in the east façade and the great court (Plates 103, 105, 106). In short, it is likely that the two most interesting and significant parts of the palace — the entrance façade and the court — were designed by Laurana, or perhaps designed by him on instructions from the Duke, aided by Alberti and perhaps also Piero. There is a close resemblance between the beautiful Composite capital of the column in Piero's *Annunciation* fresco at Arezzo (Plate 113) and those on the ground floor of the court at Urbino: the significance of this lies in the fact that the Piero fresco must be earlier than about 1460 and thus preceded the Urbino court. Apart from some consoles in the Palazzo Rucellai (Plate 67) these are the earliest examples of the use of the Composite Order in the fifteenth century, once more pointing to a close link between Alberti, Piero, and Laurana.

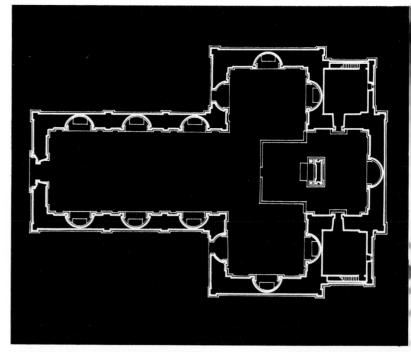

The Urbino court is important in the development of the type for two reasons. Firstly, it overcomes the difficulty experienced by Michelozzo with the angles of the courtyard of the Medici palace. At Urbino, the angles are formed by a large L-shaped pier with a half-column attached to each of the narrow end faces. Tall pilasters run up the outer faces of the piers and carry an entablature above the level of the arcade. This is visually more satisfactory than Michelozzo's single column, and it also looks back to the entablature carried on pilasters which Brunelleschi introduced over the arcade of the Innocenti (Plate 5). The second way in which the Urbino court improves on the Medici one is in the arrangement of the entablature, in which the architrave, frieze, and cornice are properly related to each other, with the frieze used to carry a long inscription cut in particularly fine Roman letters. Even in a detail such as this, the spirit of classical antiquity is recaptured better in Urbino than anywhere else. The upper storey (originally there were only two storeys) is treated in relation to the arcade below it, quite differently from the uneasy fenestration of Michelozzo's court. It is true that Laurana still sets his windows directly on the cornice, using it as a sill, but the proportion and arrangement of the openings have been carefully worked out. The big pilasters at the angles mean that the windows do not now come too close together, and each bay of the upper storey is marked off by its own pilaster and entablature corresponding to the arcade below. The top of the arch is half the total height of both storeys, while the arches themselves are 2:1 in height. This

is repeated in the rectangles of the windows, which are themselves as 1:2 in their surrounding bays. Since the columns and capitals of the ground floor equal the whole height of the upper storey, including the entablature, the proportional system is subtler than Michelozzo's and perhaps even than Brunelleschi's. The windows are also unusual in having a straight hood over sharply-profiled framing mouldings instead of the characteristic Florentine round heads (Plate 106).

The original Florentine type can be seen on the long eastern façade, where it is also clear that the relationship between void and solid has not been carefully considered. By comparison, the main entrance façade shows a maturer classicism, since in it the windows have pilasters at the sides, supporting a full entablature, the cornice of which serves as a hood to keep the rain off. Several of these windows have the FE. DUX inscription and may have been executed after Luciano had gone to Naples, but the proportions and detailing correspond so closely with the court that they can securely be attributed to the same architect. The façade is much damaged and was never completed, but enough exists to show that the original design was for a rusticated ground floor, with pilasters at the angles, pierced by three large doorways, and with three small windows in asymmetrical rhythm. Surprisingly, the *piano nobile* (perhaps also intended to be rusticated) carries four large windows so spaced that they do not coincide with the doorways on the ground floor. The rhythm of the four upper openings over three lower ones is thus irregular, although the overall effect is one of harmony and symmetry. Nothing like this can be found in contemporary Florence, although the proportions and details clearly point to Alberti and can be matched, in some respects, in the paintings of Piero della Francesca.

Francesco di Giorgio is believed to have built the small *cortile* of the palace at Gubbio, which is no more than a rather poor copy of the Urbino court. He was also strongly influenced by Alberti, since he composed a treatise on architecture and military engineering which depends equally on Alberti and on a translation of Vitruvius he owned. He had a great reputation, particularly as a military engineer, and was often consulted on problems of construction — he met Leonardo in Milan in this way — but his career is now shadowy. One of the few buildings which are certainly by him is the church of Santa Maria del Calcinaio, outside Cortona, which was commissioned in 1484. He made a model of it and building seems to have been completed shortly before he died in 1501-2.

Since this was practically his last work we may assume that it shows his fully developed style. Both exterior and interior (Plates 116, 117) confirm that he could hardly have been responsible for the court or the entrance façade at Urbino. The curious tabernacle

118. Urbino, San Bernardino, exterior.
119. Urbino, San Bernardino, interior towards the altar.
120. Urbino, San Bernardino, interior towards the entrance. ▷

windows with top-heavy triangular pediments (Plate 117), which are so marked a feature of Santa Maria del Calcinaio, bear so strong a resemblance to certain doorways at Urbino (Plate 109) that it seems plausible to ascribe these parts of the palace to him during the period from about 1475, the earliest date for his arrival in Urbino, to 1480, when the palace was virtually complete. Francesco also worked as a painter and sculptor, and his documented altarpiece of 1475, in the Accademia, Siena, shows him to have been a rather old-fashioned painter, confirming the view that he was less likely than Laurana to have been the innovator at Urbino.

One other building has been attributed to him — the church of San Bernardino, outside Urbino. This has always been a problematic building, but it has recently been suggested that it may be the work of Francesco di Giorgio at a late stage in his career, perhaps after 1482 but before 1491. In that case, the building is exactly contemporary with the church at Cortona, and it is true that there are points in common between the treatment of the exterior in both (Plates 116, 118). Nevertheless, the interior at Cortona (Plate 117), by comparison with such Brunelleschi-derived churches as Santa Maria delle Carceri at Prato (see p. 106 and Plate 147), is remarkably ill proportioned: the octagonal dome is set uncomfortably upon squinches, the internal division by two superimposed pilasters is clumsy — especially in the relationship of the taller lower Order to the upper one, which ought to be taller — and, finally and characteristically, the squat square window over the altar has a heavy and projecting triangular pediment equal in height to the window itself. The interior of San Bernardino is superior in every way. The crossing and apsis should be compared with Piero's *Brera Altarpiece,* formerly in the church, rather than with the Calcinaio (Plates 100, 117), and the undeniably Bramantesque feeling for space and volumes makes one understand how the church can be attributed to him. At the same time, the fully-modelled columns in the angles are perhaps closer to the Laurana tradition, and any attribution to Bramante has to overcome the difficulty that San Bernardino does not resemble his known work in Milan, with the exception of the treatment of the dome from outside, where it appears as a cylinder with a sloping roof and tall lantern. The cylindrical form is the one used by Brunelleschi, but the tall lantern gives it the air of a Milanese *tiburio,* so that it is close to Bramante's San Satiro, and even closer to the mingling of Florentine and Milanese traditions in the Cappella Portinari attributed to Michelozzo (Plate 160).

In the 1460s and early 70s the most significant architectural advances were being made in Urbino and in Mantua, where Alberti's two churches were rising. Florence had lost the lead for the time being, but a certain amount of interesting work was being done,

94

121. Rome, Palazzo Venezia, with the Palazzetto, in a nineteenth-century drawing.
122. Rome, Palazzo Venezia, general view.
123. Donato Bramante, Rome, Vatican, Benediction Loggia and Cortile di San Damaso, drawing by Maerten van Heemskerck (Vienna, Graphische Sammlung Albertina).

124. Rome, Palazzo Venezia, detail of façade. ▷

again directly inspired by Alberti, in Rome.

The Palazzo Venezia was begun by Cardinal Barbo in 1455 and was considerably enlarged when, in 1464, he was elected Pope and took the name Paul II. Externally, the building is a simple three-storey block (Plate 122), with a basement below and crenellations above. The very long façade is hardly articulated, and the windows are not evenly spaced. The 'Palazzetto', moved in 1911 from its original position, shows a much greater feeling for the effect of voids and solids in the double row of arcades, which are strongly reminiscent of Alberti's treatment of the side walls of the Tempio Malatestiano (Plate 73), intended to house the tombs of the *Illustri* of the Malatesta court.

The Palazzetto contained a court with a double arcade, but the main block of the palace had a second court (Plate 125), which, though never completed, is a new stage in the evolution of the type begun by Michelozzo at the Palazzo Medici and continued at Urbino. Just as Michelozzo made a rectangular court by bending Brunelleschi's Innocenti façade, so the architect of the Palazzo Venezia court took his basic design from the Colosseum (only a few hundred yards away) and adapted it to a rectangle. There was, however, an intermediate stage represented by the Benediction Loggia of Old St. Peter's. This (Plate 123) is now known to us only from drawings and engravings, but it was very probably by Alberti, and was certainly begun before the reign of Paul II. It resembled the loggia outside San Marco, which was part of the Palazzo Venezia, except that it had four bays on each of its three storeys. It derives from the Colosseum, like Alberti's Rucellai Palace, but it was closer to the prototype, since it had arched openings, with the arches supported on piers, and the piers were faced with attached columns carrying the entablatures.

The connection between it and the court of the Palazzo Venezia is evident, and in both cases the columns are set on higher bases than those of the Colosseum. For this reason, the loggia of the Palazzo Venezia has been given to Alberti, although it is known that work was being done there between 1469 and 1474 by Giuliano da Sangallo, then at the beginning of his career.

Alberti's influence can be traced in other architects active in Rome in the second half of the fifteenth century, such as Giacomo da Pietrasanta or Meo del Caprino da Settignano, whose names have been associated with the façades of the Augustinian churches of Santa Maria del Popolo (*c.* 1472-77), and Sant'Agostino (1479-83) (Plates 126, 127), as well as Meo's façade (1491-98) of the Cathedral in Turin. The plans of Santa Maria and Sant'Agostino are modernized versions of the Cistercian type introduced into Italy in the twelfth century, so that, like the prototype Santa Maria Novella in Florence, they add Albertian façades to a much older plan form. The façade of Santa

Maria del Popolo shows a close adherence to the basic scheme of Santa Maria Novella, with a well-considered relationship between the two Orders and between the voids and solids: the curved scroll-forms with garlands which mask the ends of the aisles, are, however, seventeenth-century additions (old drawings show there was nothing there originally). The façade of Sant'Agostino, which is known to be by Giacomo da Pietrasanta, shows that the scrolls invented by Alberti were adopted, and probably something similar was intended for Santa Maria. At Sant'Agostino, however, the proportions are less felicitous, and the architect has mindlessly included the attic separating the two storeys which Alberti had invented to solve the problem of matching his Orders (Plate 127).

A more interesting and more difficult problem is posed by the enormous Palazzo della Cancelleria, which incorporates the church of San Lorenzo in Damaso. It was built by Cardinal Raffaelle Riario, whose name is carved on the façade, but subsequently it became the Papal Chancery, from which it takes its present title. The palace is the work of a man profoundly influenced by Alberti, and the quality is so much higher than contemporary work in Rome that Vasari and others have attributed it, in whole or in part, to Bramante. It is, however, beyond doubt that the palace was begun before 1489, but long after the death of Alberti; the Cardinal was already living in the palace by the mid-nineties, and Bramante did not arrive in Rome until 1499. The palace is so huge that it was not completed until about 1517, so it is sometimes suggested that Bramante took part in the design and built the court after his arrival in Rome.

An additional complication is caused by the Palazzo Corneto-Giraud-Torlonia, which is a revised version of the Cancelleria, built at a time when Bramante was certainly in Rome (Plates 129, 131). (Another less successful version is the Palazzo Raimondo-Bellomi in Cremona, said to have been begun as early as 1496 by Eliseo Raimondo himself.) There is such stylistic continuity between the two façades that they are probably the work of one man, and Vasari attributes both to Bramante. He does, however, choose his words carefully, saying: 'He found himself, with other excellent architects, resolving [the problems of] a large part of the palace... which was executed by a certain Antonio Montecavallo. The palace of Cardinal Adriano Corneto was also his design...' It is now sometimes suggested that Antonio Montecavallo is to be identified with the Lombard sculptor Andrea Bregno, who had an extensive practice as a maker of tombs — including that of Cardinal Pietro Riario (c. 1474-77) — but who cannot otherwise be identified as an architect, and certainly cannot claim to be as distinguished a designer as the Master of the Cancelleria and Corneto-Giraud-Torlonia palaces.

Whoever that master was, he had learned much from Alberti and was able to extend what he had learned to create something new. To begin with, the Cancelleria has an enormously long façade — 295 feet — and is proportionately high, so that it was necessary to break up this great mass of masonry both vertically and horizontally. The prototype was Alberti's rusticated Palazzo Rucellai in Florence, which in turn derived from the Colosseum. The Palazzo Rucellai, however, would be about 90 feet wide if completed, and is 65 feet high; it was thus possible to break up the façade into three horizontal layers by means of the entablatures, and to obtain all the relief necessary in the vertical plane by single pilasters. The door-bays are slightly wider than the others, but that is all. In the Cancelleria the same horizontal division is retained, but the great length is diversified by the introduction of salients at each end. In fact, however, the projection of these bays is so small (something like two feet) that it has no effect on the huge bulk of masonry. The main entrance to the palace and to the church of San Lorenzo, which are the other focal points, are both sixteenth-century additions, and we do not know the original architect's intentions.

The great novelty, and one which was significant for the future, was the introduction of triplet bays — the alternating bay scheme which Alberti had used at Sant'Andrea in Mantua — as a means of articulating the façade. Where the bays of the Palazzo Rucellai are all the same width, except for a slight increase in the third and sixth, and are separated by single pilasters, giving a rhythm which may be expressed as *A.A'.A...*, the bay-scheme of the Cancelleria depends on a rhythm of pilaster, blank wall, pilaster, window, pilaster — or *a.A.a...* The salient at each end consists of one of these triplets, showing that they are intended to be read as a unit. This is more easily seen in elevations than in photographs (Plates 128, 129).

Looked at in detail, the bays show another interesting advance over Alberti's prototype, since the proportions of the whole bay are now more fully worked out. The space between each pair of pilasters is related to the space containing the window in the irrational proportion known as the Golden Section, and this same proportion can be traced in many other parts: for example, in the relationship of height to width in the windows of the top floor, and in other voids and solids. The three storeys are also more carefully differentiated than in the Palazzo Rucellai. The ground floor is set upon a high podium, which has small windows to light the basement. The ground floor itself has a rusticated surface with evenly channelled blocks and rather small round-headed windows in a rectangular frame, but without an Order. The *piano nobile* has an apron of smooth walling as a base both for the windows and for the cou-

125. Giuliano da Sangallo, Rome, Palazzo Venezia, court.

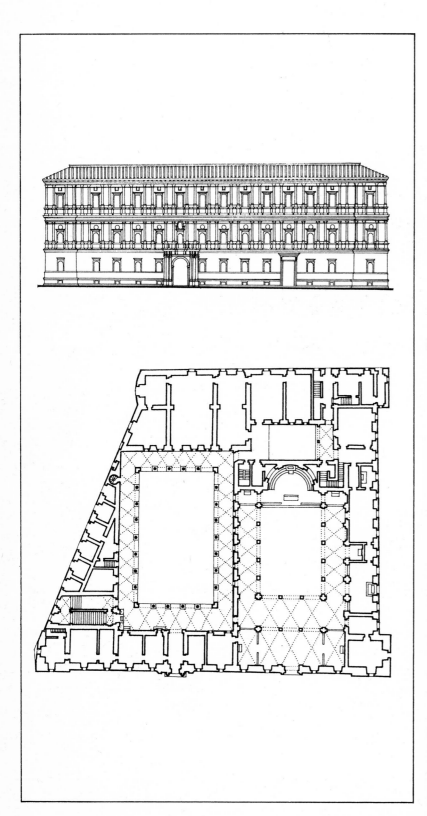

pled pilasters, while the windows of this floor are emphasized by having round-headed openings set in a rectangular frame with a projecting cornice, the spandrels of which are decorated with *paterae*. This is a form used in ancient buildings, but it is used here for the first time in the fifteenth century. The top floor is similar to the *piano nobile*, except that the windows are smaller and rectangular, and have small round-headed attic windows above them. The rustication is even all the way up the façade, and no attempt was made to give a more massive air to the ground floor by heavier rustication like that of contemporary Florentine palaces.

The *cortile* of the Cancelleria has very marked affinities with the court at Urbino, particularly if one looks only at the two upper storeys (Plates 106, 130). The use of an L-shaped angle pier is common to both, and differs from the Colosseum type of arcade introduced at the Palazzo Venezia. This fact alone gives some substance to the attribution of the court to Bramante, which is also possible on chronological grounds. In order to accept the ascription one must, however, be satisfied that the Cancelleria court fits into the sequence of Bramante's work exemplified by the cloisters in Milan (*c.* 1497) and the cloister at Santa Maria della Pace, completed by 1504 (Plate 193).

The period between Alberti and Bramante is spanned by the career of Giuliano da Sangallo, eldest of the three famous members of the family. He was born in Florence, but was working in Rome by about 1465, according to the date inscribed in the collection of his drawings of Roman and other antiquities known as the *Codex Barberini* (Plate 278). He would thus have known the work of Alberti in both cities, and his own works in Tuscany, at Prato, and at Poggio a Caiano, as well as in Florence, all show a combination of Albertian and Brunelleschian ideas; yet these are sufficiently old-fashioned in expression that when, at the beginning of the sixteenth century, he hoped to become the architect of the New St. Peter's, he found himself superseded by Bramante, in spite of his own long-standing connection with Julius II. In 1515, just before he died, he made designs for the façade of San Lorenzo in Florence and was again superseded by Michelangelo, although these designs show considerable awareness of the change in taste. One of them (Uffizi A. 280: Plate 133) probably even reflects an early project by Bramante for St. Peter's.

Giuliano's major works are the church at Prato, the Sacristy of Santo Spirito, the Villa Medici at Poggio a Caiano, near Florence, and his Florentine palaces. The villa at Poggio seems to be the earliest attempt to recreate a classical *villa suburbana* based on the texts of Pliny and Vitruvius although the plan, with its great central barrel-vaulted hall, derives from a study of Roman thermae. His plan for a royal palace in Naples, in the *Codex Barberini*,

131. *Rome, Palazzo Corneto-Giraud-Torlonia, façade.*
132. *Rome, Palazzo Corneto-Giraud-Torlonia, detail of façade.*
133. *Giuliano da Sangallo, Florence, San Lorenzo, project for façade,*
A. 280 (Florence, Uffizi, Gabinetto dei Disegni e Stampe). ▷

is even closer to Roman baths. The portico at Poggio a Caiano ante-dates Palladio's use of the motif as a distinguishing feature of his villas by some seventy years (Plate 136).

In Florence itself, the tradition of palace design was still overwhelmingly influenced by Michelozzo's Palazzo Medici, and Alberti's introduction of the Orders at the Palazzo Rucellai remained unique, although Giuliano himself followed this example in the palace he built at Savona for the future Julius II. In Florence he built the Palazzo Gondi from about 1490 (Plate 138), which is hardly more than a prettified version of the Palazzo Medici, with the rustication smoothed out and laid in even courses in a manner exactly parallel to the soft, smooth forms of sculptors like Mino da Fiesole or Benedetto da Maiano. Giuliano also made the wooden model — one of the few to have been preserved — for the Palazzo Strozzi, the largest and grandest of all the descendants of the Palazzo Medici (Plate 55). It is not certain that Giuliano himself actually designed the palace, since he may have been employed as a skilled woodworker to make the model, and Benedetto da Maiano may have been the actual designer. The position is also complicated by the fact that Il Cronaca certainly acted as executant for part of the palace and designed the great cornice about 1500, finishing it in 1504. Another case of a possible collaboration between Giuliano da Sangallo and Cronaca is provided by the vestibule and sacristy of Santo Spirito in Florence, which the *operai* decided to build from Sangallo's model in 1489. Here, in adding to one of Brunelleschi's most famous buildings, and one that was regarded as a norm of good architecture, both architects felt constrained to follow Brunelleschian forms, but the sacristy (Plate 142) is clearly modelled on the Florentine Baptistery (which was presumably still thought of as antique), although the vestibule, in which Cronaca was concerned, is far closer to Roman forms and is reminiscent of the *romanitas* of the hall at Poggio a Caiano.

At the same moment, Giuliano was engaged on the choir of Santa Chiara in Florence (1493-1500), now preserved in the Victoria and Albert Museum, London (Plate 144). Here the decorative feeling is much more evident, especially in the frieze with its coloured della Robbia terracottas, and it is this aspect of the Brunelleschian heritage which, crossed with the Albertian Greek cross plan-form, gave rise to the church of Santa Maria delle Carceri at Prato. In his *Diary* for July 1484, Luca Landucci noted censoriously that a great veneration of an image of the Virgin had begun at Prato: 'People rushing there from all the country round. It worked miracles like that at Bibbona, so that building was begun and great expense incurred'.

The Greek cross shape of the church was thus due to its function, since the connection between centrally-planned churches and *martyria* goes back to Early Christian times, and, only a few years

quello disegnio
pe mdapoe 49 1946

134. *Giusto Utens, Poggio a Caiano, Florence, Villa Medici (Florence, Museo Topografico).*
135. *Poggio a Caiano, Florence, Villa Medici, plan.*

136. *Giuliano da Sangallo, Poggio a Caiano, Florence, Villa Medici, façade.*
137. *Giuliano da Sangallo, Poggio a Caiano, Florence, Villa Medici, ceiling of salone.*

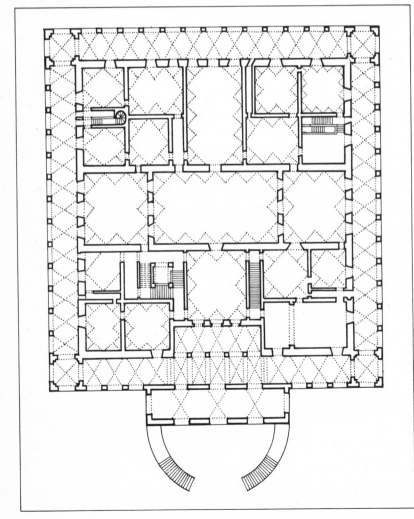

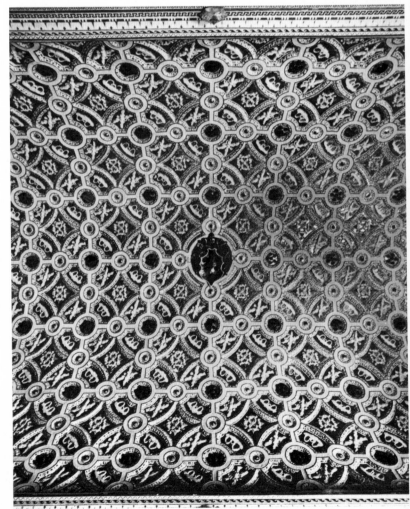

141. *Giuliano da Sangallo, Florence, Santo Spirito, Sacristy, dome.*
142. *Giuliano da Sangallo, Florence, Santo Spirito, interior of Sacristy.*
143. *Giuliano da Sangallo, Florence, Santo Spirito, Sacristy, ceiling of vestibule.*

144. *Giuliano da Sangallo, Florence, Santa Chiara, chapel (now in London, Victoria and Albert Museum).*

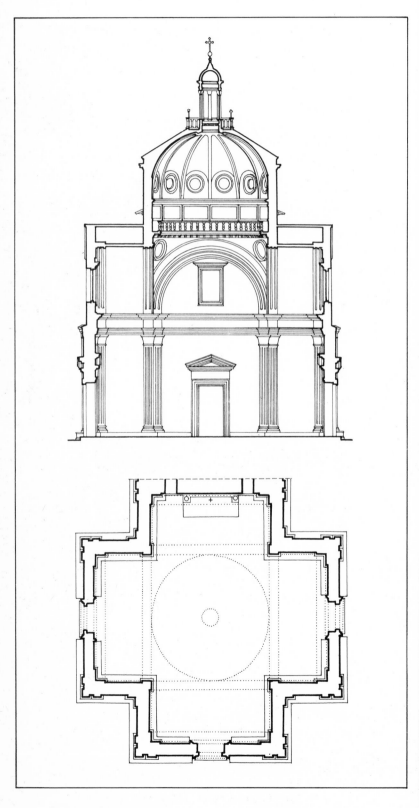

later, it was to be the underlying inspiration of the New St. Peter's, at least in the Greek cross form planned by Bramante. Once the form had been decided for Santa Maria delle Carceri, Giuliano adapted the prototypes provided by Brunelleschi and Alberti: the latter's San Sebastiano at Mantua for the Greek cross shape, and the former's Old Sacristy and Pazzi Chapel, and, perhaps, his Angeli as well, as examples for the detailed treatment. In the interior, Giuliano managed to solve the problem of the pilasters at the inner corners, which Brunelleschi had never really been able to deal with — his pilasters seem to disappear into the wall-surface, even in the Pazzi Chapel. Nevertheless, Giuliano found himself without a Brunelleschian precedent for the exterior, with its right angles and comparatively high walls, ill-suited to a single Order and not really high enough for two (Plate 146). Like Francesco di Giorgio in the exactly contemporary church at Cortona, he produced an unhappy compromise. This, more than anything else, shows that Giuliano was the last exponent of a tradition going back to Brunelleschi, not the innovator the age was awaiting.

During the first half of the fifteenth century, Milanese architecture remained fundamentally Gothic, in spite of the fact that Brunelleschi is known to have visited the city (where, indeed, the *porticus* at San Lorenzo, dating from Roman times, may have inspired his own colonnade at the Pazzi Chapel). In the second half of the century the situation changed dramatically. From 1450 to 1499, the Sforzas ruled the city, and for most of the time there was an alliance between Milan and Florence. More important, a number of Florentine artists worked in the city and introduced the new ideas — Michelozzo, Filarete, and above all Leonardo. As far as we can now reconstruct it, the work of Michelozzo and Filarete was profoundly modified by local conditions, so that it would have seemed unrecognizably Gothic to their Florentine contemporaries: on the other hand, the architecture of Milan itself may have influenced all three Florentines in an unexpected way. During the later sixteenth and seventeenth centuries, a great deal of Milan was rebuilt, but we know that in the fifteenth century there were still a great many remains of late Roman and early medieval buildings in the city — indeed, the first archaeological survey was made in the fifteenth century. Very few of these buildings have survived, but the greatest of them all, the Basilica of San Lorenzo, though rebuilt since Bramante knew it, survives in a form which enables us to guess at the crucial role it played in the development of Renaissance architecture. Another, much later, example is the tiny chapel of San Satiro, recast by Bramante himself, but dating in its original form from the late ninth century. Both these churches are representative of the large number of centrally-planned buildings still extant in the fifteenth century. The impetus given to the theory of the centrally-planned church in the fifteenth and sixteenth centuries can be directly linked with the presence in Milan of Filarete, and from about 1482, of Leonardo da Vinci.

Filarete, whose shortcomings as an artist should not be allowed to obscure his importance as a propagandist, arrived in the city in 1451 on the recommendation of Piero de' Medici, but his most important work was done during his second stay, in the sixties, when he was designing the Ca' Grande or Ospedale Maggiore, a project to unite all the numerous charitable foundations and hospitals into one great complex in the centre of the city, to provide a unified medical service. Architecturally, the project did not match the revolutionary nature of the undertaking. Filarete was working there between 1461 and 1465, at the same time as he was composing his treatise, and there is a drawing in it which shows his strength and his weakness. The hospital was designed as a centrally-planned complex of courts and buildings, with a tall centrally-planned chapel at the focal point (Plates 155, 158). Both the drawings and

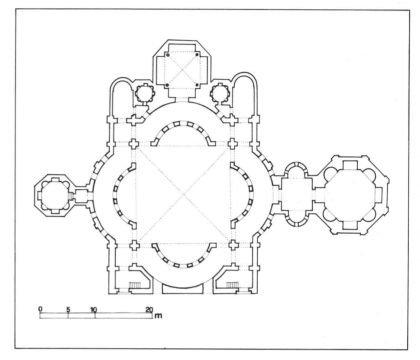

149. *Milan, San Lorenzo, plan.*
150. *Milan, San Lorenzo, exterior.*

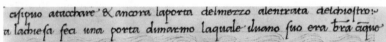

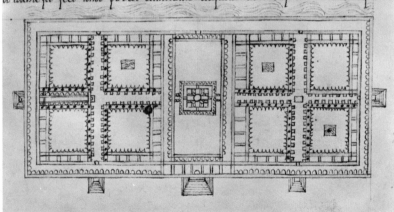

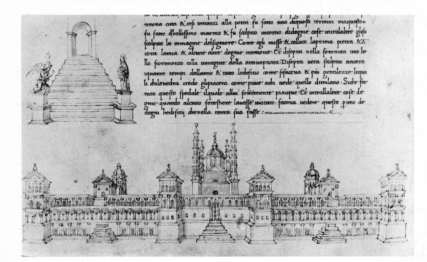

the surviving parts of the building (Plates 155, 156, 158, 159) show very clearly how great a gap there was between Filarete's theory and the practice he was able to impose upon Milanese contractors; and the fierce denunciations in his treatise of the barbarous modern manner — by which he meant Gothic, as opposed to ancient — show the strength of the opposition to the antique style of Brunelleschi which he hoped to introduce into Milan.

His treatise also contains a drawing (Plate 154) of the Medici Bank in Milan, designed by Michelozzo, of which only the doorway survives (Plate 157). Although it was designed by a Florentine for a Florentine, the Milanese craftsmen have modified the classical purity of the design almost beyond recognition, and for this reason the attribution of the Portinari Chapel of Sant'Eustorgio to Michelozzo must remain problematical. The chapel was built about 1462 by the manager of the Milanese branch of the Medici Bank and is distantly reminiscent of the Florentine Baptistery as well as Brunelleschi's Old Sacristy, although once more the execution by local craftsmen shows a lack of understanding of classical formal ideals. Another Florentine, Benedetto Ferrini, also worked as an architect in Milan and on the Certosa at Pavia, and some elements of his style can be seen in the Portinari Chapel.

More characteristic of the taste for elaborate decoration is the Colleoni Chapel at Bergamo, designed by Amadeo in the early 1470s and resembling some of the minaret-like structures in Filarete's drawings. A similar combination of a basically simple and classical form with exuberant decoration is to be found on a larger scale at the Certosa of Pavia (Plates 163, 164), and there are still echoes of it in the model for Pavia Cathedral, with which Bramante himself was concerned (Plate 167).

Neither Filarete nor even Michelozzo was an architect of sufficient stature to impose his style or his conception of the antique on the Lombard capital. The most significant date in the conversion of Milan is probably 1481-82, when Bramante was certainly in the city. He was to remain there until the French invasion of 1499, and within a few months, he was to be joined by Leonardo. For some seventeen years, the Sforzas employed the two greatest artists of the age.

When Bramante arrived in Milan, he was a fully-formed artist. He was born at Fermignano, near Urbino, apparently in 1444, but he is first documented in 1477 when he painted the *Chilon* fresco in Bergamo. Probably at this time he began his first architectural work, at Santa Maria presso San Satiro in Milan, and he was certainly in the city in 1481, when he made the drawing for an engraving of *Ruins and Figures* — *stampam unam cum hedifitiis et figuris* (Plate 169). According to his contemporary Sabba Castiglione,

he was trained as a painter by Piero della Francesca and Mantegna, and this is confirmed by his frescoes in the Brera. Another engraving which bears his name (Plate 170), although not always accepted as his, seems to support this, since it is close in spirit to the *Ideal City* at Urbino (Plate 87). It is also very close to the *tarsie* of the doors of some of the state rooms — notably that of the door leading to the Sala delle Udienze (Plate 111), which dates from after 1474, since it is inscribed FE. DUX. If Bramante came from Urbino and was trained by Piero it would not be unreasonable to connect him with the building of the palace, perhaps in the period between 1472, when Laurana went to Naples, and 1475, the earliest date for the arrival of Francesco di Giorgio. Bramante would have been about thirty then, so it is not surprising that some parts of the palace, particularly the Cappella del Perdono, have been attributed to him: unfortunately, the style of the 1481 engraving and that of his work at San Satiro agree between themselves, but do not correspond to anything at Urbino. The Cappella del Perdono has often been compared with the imaginary church in Piero's *Brera Altarpiece* (Plate 100), which dates from the same time, the middle seventies.

His work at San Satiro is naturally less fantastic than the engraving, with its romantic Early Christian overtones, but it still shows his debt to his training as a painter, since the main effect is due to perspective — the choir is little more than a few feet deep, for the street outside limited its construction (Plate 172). Effective as it is, it is not architecture in the sense in which Bramante himself was to understand it only a few years later, and the change from a pictorial, scenographic outlook to one which is not only classical but organic as well is probably due more to Leonardo than to any other single factor. Leonardo's *Last Supper* in the refectory of Santa Maria delle Grazie is often regarded as the first work of the High Renaissance, and it was painted while Bramante was building the tribune of the church on a Brunelleschian scheme (Plates 176-82). The maturity of Bramante as an architect — the cloisters of Sant'Ambrogio (Plates 190, 191) — is contemporary with Leonardo's work at the Grazie, and this is not a coincidence.

Leonardo's own interest in architecture must have been due to Bramante, since he began to write a treatise on the subject, the draft for which (MS B) is now in Paris, and the greater part of the work seems to have been done in the 1480s and 90s, at a time when he was in daily contact at the Sforza court with Bramante, whose own style was developing to maturity over nearly twenty years. The elements which make up Bramante's style can therefore be defined as the Brunelleschian tradition in its modified form exemplified by Filarete and Michelozzo; the classical inheritance of

the late Roman buildings surviving in Milan, as exemplified by San Lorenzo; the studies made by Leonardo in connection with the problems of the centrally-planned building; and, above all, the technique of drawing evolved by Leonardo primarily for use in his anatomical studies, but which could be applied to the architectural forms studied in MS B.

It seems that Leonardo's interest in anatomy, which he pursued with zeal during his years in Milan, may well have inspired him to begin a treatise on this subject in the 1480s. A series of celebrated drawings at Windsor Castle, from Anatomical Notebook B, belong to the late eighties, one of the drawings being dated 2 April 1489, although other parts of the notebook are now dated as late as 1506-9. In his miscellaneous notes, Leonardo makes it clear that the purpose of his treatise was to make the study of anatomy both simpler and much more accurate than it had ever been before, and, in what is perhaps a draft Introduction to his treatise, he describes the drawings he intends to make as, in some respects, superior to an actual dissection: 'by my plan you will become acquainted with every part and every whole by means of a demonstration of each part from three different aspects... just as though you had the very member in your hand and went on turning it from side to side until you had a full understanding of all that you desire to know.

'And so in like manner, there will be placed before you three or four demonstrations of each member under different aspects... And you who say that it is better to look at an anatomical demonstration than to see these drawings, you would be right, if it were possible to observe all the details shown in these drawings in a single figure, in which, with all your ability, you will not see nor acquire a knowledge of more than some few veins...' (Leonardo, *Quaderni d'Anatomia*, I).

From this passage and from the numerous drawings of this type (Plate 184) it may be seen that Leonardo was not only a better anatomist than any of his contemporaries, but that he had evolved a new means of technical drawing which could convey the maximum amount of information about a three-dimensional object, and the application of this technique to architecture was equally revolutionary. In the great majority of the drawings in the architectural treatise, Leonardo presents a plan and a bird's-eye view, so arranged that the maximum amount of information about a building, both externally and internally, is given in two drawings, neither of which is a representational drawing in the ordinary sense of the word. The plan as a diagram was something that had been known for centuries, but architectural draughtsmanship before Leonardo does not seem to have advanced beyond the plan and elevation, of the type familiar from the sketchbook of Villard de Honnecourt. Leo-

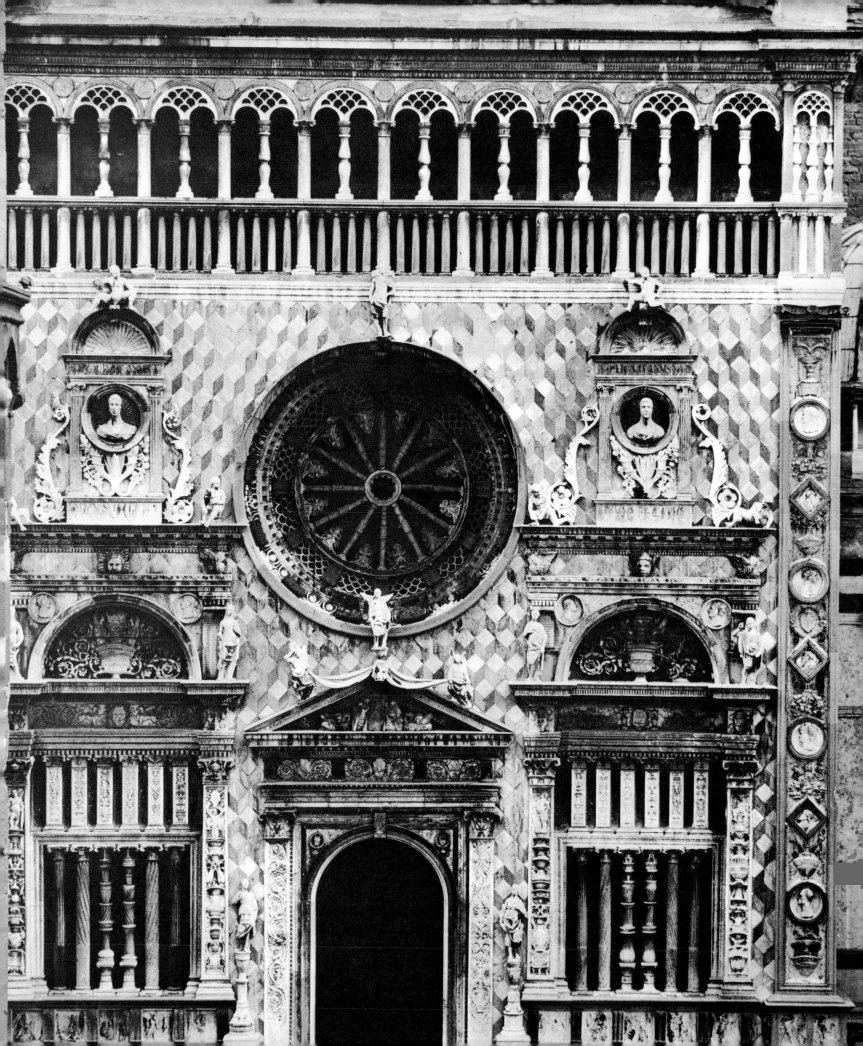

163. *Giovanni Amadeo, Pavia, Certosa, façade.*
164. *Giovanni Amadeo, Pavia, Certosa, small cloister.*
165. *Giovanni Amadeo, Pavia, Cathedral, interior.*

166. *Giovanni Amadeo, Pavia, Cathedral, interior of dome.*
167. *Pavia, Cathedral, wooden model (Pavia, Museo del Castello).*
168. *Luciano Laurana, Urbino, Palazzo Ducale, Sala degli Angeli, detail of tarsia of a door.*

169. *Bernardo Prevedari, engraving of Ideal Architecture after a Bramante drawing, 1481, detail (Milan, Perego di Cremnago Collection).*
170. *Donato Bramante, Street Scene, engraving, c. 1500 (London, British Museum).*

171. *Milan, Santa Maria presso San Satiro, section and plan.*

172. *Donato Bramante, Milan, Santa Maria presso San Satiro, exterior.*
173. *Donato Bramante, Milan, Santa Maria presso San Satiro, detail of interior.*
174. *Donato Bramante, Milan, Santa Maria presso San Satiro, detail of choir.* ▷

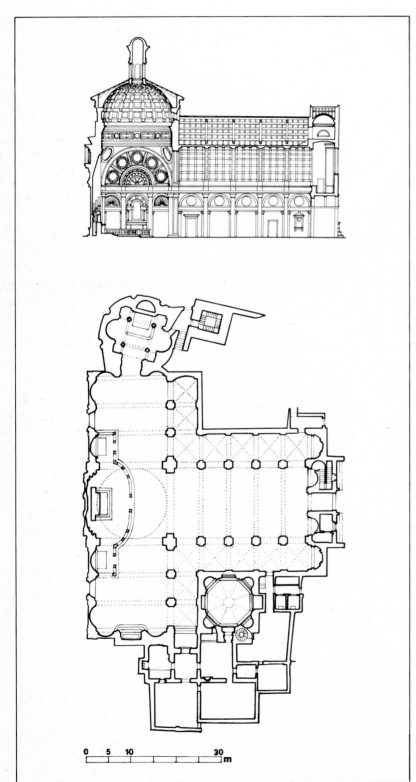

175. *Milan, Santa Maria delle Grazie, section and plan.*

176. *Donato Bramante, Milan, Santa Maria delle Grazie, exterior.*
177. *Donato Bramante, Milan, Santa Maria delle Grazie, detail of exterior of apse.* ▷

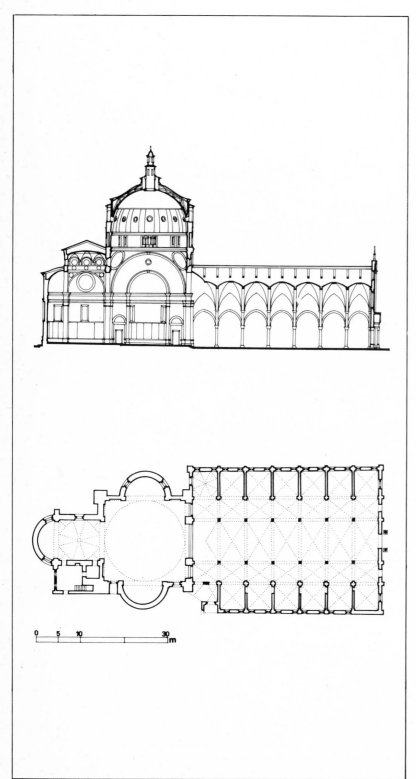

183. *Leonardo, architectural drawing from the Codex Atlanticus, f. 271v (Milan, Biblioteca Ambrosiana).*
184. *Leonardo, anatomical drawing (Windsor Castle, Royal Library).*

185. *Leonardo, architectural drawing, ms B.N. 2037, f. 3v (Paris, Institut de France).*
186. *Leonardo, architectural drawing, ms B, f. 19r (Paris, Institut de France).*

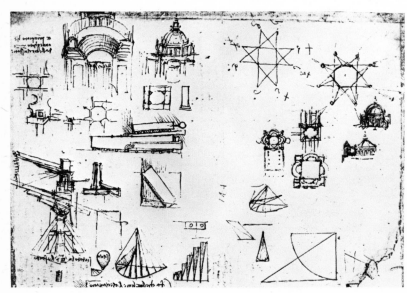

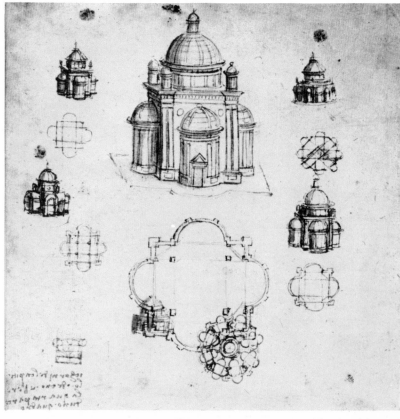

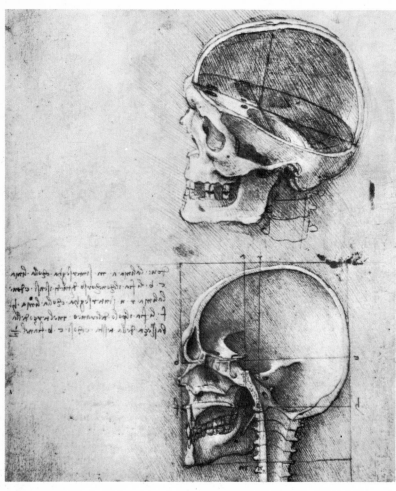

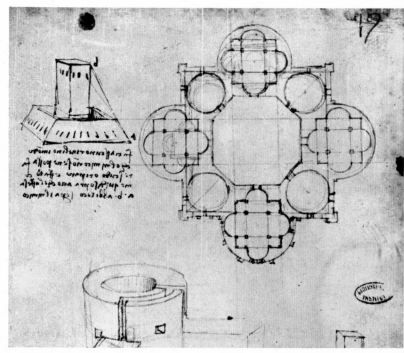

187. Leonardo, architectural drawing, ms B, f. 22r (Paris, Institut de France).

188. Leonardo, architectural drawing from the Codex Atlanticus, f. 362v (Milan, Biblioteca Ambrosiana).

189. Leonardo, architectural drawing, ms B, f. 25v (Paris, Institut de France).

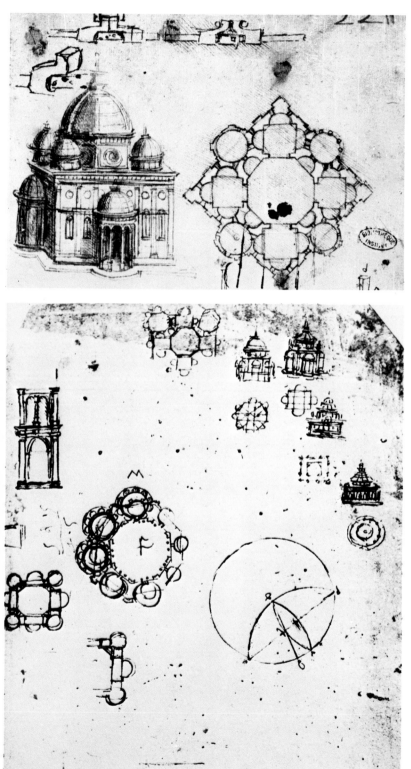

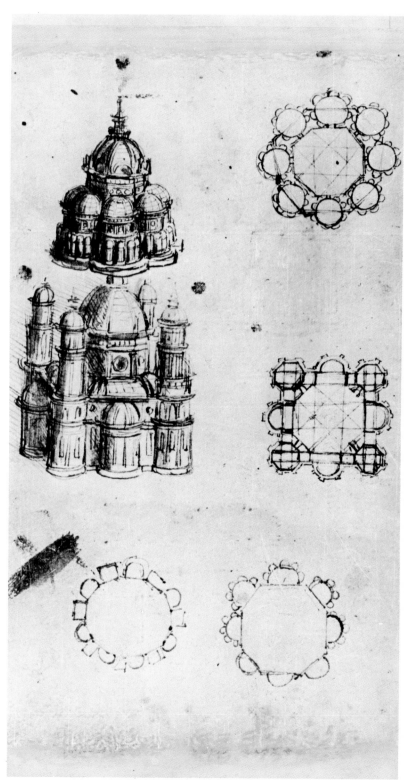

nardo's invention of the bird's-eye view type of drawing, which is neither a completely conventional type of representation like a plan, nor a normal ground-level view, opened a whole field of new possibilities, and it is probable that Bramante inspired him to invent this new form of draughtsmanship in connection with architecture. In turn, Bramante's whole cast of thought would have been influenced by the new technique of visualization.

Another significant factor in the drawings in MS B is that they are almost exclusively centrally-planned churches with multiple domes, giving a rather Byzantine appearance. Leonardo's interest in architecture does not seem to have extended to an interest in ancient Roman forms, and in this, as in so much else, he differed from most of his contemporaries. He did, however, know the text of Vitruvius, since there are several references in his notebooks — but they refer to problems of engineering, and, in particular, human proportion, rather than to architecture. The famous drawing in Venice was his solution to the problem of human proportion, and this certainly had an indirect bearing on architectural theory.

The presence in Milan of so many late Roman buildings provided a repertory of forms quite different from those in Leonardo's drawings, but common ground occurs in such centrally-planned buildings as San Lorenzo. There are other drawings in MS B which seem to provide a link between Leonardo and Bramante; for example, the drawing (MS B 19 *recto*: Plate 186) which looks very like San Satiro, or, prophetically, plans (Plates 185, 188) which look forward many years — in one case to St. Peter's and in the other still further ahead to a building only loosely connected with Bramante, Santa Maria della Consolazione at Todi (Plates 228-31).

For Leonardo the problems of architecture were either straightforward engineering problems, such as the *tiburio* of Milan Cathedral, or else a development in a functional sense of the forms implicit in a given mathematical plan: in neither case was he concerned with stylistic or aesthetic problems, or with the imitation of antique prototypes. This can be seen in MS B 22 *recto* and 25 *verso* (Plates 187, 189), where there are five plans, four of which are developed from a basic octagon. The two simplest — 25*v*, top and bottom — are octagons with identical openings on all sides, first experimented with as semicircles and then, in the other drawing, as full circles. The external elevation is worked out as a series of half-cylinders, each abutting against a larger one until a central core is reached. (The effect should be compared with the tribune of Bramante's Santa Maria delle Grazie; Plate 176.) Leonardo's church is crowned with a ribbed dome, partly Lombard and partly reminiscent of Florence Cathedral, but the actual forms of this structure show no awareness of any architecture later than Brunelleschi. The

interior of the building is developed exclusively in terms of the plan. There is no entrance; but, once inside the building, one would find oneself in a single, cylindrical, chapel space with small niches all round the walls, one of which presumably leads to the main, central, domed octagon, the transition from one spatial effect to the next being abrupt and effected by a narrow (and therefore low) doorway. The plan shows an exterior made up of half-cylinders separated by masonry angles corresponding to the angles of the octagon; from this one may conclude that the half-cylinders were covered by half-domes abutted against the very thick octagon core. From the inside, the chapels presumably gave the effect of having a complete hemisphere as a dome, but lit from one side only. The drawing is not clear, but it seems possible that the intention was to have complete domes, Byzantine in appearance, yet perhaps not unsympathetic to Lombard taste.

The other two plans abandon this problem and start a fresh train of thought. Here, in the central part of 25*v*, the basic octagon has every alternate side pierced by a large arch which leads into the half-circular chapel used in the previous designs, so that a Greek cross with rounded arms is superimposed on the octagon. The remaining four sides develop the fully-circular chapel shape, transforming it into a minor octagon, so that a true elevation would present the same sequence of half-cylinders. If the prototype for these designs was San Lorenzo, it is evident that Bramante and Leonardo were thinking on different lines, yet these and other drawings in MS B show that some of the formal problems which were to arise in connection with St. Peter's had been stated, if not solved, before Bramante left Milan, and long before Julius II was even elected Pope.

Yet Bramante's vision of the New St. Peter's was grander than these formal problems of geometry. He was concerned to build something that would replace the Constantinian Basilica on its own terms, something that would be charged with the same meaning — *Templi Petri instauracio* — and be in as pure a Latin: in other words, he desired an antique form as much as he desired a geometrical one. If we compare a drawing by Leonardo of an arcade (Plate 188) with Bramante's cloister at Sant'Ambrogio in Milan, built during the 1490s (Plate 191), it is evident that the amplitude and spaciousness of the cloister is due to calculated proportions, simplicity of form, and horizontal emphasis. These lessons could best be learned in the late fifteenth century from the study of antiquity combined with the search for Vitruvian proportion (which interested Leonardo as much as anyone else), yet the pupil of Piero della Francesca and Mantegna was equipped as no Florentine of his generation could have been. Before Bramante could design St.

Peter's anew, it was necessary that he should experience the classic art of Mantegna, Piero, and Laurana; the romantic antiquity of Lombard art of the fifteenth century, expressed in his own *Ruins*; the mechanical and cerebral architecture of Leonardo, something of which he expressed in the solid geometry of Santa Maria delle Grazie (Plates 176-182); and finally the Roman buildings that had come down from the age of Ambrose and Augustine. Even this had still to be consummated by intense study, structural and aesthetic, of the ruins of Rome itself before he was ready to attempt the grandest Roman building of all, the 'Pantheon over the vaults of the Temple of Peace'.

The Rome of Julius II began in 1500 when the future Pope, then still Cardinal Giuliano della Rovere, was living in exile to avoid Alexander VI Borgia. His own pontificate, from 1 November 1503 to 21 February 1513, can be equated with the brief duration of the High Renaissance, but the first works of the Roman Renaissance were created by Bramante in the years between his own arrival in Rome as a refugee from Milan in the winter of 1499-1500, and the election of Julius, who, more than any other single man, brought about the full flowering of the Renaissance by discerning the talents of Bramante, Raphael, and Michelangelo, and then driving them to the limits of even their marvellous capabilities.

Bramante was a comparatively old man — about fifty-six — when he arrived in Rome and found himself forced to seek new patrons. Fortunately for him, there was very little competition, since the only major architect with Roman experience and connections was Giuliano da Sangallo, who was probably a few years older than himself. It is difficult to imagine Giuliano as a serious rival to Bramante, yet he was in fact the architect to Cardinal della Rovere and might therefore reasonably have hoped for great commissions when the Cardinal became Pope. Hard as it was on Giuliano when he was dropped in favour of Bramante, posterity must endorse Julius's action, if only because Bramante had given proof in the years 1500-3 that he was capable of architecture of an imaginative grandeur far beyond Giuliano. When he arrived in Rome, so Vasari tells us, he lived on his savings while he made measured drawings of all the antiquities in Rome and the Campagna, as far south even as Naples, and including Tivoli and Hadrian's Villa. His studies were pursued *solo e cogitativo*, but they brought him to the attention of the Cardinal of Naples, who gave him the commission for the cloister of Santa Maria della Pace. There is every reason to believe this account, since a document of 1500 mentions Bramante, and the cloister bears an inscription in beautiful Roman letters, similar to those in the frieze at Urbino, with the name of Cardinal Carafa and the date 1504.

The Pace cloister is immediately comparable with the Doric cloister of Sant'Ambrogio in Milan, and both the differences and similarities make clear exactly what Bramante had learned from his meditations among the ruins of Rome, so much grander and more extensive than anything he had formerly been able to study in detail. It is possible that he had visited Rome before, but he had never had the opportunity to devote himself at length to the study of the antiquities, and, in any case, it is probable that his knowledge of Vitruvius, acquired in Milan, meant that he was not really prepared before 1500. What is common to both cloisters is the division into two storeys, with two openings on the upper floor

192. Donato Bramante, Rome, Santa Maria della Pace, engraving of the cloister (from Letarouilly).
193. Donato Bramante, Rome, Santa Maria della Pace, cloister.

194. *Donato Bramante, Rome, Tempietto of San Pietro in Montorio, wood-cut of section and elevation (from Palladio).*
195. *Donato Bramante, Rome, Tempietto of San Pietro in Montorio, wood-cut of plan (from Serlio).*

196. *Donato Bramante, Rome, Tempietto of San Pietro in Montorio, ex-terior.*
197. *Donato Bramante, Rome, Tempietto of San Pietro in Montorio, draw-ing attributed to Bramante (Florence, Uffizi, Gabinetto dei Disegni e Stampe).* ▷

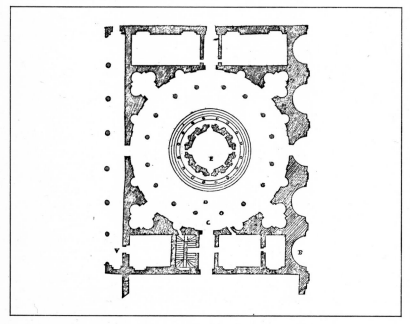

198. *Donato Bramante, Rome, Tempietto of San Pietro in Montorio, detail of frieze.*
199. *Rome, Temple of Vespasian, frieze (from an engraving by Giovanni Battista Piranesi).*
200. *Tivoli, Temple of Vesta, section (from Palladio).*

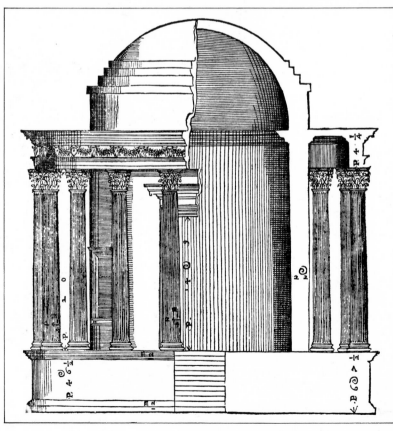

201. Cristoforo Caradosso, Rome, St. Peter's, Foundation Medal (London, British Museum).
202. Donato Bramante, Rome, St. Peter's, drawing of plan for first project (Florence, Uffizi, Gabinetto dei Disegni e Stampe).
203. Giuliano da Sangallo, Rome, St. Peter's, plan, A 8r (Florence, Uffizi, Gabinetto dei Disegni e Stampe).

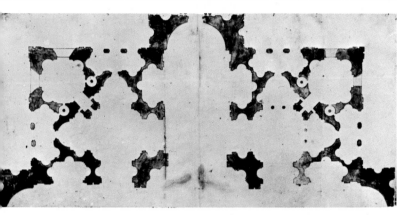

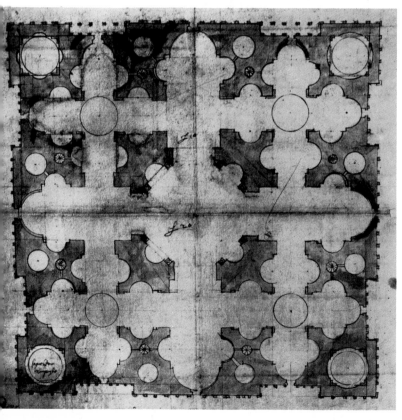

corresponding to each bay of the ground floor. There is an antique prototype for this division, the so-called Crypta Balbi in Rome, known from Giuliano da Sangallo's *Codex Barberini*, but now surviving only in very fragmentary form. Vasari criticizes the Pace cloister as 'not a work of perfect beauty', and this is often thought to refer to the proportions and the presence of a small column over the crown of the arches of the arcade. In the Milanese cloister this solid-over-void effect is less noticeable, since the upper storey is a continuous wall, articulated by pilasters and arches. The important point, in both cases, is the proportion of the lower to the upper storey and the consequent relationships of the sub-divisions. At Sant'Ambrogio the lower arches are very large and therefore the upper arches and pilasters are very small, so that the whole can be sustained on single columns, like Brunelleschi's Innocenti, without appearing top-heavy: the upper part is very similar to the Crypta Balbi, and the proportion of the upper pilasters to the actual columns of the ground floor is also similar — but Bramante has used arches rising from the columns instead of the Roman type of arcade with applied half-columns. The result is airiness and spaciousness at the expense of gravity. His Roman studies must have taught him, above all else, the dignity and weight of the best ancient architecture, and the fact that decorative elements must be minimized if these virtues are not to be lost.

At the Pace Bramante returned to the Crypta Balbi division into two almost equal storeys — the height to the top of the ground-floor arch being equal to the whole height of the upper floor — but this time he abandoned the upper arcades and substituted a rather complex arrangement with a pilaster over the ground floor pilaster (not a column) and a section of wall behind it. The wall is then made discontinuous, so that the centre of the bay can be filled by a colonnette, supporting the entablature and making a contrast, by its slender, cylindrical shape, with the bulky rectilinear forms of wall and pilaster.

At the same time as he was designing the cloister at Santa Maria della Pace, Bramante was engaged on an even more important work, the Tempietto of San Pietro in Montorio. This, although very small, is perhaps the norm by which to judge Bramante's architectural ideals and the whole concept of the High Renaissance in Rome as it was recognized in the sixteenth century by Serlio and Palladio. Serlio describes it as: 'made for the sole purpose of commemorating St. Peter the Apostle, on the spot where, it is said, he was crucified'. He includes it in his Third Book, along with St. Peter's, although the Book is headed *Delle Antichità*. Palladio, in 1570, is more explicit: 'Since Bramante was the first to bring to light the good and beautiful architecture that had been concealed since the

204. *Donato Bramante, Rome, St. Peter's, drawing of plan, A 20 (Florence, Uffizi, Gabinetto dei Disegni e Stampe).*

205. *Menicantonio de' Chiarellis, Rome, St. Peter's, elevation and section (Upperville, Virginia, Paul Mellon Collection).* ▷

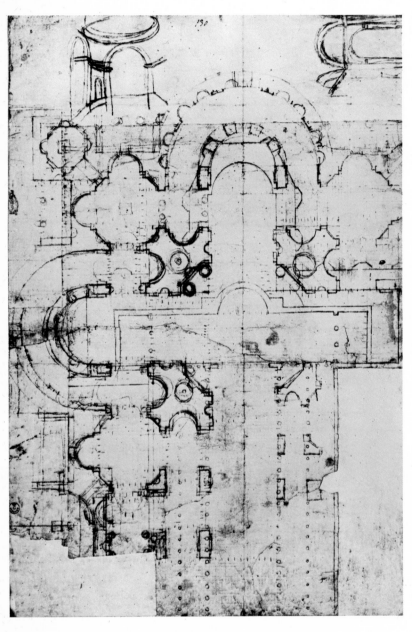

time of the Ancients, it seemed to me to be reasonable to include works by him among those by the ancients, and that is why I have put in this Book the following Temple, erected by him on the Janiculum; and because it was built to commemorate St. Peter the Apostle, who is said to have been crucified on this spot, it is called San Pietro in Montorio...' (*I Quattro Libri*, IV, XVII).

During the fifteenth century, the place of Peter's martyrdom, *inter duas metas*, came to be interpreted as halfway between the Obelisk of Nero and the Meta Romuli; that is, a spot on the top of the Janiculum, *in monte aureo sive janiculo*, later known as Montorio. The importance of this identification lies in the fact that the Tempietto was erected for the sole purpose of commemorating this spot, and an inscription with the date 1502 in the crypt confirms this. The date 1502 has usually been taken to refer to the completion of the Tempietto, but some recent writers have suggested that the style is more advanced than that of the Pace cloister, and, therefore, the date should be taken to mean no more than that of the decision to build, the actual construction being perhaps as late as about 1510. This seems to be going too far, since there is a close relationship between the form and function of the Tempietto and the rebuilding of St. Peter's, which was certainly in progress by the end of 1505.

The Tempietto was conceived from the beginning as a *martyrium*, and was therefore designed on a central plan, based on ancient peripteral temples. It is also one of the earliest examples of the consistent use of the Doric Order, which is significant because it conforms with the account given by Vitruvius of the relationship between the Order and the nature of the divinity to whom the temple is dedicated. Thus, Corinthian is suitable for Vesta — and Bramante used the Temple of Vesta at Tivoli as one of his sources — because she was a virgin goddess, while the Doric Order is suited to heroic male gods, such as Hercules or Mars. Hercules was often used in the Middle Ages as a symbol of Fortitude, so Doric would obviously be the Order suited to St. Peter. The choice was thus not a question of aesthetics, but, one might also say, of liturgy, and this search for classical formal equivalents for new iconographical requirements made the Tempietto a revolutionary building and an essential precursor of the rebuilding of St. Peter's.

In its present state the Tempietto has a dome which is not original, and it stands rather forlornly in a courtyard which seems too small for it (Plate 196). The original dome can be seen in the woodcuts of Serlio and Palladio (Plates 194, 195), and Serlio also reproduces Bramante's original design for the courtyard as a whole with a second colonnade encircling the Tempietto, and with four small centrally-planned chapels in each of the corners of the square

cant. 90. fa bisogn

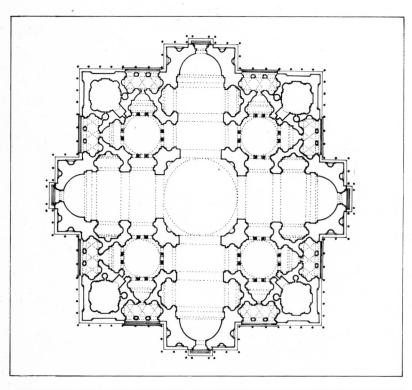

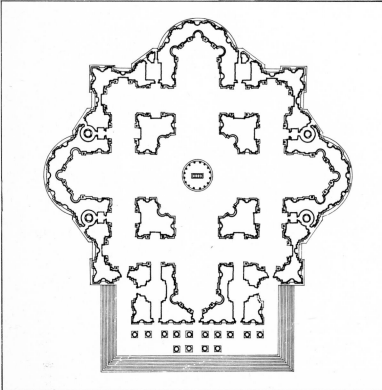

court. The total effect is significantly close to the basic design for New St. Peter's.

In the Uffizi there is a drawing (Plate 197) which has been regarded as Bramante's original design, although this seems stylistically improbable. It shows several variations from the executed building, by far the most important being the treatment of the frieze. In the drawing the frieze is a correct classical arrangement of alternating metopes and triglyphs, with a *patera* in each metope. The executed building is more interesting (Plate 198), because it carries a frieze of reliefs representing the liturgical instruments of the Mass and the symbols of St. Peter — the Keys, a chalice and paten, the incense-boat, the tabernacle — and there is a direct classical prototype for this in the frieze of the Temple of Vespasian (Plate 199), which has similar carvings of the instruments of the pagan cults. This deliberate symbolism makes it clear beyond doubt that Bramante designed the Tempietto as an essay in the recreation of an Early Christian prototypal *martyrium*, an ideal building of a type which must once have existed, rather than as a copy of any actual building. He knew examples such as Santa Costanza, and he was trying to create something with the same meaning but even more classical in form. In this connection, the frieze in the Prevedari engraving may be relevant.

If this interpretation is correct, then the essential fact about the Tempietto is not so much that it is a modern version of the round temple near the Tiber ('Hercules Victor'), or of Vesta, or of any other ancient prototype: it is that it provides the key to the understanding of Bramante's designs for New St. Peter's.

The designs prepared in the eight years (*c.* 1505-14) when Bramante was working on St. Peter's are extremely difficult to interpret. There are very few established facts, and the whole enterprise seems to have been run with a degree of inefficiency difficult to understand, except in terms of Julius's impatience to see results. We know that the foundation stone was laid on 18 April 1506, and we have two accounts by eye-witnesses of the ceremonies, which make it clear that much preliminary work must have been done before then. Julius II was elected on 1 November 1503, and in 1505 he was still concerned with his own tomb, to be built in Old St. Peter's; yet, by the late summer or autumn of 1505 the decision must have been taken (though never formally recorded) to pull down the Constantinian Basilica and to rebuild it anew. Bramante died on 11 April 1514, only fourteen months after Julius, and at his death there was confusion in the Fabbrica, since no definitive plan had been made. A whole series of alternative designs can be dated in the years after 1514.

208-211. *Maerten van Heemskerck, Rome, St. Peter's, in construction, four views (Berlin, Kupferstichkabinett).*

212. Raphael, *The School of Athens*, detail (Rome, Vatican).
213. Maerten van Heemskerck, *Rome, Vatican and St. Peter's, in construction* (Berlin, Kupferstichkabinett).

214. Baldassare Peruzzi, *Rome, St. Peter's, axonometric drawing, A 2* (Florence, Uffizi, Gabinetto dei Disegni e Stampe).
215. *Rome, St. Peter's, dome, section and elevation, as in Bramante's project* (from Serlio).

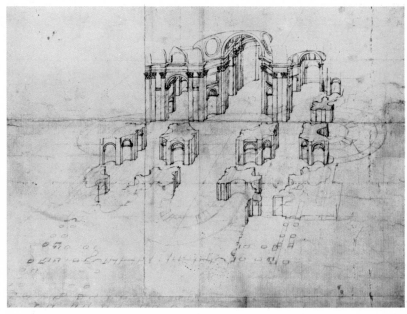

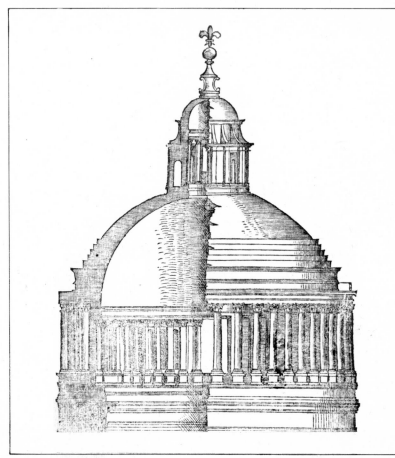

212. Raphael, *The School of Athens*, detail (Rome, Vatican).

216. *Rome, Santa Maria del Popolo, apse.*
217. *Donato Bramante, Rome, Sant'Eligio degli Orefici, interior of dome.*
218. *Donato Bramante, Rome, Sant'Eligio degli Orefici, exterior.*

216. *Rome, Santa Maria del Popolo, apse.*
217. *Donato Bramante, Rome, Sant'Eligio degli Orefici, interior of dome.*

218. *Donato Bramante, Rome, Sant'Eligio degli Orefici, exterior.*

219. *Raphael, Rome, Santa Maria del Popolo, Chigi Chapel, interior of dome.*
220. *Raphael, Rome, Santa Maria del Popolo, Chigi Chapel.*

What emerges is that during this first phase, 1505-14, New St. Peter's was never designed in the modern sense, beginning with a clear assessment of the needs and the means available to meet them. There was no formal contract by which a definitive design was prepared and the old building demolished to make way for the new. Rather, in a way curiously reminiscent of the Sistine Ceiling, the building grew under the hands of Bramante and Julius. It seems very probable that they deliberately avoided a formal decision to pull down Old St. Peter's, which, although by then in a very dilapidated state, was still usable and was hallowed by twelve hundred years of history, reaching back to the time of Constantine himself. In various letters and Briefs (including one of 6 January 1506 to Henry VII of England), Julius is careful to explain that the old basilica is on the point of collapse, and that it really is necessary to take drastic action.

A medal by Caradosso (Plate 201), cast in 1506 and buried under the foundation stone on 18 April, is the key to the whole philosophy of the new building. This medal must have been made early in 1506 and therefore represents the design in an early stage: it, and the plan on parchment (Uffizi A 1) are the only two pieces of evidence that can be securely associated with Bramante and with the project at this early date. At this time, the project was not concerned with the amount of accommodation, the number of chapels and altars, or similar questions; essentially, it was to evolve a building to fulfil three ideological requirements. Firstly, it had to be colossal in order to be a suitable successor to the Constantinian Basilica; secondly, like the Tempietto, it had to be a symbol of the Petrine Primacy and of the antiquity of the church in Rome; and, thirdly, arising from these needs, it had to be expressed in purely classical forms — in, as it were, modern antique. All of these aims and aspirations are expressed in the one phrase used on the Foundation Medal: *Templi Petri Instauracio*. The choice of the word *instauracio* is fundamental. It is a public statement of the intention to recreate St. Peter's afresh, not to destroy it. In pagan Rome the word *instaurare* had a sacral meaning: when a sacrifice was incorrectly performed, it was necessary for the priest to repeat it from the beginning and the technical word for this was *instauratio*. The idea of renewal, almost of rebirth, was retained in the Vulgate, for example in the Book of Kings: 'Vocavitque rex Joas Joiadam pontificem et sacerdotes, dicens eis: Quare sartatecta non instauratis templi?...' (*Lib. Regum*, IV, 12, 7. Authorised Version: II *Kings*, 12, 7: 'Then King Jehoash called for Jehoiada the priest, and the other priests, and said unto them, Why repair ye not the breaches of the house?...'); or, perhaps even more appositely, in the Epistles of St. Paul, as in *Romans*, 13, 9: 'et si quod est

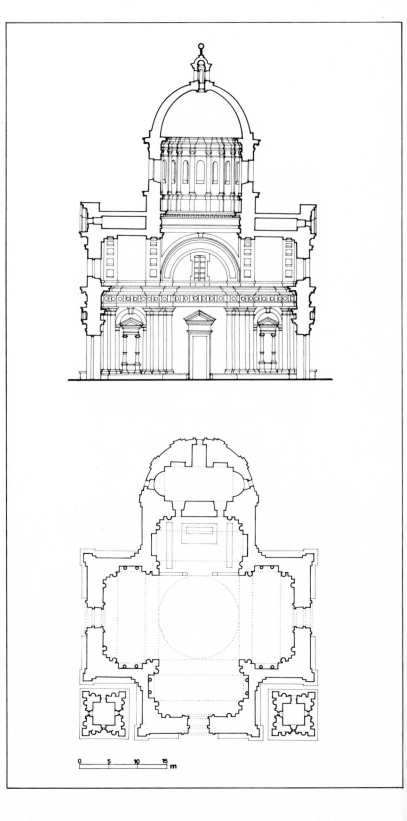

223. *Antonio da Sangallo the Elder, Montepulciano, San Biagio, detail of dome and campanile.*
224. *Antonio da Sangallo the Elder, Montepulciano, San Biagio, interior.*
225. *Antonio da Sangallo the Elder, Montepulciano, San Biagio, pendentive of dome.*

aliud mandatum, in hoc verbo instauratur: Diliges proximum tuum...'
(A.V.: and if there be any other commandment, it is briefly com-
prehended in this saying, Thou shalt love thy neighbour...), or in
Ephesians, 1, 10: 'in dispensatione plenitudinis temporum, instaurare
omnia in Christo...' (A.V.: in the dispensation of the fullness of
times he might gather together in one all things in Christ...) and
the same idea was present to the writer of the Collect for the Feast
of the Kingship of Christ (instituted in 1925) when he used the
phrase *omnia instaurare voluisti*.

Like the old basilica, the new one was erected over the Tomb
of the Apostle, and was therefore a *martyrium*. The celebrated
story, told by Egidius of Viterbo, of Julius's explosion of wrath at
the mere idea of moving the tomb, shows the importance of the
martyrium, but, again like Old St. Peter's, the new basilica had to
be a combination of a *martyrium* with a shape capacious enough
for the enormous crowds present at the greater ceremonies: this
question of accommodation was the cause of the ultimate adoption
of the Latin cross plan in the seventeenth century.

Old St. Peter's was not the only combination of *martyrium* and
basilica, rare though it is. Two other examples, also founded by
Constantine, were the Holy Sepulchre and the Church of the Nativ-
ity, both in the Holy Land. In the early sixteenth century both of
these, as well as the greatest monument of the Eastern Church,
Santa Sophia in Constantinople, were in the hands of the infidel.
The New St. Peter's had, therefore, to act as a symbol for them all,
and not merely as a monument to the pontificate of Julius II. This
'political' conception probably did not arise at the beginning, but
it may well have evolved over the years, in the same way as Bramante's formal solutions to the problems certainly evolved, even
though we have almost no evidence for their chronological sequence.

The Parchment Plan is attested as Bramante's by an inscription
on the back in the hand of Antonio da Sangallo the Younger, who
worked as an assistant in the Fabbrica. Nevertheless, it is only a
half plan (Plate 204), although it is usually reproduced in the form
of a complete Greek cross building (Plate 206). Since the Foundation
Medal cannot be explicit but seems to represent a centrally-planned
building, it is very likely that the original 1505 design was of this
form. Strong confirmation of this is supplied by a number of copies and adaptations, such as the one by Giuliano da Sangallo (Uffizi A 8r: Plate 203). It should be observed, as an indication of the
fluidity of the design, that the Parchment Plan does not coincide
exactly with the elevation of the medal. Another problem raised by
the Foundation Medal is that of the campanile flanking the entrance.
It seems most likely, in view of all the evidence, including the
fresh light thrown by the sketchbook of Menicantonio de Chia-

rellis (Paul Mellon Collection: Plate 205), that Bramante intended
only two campanili, marking the principal entrance, while the corresponding spaces at the other side were to be domed.

While the design was still being discussed in this way, work was
proceeding on the actual building, with results of the greatest significance for the future. When the ceremony of 18 April 1506 took
place, it determined the position of one of the great piers intended
to support the dome, and the founding of a second pier followed
very rapidly: thus, the central space, over the tomb, was defined
by Bramante, and, because the distance between the piers would
affect their height, he also circumscribed the general layout of the
whole design. Even in Bramante's time it was necessary to enlarge
the piers, as it was soon obvious that the thickness of those in the
Parchment Plan would be insufficient to support a dome of the
magnitude implied by the width between the centres of the piers.
In fact, the piers were thickened by Antonio da Sangallo and again
by Michelangelo, whose redesign (Plate 207) of the plan took account
of the statical problem which Bramante seems hardly to have
grasped, since the scale of the undertaking was so much greater
than anything in his experience or that of the masons he employed.
A drawing in the Uffizi (A 20: Plate 204), which must come from
the Fabbrica, shows the evolution of the piers and their relative
positions.

Bramante also succeeded in fixing the general arrangement of the
coffered arches supporting the dome. There is a series of drawings
by the Dutch artist Maerten van Heemskerck, who was in Italy
between 1532 and 1535, which, although made twenty years after
Bramante's death, are still the best evidence available for the state
of St. Peter's in the early sixteenth century. From Heemskerck's
drawings (Plates 208-11) we can see what Bramante's temporary
shrine, built to protect the Tomb of St. Peter, looked like, as well
as glean information about the crossing arches and the shell half-
dome in the choir. This detail, reminiscent of Santa Maria delle Grazie
and San Satiro, can also be seen in the apse of Santa Maria del Popolo in Rome (Plate 216), together with the Pantheon-type coffering
designed by Bramante as an experiment for the crossing of St. Peter's.
This work was paid for in 1509, the year in which *The School of
Athens* (Plate 212) was painted, and the architecture in the fresco is
traditionally attributed to Bramante; certainly, if one takes it in
conjunction with the drawings by Heemskerck and the actual work
executed at Santa Maria del Popolo, one can get an impression of
what Bramante intended for St. Peter's. The elevation of the dome,
preserved by Serlio (Plate 215), completes the impression of the Pantheon-like conception, and it is relevant that the Pantheon itself had
been made into a *martyrium*, Santa Maria ad Martyres.

226. *Antonio da Sangallo the Younger, Rome, St. Peter's, wooden model,
detail of façade with towers (Rome, Musei Vaticani).*

227. *Todi, Santa Maria della Consolazione, plan.*
228. *Todi, Santa Maria della Consolazione, exterior.*

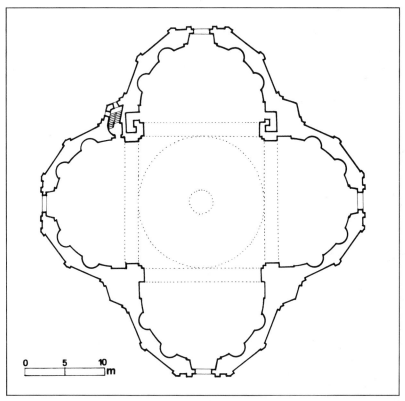

229-231. *Todi, Santa Maria della Consolazione, views of the interior.*

160

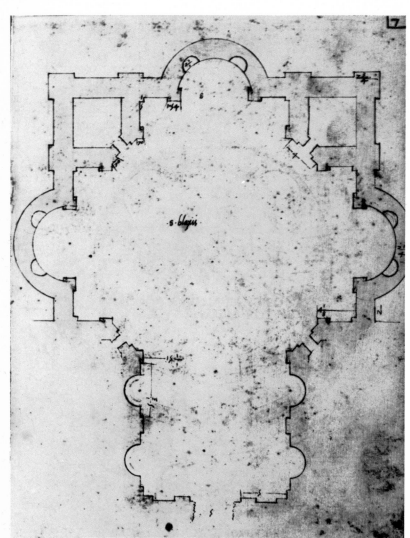

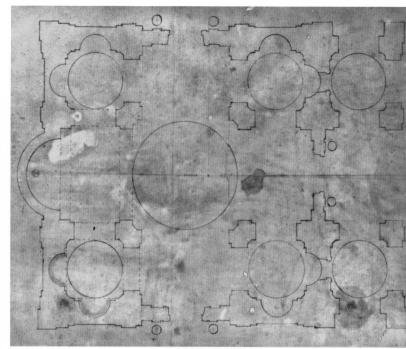

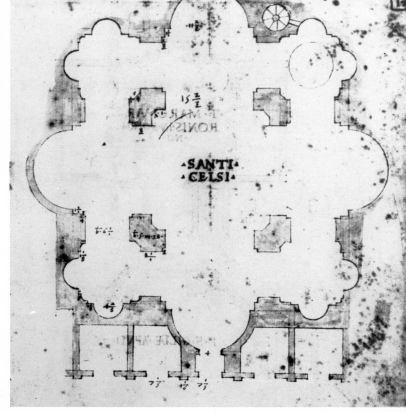

232. *Rome, San Biagio alla Pagnotta, plan (from Codex Coner, London, Sir John Soane's Museum).*

233. *Antonio da Sangallo the Younger, Rome, Santi Giuliano e Celso, plan, A 4037 (Florence, Uffizi, Gabinetto dei Disegni e Stampe).*

234. *Rome, Santi Giuliano e Celso, plan (from Codex Coner, London, Sir John Soane's Museum).*

Serlio also says that Bramante left an unfinished model — 'I not only leave the fabric unfinished, but even the model was left unfinished in several parts...' — and there is an explicit reference to a wooden model in the *De rebus antiquis... basilicae Sancti Petri* written by Onofrius Panvinius about 1566-72: 'Then Bramante, having made a wooden model of the new temple... and having left even the wooden model unfinished...'

At Bramante's death there were two main projects for the basilica — a Greek cross, derived from the Parchment Plan but modified to allow for greater strength, and a Latin cross type, with the Parchment Plan design added to a nave, rather in the way the tribune had been added to the nave of Santa Maria delle Grazie. There can be no doubt that the Parchment Plan, if it could have been built, would have had a beauty unlike anything ever seen before, largely because of the pure geometrical harmony of the plan and of the way in which the small Greek crosses would have built up to the climax of the dome, with space flowing freely around and between the points of support. The proportion of these solids to the total space would have been too small, and this was the reason why it was never put into execution.

The spatial disadvantages of the long plan are obvious, and the loss of perfect bi-axial symmetry would have been felt as grievous, but there is no doubt that the Latin cross is far more practical when it is necessary to accommodate many thousands of people and to organize great processions. (Confirmation can be found in the way in which Wren was forced to abandon a Greek cross plan for St. Paul's). A drawing, by Bramante's assistant, draughtsman, and successor, Baldassare Peruzzi, shows an ingenious compromise (Uffizi A 2: Plate 214), with the Greek cross modified and given a directional emphasis by the addition of a narthex on the entrance side. (In Maderno's present building something of this can still be seen.)

Part of the confusion arising at Bramante's death was undoubtedly due to the experiments made with all these forms, either by Bramante himself or by others directly inspired by him. The Greek cross experiments include some of the masterpieces of Italian architecture — Sant'Eligio degli Orefici in Rome, San Biagio at Montepulciano, Santa Maria della Consolazione at Todi, and the designs for Santi Giuliano e Celso in Rome, now entirely rebuilt.

Sant'Eligio (Plates 217,218) is one of the most austerely beautiful realizations of the harmony obtainable from a simple hemisphere supported on the arms of a Greek cross. It was probably designed by Bramante, perhaps about 1509, and Raphael's name has often been associated with it. It was finished by Peruzzi or his son after the deaths of both Bramante and Raphael, but the purity of the shapes makes it reasonable to think of it as an experiment by Bram-

237. *Giovanantonio Dosio, Rome, Vatican, Cortile del Belvedere, drawing (Florence, Uffizi, Gabinetto dei Disegni e Stampe).*
238, 239. *Sebastiano Serlio, Rome, Vatican, Cortile del Belvedere, drawings.*

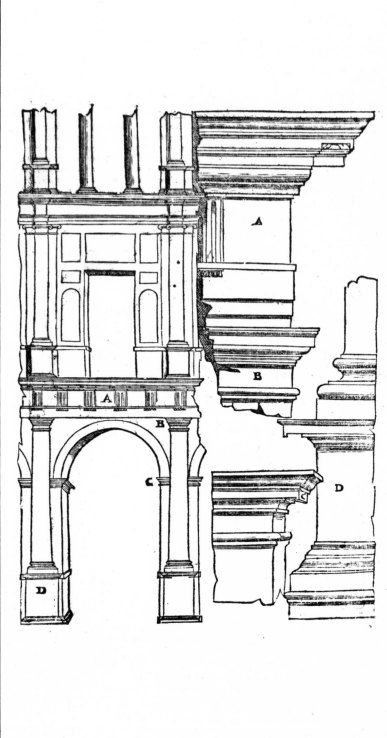

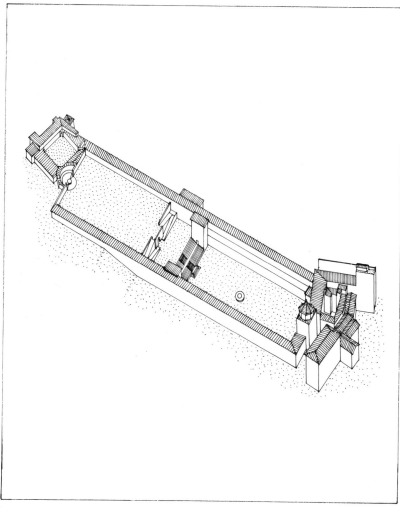

ante, perhaps with Raphael already in mind as his successor at St. Peter's. There is a close likeness to *The School of Athens* (Plate 212), and, just as Raphael developed towards a stronger chiaroscuro and a more dramatic characterization in frescoes like the *Heliodorus* or the *Mass of Bolsena*, so in architecture he developed a taste for greater richness and ornament, as is shown by his Cappella Chigi in Santa Maria del Popolo, completed in 1516 (Plates 219, 220), as well as by his statement on ancient architecture in which he criticizes Bramante's austerity by implication.

The pilgrimage church of San Biagio, just outside Montepulciano, was designed by Antonio da Sangallo the Elder, the brother of Giuliano and uncle of Antonio the Younger, and built between 1518 and 1545 (Plates 222-25). The close relationship to St. Peter's is evident in the campanili flanking the dome, as well as in the Greek cross plan, here modified to give the directional emphasis that Bramante needed at St. Peter's. A comparison between the campanili of St. Peter's as drawn by Menicantonio, the campanili at Montepulciano, and those in the model made by Antonio da Sangallo the Younger some twenty years later when he became *Capomaestro* at St. Peter's, shows the constant thread of a Doric monumentality, first established by Bramante at the Tempietto (Plates 194-98). Perhaps the most striking proof of the intervention of Bramante, and of the overwhelming influence he had on the men in his immediate circle is afforded by a comparison between Antonio the Elder's San Biagio and his brother's similar *martyrium* at Prato (Plates 146, 223). Such a comparison defines the difference between the Early and the High Renaissance.

The church at Todi is even simpler in form, since the square has only four semicircular apses and there is nothing to distract the eye from the soaring dome. The plan is almost identical with a drawing in Leonardo's MS B (Plate 186), and it is usually thought that the idea is Bramante's (or perhaps Leonardo's), although it is known that the execution is due to the otherwise almost unknown Cola da Caprarola, with Peruzzi intervening and with the dome not completed until the seventeenth century. Bramante's own design for the church of Santi Giuliano e Celso in Rome is known to us from drawings, including two variant plans, one in the *Codex Coner* in London (Plate 234), and one by Antonio da Sangallo the Younger (Uffizi A 4037: Plate 233), both of which show a direct connection with St. Peter's.

The experiments with a Greek cross extended on one side can be seen in the Sangallo version of Santi Giuliano e Celso as well as in Peruzzi's drawing (Plate 300), and there can be no doubt that Bramante had a Latin cross plan for St. Peter's constantly in mind, although he probably intended a directional central plan rather than

165

242. *Donato Bramante, Rome, Vatican, Loggie of Raphael, interior.*

243. *Donato Bramante, Rome, House of Raphael (engraving by Lafréry).*
244. *Donato Bramante, Rome, House of Raphael, drawing attributed to Palladio (London, Royal Institute of British Architects).*

he very long nave of the true Latin cross designs prepared by his immediate successors, Fra Giocondo and Raphael (Plate 301). Apart from being ugly, neither seems to take account of the huge scale, and Bramante's own version, in his design for San Biagio alla Pagnotta in Rome, known from drawings such as the plan in the Codex Coner (Plate 232), shows his constant struggle to preserve the dominance of the dome which was the essence of his conception of a *memoria*.

Sangallo's model for St. Peter's (Plates 226, 235, 236) has always been disliked since the day when Michelangelo referred to it as a pasture for oxen, yet he did at least try to combine Bramante-like campanili with a great dome, and his solution of the Greek-Latin cross difficulty was to add a vestibule to a Greek cross, in the way that Bramante had already indicated as a possible solution. It is a measure of Bramante's greatness that even a skilled and conscientious architect (as Sangallo was) was unable to follow his ideas and totally unable to grasp the cyclopean scale of his basilica. Bramante's feeling for the grandiose is demonstrated by other schemes such as the Belvedere and the Cortile di San Damaso, both in the Vatican Palace, or the projects for the Palazzo dei Tribunali, of which nothing now remains except a few blocks of rusticated masonry, of a size unequalled since the Pitti and Strozzi palaces, and some drawings and a medal of the project originally planned.

The Belvedere was a scheme, hundreds of feet in length, to unite the Vatican Palace with the Villa di Belvedere built by Innocent VIII on the top of a slight hill. It was based on a classical amphitheatre and consisted of a series of arcuated bays, starting with three storeys, diminishing to two at the first terrace marking a change of level, and ending with a single storey and a huge exedra at the Belvedere end. Drawings (Plate 237) show the impressive character of the original design, now ruined by the building of part of the Vatican Library across the middle of it. The great exedra was also completely changed by Michelangelo and Pirro Ligorio. It was originally based on the Temple of Fortune at Palestrina, but Michelangelo's reworking of the stairs and the addition of the Early Christian bronze pine-cone from Old St. Peter's modified the whole character of the design. In the same way, the Cortile di San Damaso, which contains the Loggie painted by Raphael and his assistants in the manner of ancient 'grotesque' decoration, has been altered by the glazing of the open arcades, so that the reference to the Colosseum is no longer obvious (Plates 241, 242).

More important than any of these, however, was the Palazzo Caprini, bought by Raphael in 1517 and usually called the House of Raphael. It was destroyed in the rebuilding of the area around St. Peter's and is known only from drawings such as the one, at-

245. *Raphael, Rome, Palazzo Vidoni-Caffarelli (reconstruction by Geymüller).*

246. *Raphael, Rome, Palazzo Vidoni-Caffarelli, detail of rustication.*
247. *Raphael, Rome, Palazzo Branconio dell' Aquila (engraving by Ferrerio).*
248. *Rome, Palazzo Spada, detail of façade.* ▷

249. *Baldassare Peruzzi, Rome, Palazzo Massimo alle Colonne, entrance portico.*
250. *Baldassare Peruzzi, Rome, Palazzo Massimo alle Colonne, vault of atrium.*

251-253. *Baldassare Peruzzi, Rome, Palazzo Massimo alle Colonne, façade.*

254. *Baldassare Peruzzi, Rome, Palazzo Massimo alle Colonne, court.*
255. *Baldassare Peruzzi, Rome, Palazzo Massimo alle Colonne, Loggia.*

256. *Giulio Romano, Rome, Palazzo Cicciaporci.* ▷

tributed to Palladio, in London (Plate 244), and engravings like Plate 243. Nevertheless, the House of Raphael was the most important palace design of the sixteenth century. Almost every later palace either copied its main ideas or was a variation on it, and its influence can be seen in the work of Raphael himself, Giulio Romano, Sanmichele, Sansovino, and Palladio.

The palace type established by Brunelleschi, Michelozzo, Alberti and the Cancelleria Master had consisted of a detached block with a ground floor, usually rusticated, and two other storeys above it. In general the storeys were separated by cornices or string-courses, but not usually by distinguishing Orders. The importance of the House of Raphael is that it reduced the palace design to a type consisting of only two storeys, sharply differentiated by the use of rustication on the ground floor only, and an Order on the *piano nobile*, without an upper floor to compete with it (although the windows of an attic storey can be seen in the entablature). In practice, most families would have needed at least one storey above the *piano nobile*, but the House of Raphael was intended as a type rather than a dwelling. The basic idea was derived (like the Palazzo Davanzati in Florence and its successor, the Palazzo Medici) from the ancient *insula*, a block of flats with shops on the ground floor. To distinguish the residential from the commercial part, the upper floor of the House of Raphael has an Order, but the principles of design are to distinguish one element from another — rusticated ground floor from ashlar-and-Order *piano nobile* — and to observe exactly each element of the repetitive design. Thus, each bay has two identical columns and a pedimented window, and each window has a triangular pediment. The first variation on such a scheme would be to alternate triangular and segmental pediments in a search for richer textures.

Raphael's desire for greater richness found expression in the letter to Leo X on the antiquities of Rome and also in his own version of the palace type. The Palazzo Vidoni-Caffarelli is often denied to Raphael on the ground that it is too late to have been designed by him, but it certainly shows (Plates 245, 246) a direct descent from the Bramante prototype. The Palazzo Branconio dell'Aquila, on the other hand (Plate 247), was certainly by Raphael, but has little kinship with the House of Raphael. Some idea of its original appearance can be gained from the Palazzo Spada (Plate 248), a mid-sixteenth-century Roman building obviously inspired by the ideas of richness and textural variation which distinguish the Palazzo Branconio from the House of Raphael and from Bramante's work in general. The Palazzo Branconio, however, has one novel feature, which is the placing of the only Order on the ground floor instead of the *piano nobile*, thus reducing the importance given to the upper floor

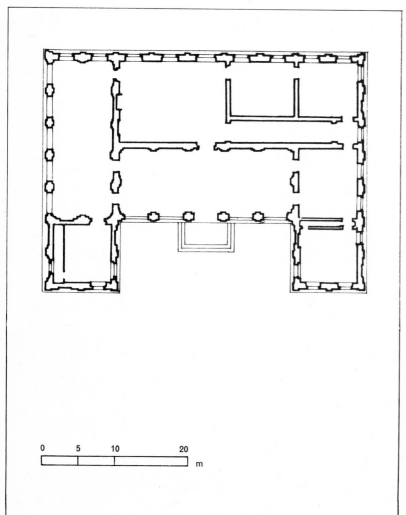

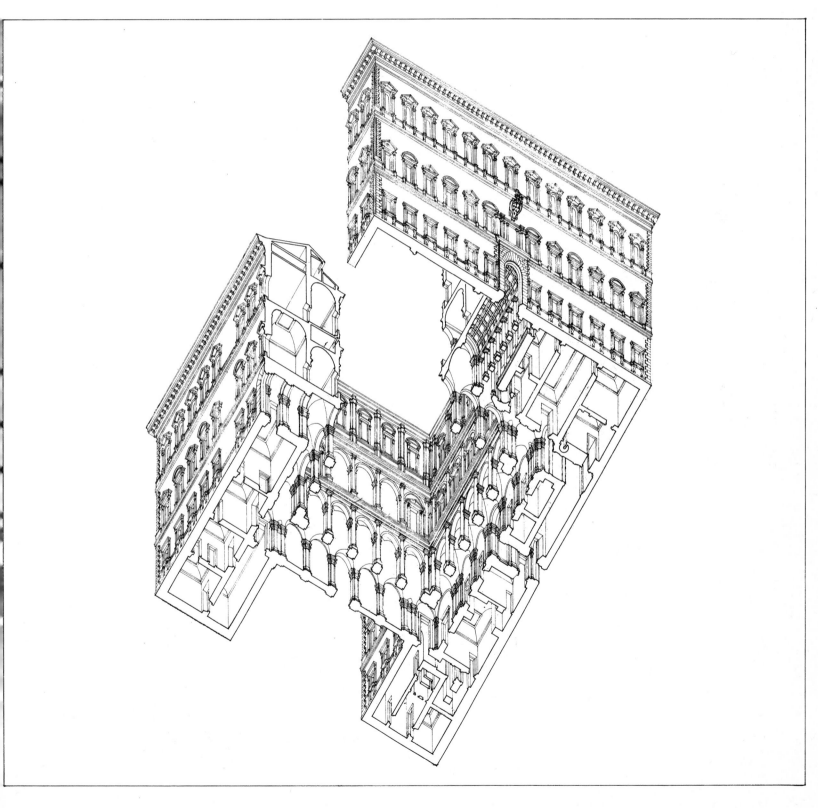

263. *Antonio da Sangallo the Younger, Rome, Palazzo Farnese, façade.*

— yet the ground floor clearly remains the less important, since it contains shops. The Palazzo Massimo alle Colonne, built by Peruzzi in the 1530s, repeats the theme of the Order on the ground floor without the shops, but Peruzzi was faced with a problem of siting, since the façade had to be curved (Plates 251-53) and a normal *piano nobile* would have lost its effectiveness. He redesigned his palace to contain a Roman portico *in antis*, severely classical (Plate 249), and continued the theme in the atrium and the loggia of the first floor (Plates 254, 255). The Massimo claimed descent from Fabius Maximus, and were therefore open to ideas of this kind, but in general Raphael's use of a ground-floor Order met with little response. The two palaces attributed to his pupil, Giulio Romano, are both variations on the Bramante theme.

Peruzzi's other, earlier, work in Rome, the Villa Farnesina, was built for the Sienese banker Agostino Chigi about 1509 (Plates 258-60) and is even more important as a very early example of a *villa suburbana* on the lines of those described by Pliny the Younger in his *Letters* (first century A.D.), which were to be worked out in detail by Raphael, Giulio Romano, Vignola, and Palladio.

The town palace tradition was continued in Rome by Bramante's followers and assistants, notably Antonio da Sangallo the Younger, whose academic cast of mind led him to a Vitruvian formulation in the early Palazzo Baldassini as well as in his masterpiece, the pre-Michelangelo design of the Palazzo Farnese in Rome. This was unfinished at Antonio's death in 1546, when Michelangelo took over, adding the great cornice, altering the whole disposition of the central part, and designing a new, and very un-Vitruvian, upper floor on the court side (Plate 266). The sheer mass of the façade of the Palazzo Farnese (and, even more, the entrance tunnel and lower parts of the court) has something of the quality of ancient Roman building and shows that Antonio had not entirely failed to grasp the monumentality of Bramante's St. Peter's; but, by 1546, taste had changed and Michelangelo had altered the whole repertory of architectural forms.

In the last fifty years it has become customary to refer to almost all architecture of the latter part of the sixteenth century as 'Mannerist', and, as a stylistic category, Mannerism seems now to be firmly established, like Renaissance or Baroque. There are disadvantages in this which are not always obvious and it is perhaps time to review the use of the word 'Mannerism' and to redefine, from the works of art themselves, the characteristics which separate a Mannerist work from its predecessors and successors. In the first place, if one looks at works of art outside Italy, it is evident that there are features of the Gallery of François I at Fontainebleau, or the portraits of Queen Elizabeth of England, or the architectural fantasies of Flemish and German designers, which are difficult to reconcile with the idea of Mannerism as a development from, or even a reaction against, the style of the High Renaissance. The situation in these countries is perhaps best summed up by the Chapel of Henry VII in Westminster Abbey. Here, the tomb of the King by Torrigiano was completed in 1518 and stands in a chapel, specially built to receive it, which is one of the greatest works of the last, most exuberant, phase of Perpendicular Gothic. The two styles simply co-exist, with no point of contact between them. Much the same is true of many of the works of architecture produced in the Northern countries more or less in reaction against Gothic ideals, and lacking that grounding in antiquity and in theory which was the essential foundation of the High Renaissance in Italy. Inigo Jones in England was one of the few artists who had truly absorbed the spirit of Italian classicism, but it is significant that his works belong to the first quarter of the seventeenth century rather than to the sixteenth, and it was more than a hundred years after the death of Bramante when he began the Banqueting House in Whitehall.

Even in Italy the development is far from simple and the style of Sansovino, or even of Palladio, can hardly be called Mannerist in the sense in which the word may be used of Giulio Romano or Michelangelo. The idea that the complexities which are an essential characteristic of any definition of Mannerism can be directly related to political upheavals in Italy (and specifically the Sack of Rome in 1527) must be abandoned. Not only were revolution, war, plague, and famine ordinary concomitants of life in the fourteenth and fifteenth centuries, but it can be demonstrated that a new style, different from that practised by Bramante, Raphael, and Michelangelo in the years around 1510, arose in the early 1520s, several years before the Sack of Rome took place.

The two principal exponents of this style were Giulio Romano and Michelangelo acting, so far as can be seen, independently of one another. Michelangelo seems to have developed a new style in

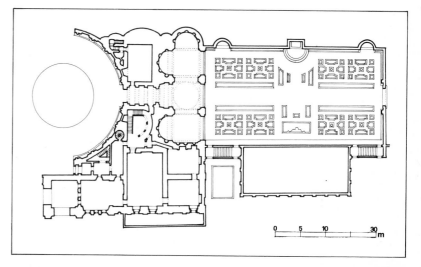

267. Rome, Villa Madama, plan.
268, 269. Giulio Romano, Rome, Villa Madama, views of exterior.

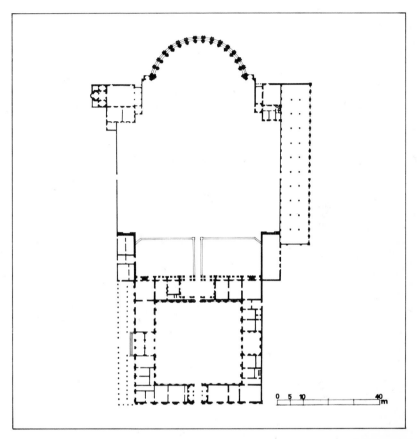

an Lorenzo in response to the inner logic of his own creative powers, but it may reasonably be said that Giulio Romano was acting under an external stimulus in so far as he was consciously trying to do something different from Raphael's late works. In this context, Mannerism is an aesthetic rather than a social phenomenon, but it is certainly social in the sense that the works produced were intended for the appreciation of a cultivated and sophisticated audience, and the element of virtuosity which is an essential component of Mannerist art always lies close to the surface.

When Raphael died in 1520, it was evident that his style had been about to enter a new phase. The desire for greater richness and expressiveness, already noted in the Palazzo Branconio dell'Aquila or the Cappella Chigi, can be seen even more explicitly in his last work, the enormous altarpiece of the *Transfiguration*. It is well known that this was exhibited in the room in which his body lay in state and this must imply that, although the picture was unfinished, it was sufficiently far advanced to be worthy of public exhibition on such an occasion. The twisted poses and melodramatic gesticulation of many of the figures must therefore be due to Raphael himself, and they indicate the path which was to be taken by his pupil and artistic executor, Giulio Romano. Paintings like the *Madonna and Saints* in Santa Maria dell'Anima, or the *Stoning of Saint Stephen*, show Giulio Romano working in a very similar vein in the years 1520-24. During the same period he completed the frescoes in the Vatican and also worked on the Villa Madama just outside Rome (Plates 268,269). This villa, begun about 1516, was one of the most important works of the Raphael circle. It was a full-scale attempt to recreate a classical villa complete with a circular court, an atrium, and *grotteschi* copied from those which had recently been rediscovered in the Golden House of Nero. Giulio's decorative paintings show that he was fully in sympathy with the classicising aims of Antonio da Sangallo and Raphael, and his experience at the Villa Madama was an essential preparation for his masterpiece, the Palazzo del Te in Mantua.

Giulio left Rome in 1524 to work for the Gonzaga family in Mantua, where he remained for the rest of his life. Soon after his arrival he began to work on the palace, which was under construction by the end of 1526 and completed by about 1534. Since the Gonzagas already possessed the enormous Reggia in Mantua, the Palazzo del Te was never intended to be anything but a *villa suburbana*. It is laid out as a hollow square with a large garden on the eastern side. The main entrance front, however, is at right angles to the axis of the garden front, and the treatment of the entrance, western, and eastern fronts differs in each case (Plates 272-77). The entrance (south) front has a three-bay portico in the middle, flanked

273. *Giulio Romano, Mantua, Palazzo del Te, side view.*
274. *Giulio Romano, Mantua, Palazzo del Te, detail of side door.*
275. *Giulio Romano, Mantua, Palazzo del Te, vestibule.*

on either side by windows with exaggeratedly rusticated keystones set in a rusticated wall and separated by Tuscan pilasters. The end bays of this façade are marked off from the rest by paired pilasters, and by the introduction of a small niche between the inner pair of pilasters. The rhythm of the whole front is thus fairly complex, but it is not repeated on the western side, where the first variation on the theme occurs. This has a central entrance with a single arch flanked on either side by niches, giving a triumphal arch effect. The main rhythm of windows and pilasters is repeated from the entrance façade, but the termination is again different.

Once inside the court, the spectator is confronted by a similar arrangement of niches, rusticated stonework, and a Tuscan Order; but the pilasters have become columns, the window frames have received a curious form of triangular pediment, set on top of the rusticated keystone, and, strangest of all, at regular intervals the Doric triglyphs appear to have slipped down into the zone below the entablature. This odd feature (Plates 276, 277) can almost certainly be traced back to an actual Roman ruin in which the frieze had broken up, and a drawing in the *Codex Barberini* (Plate 278) suggests a possible derivation. This shows that Giulio, like Raphael, had looked keenly at ancient buildings in his search for classical prototypes. The difference between Bramante on the one hand, and Raphael and Giulio on the other, lies principally in the buildings they chose as models.

The garden front, as befits its more private character, differs sharply from the main and western façades in that it has a much larger proportion of voids to solids and has smooth ashlar stonework (actually stucco) in place of rustication (Plate 279-81). Nevertheless, the central part of the façade has three arched openings, corresponding to the arches on the entrance front, and the wings are articulated by means of a succession of two Palladian motifs followed by two arched openings framing a small niche, giving a sort of reversed triumphal arch effect. In short, the theme stated in the main façade has been modulated into a different key, but is still recognizable by those who look hard enough at the building. This appeal to an educated, one might almost say professional, audience is again an enduring characteristic of Mannerist art. It possesses a slightly show-off quality which, one feels, would not have appealed to Bramante. Nevertheless, as a piece of superb princely decoration, the Palazzo del Te was obviously a great success, and the interior of the atrium shows that when he put his mind to it, Giulio could compete on level terms with Raphael himself in the creation of a splendid classical portico like the one at the Villa Madama (Plate 268). Inside the Palazzo del Te, the painted decorations vary from Raphaelesque classical mythologies reminiscent of those

279. *Giulio Romano, Mantua, Palazzo del Te, garden façade.*
280, 281. *Giulio Romano, Mantua, Palazzo del Te, views of interior of Loggia.*

in the Farnesina (Plate 261), through some extraordinarily illusionistic portraits of horses, to the Sala dei Giganti (Plate 282), in which Giulio combined the arts of painting and architecture in a triumph of theatrical illusionism which surpasses anything achieved earlier, even the Camera degli Sposi by Mantegna, his predecessor as Court Painter at Mantua.

Vasari visited Giulio in Mantua a few years before the latter's death in 1546, and his description and praise of Giulio's works must therefore be given due weight as evidence of informed contemporary opinion. Vasari says: 'The Marquis had a property with some stables, called the Te, where he kept his stud... He said he wanted to have, without destroying the old walls, somewhere to go to for recreation or for supper from time to time... Thereupon Giulio made a very beautiful model, entirely rusticated, both within and without the court... After passing through the great Loggia, which is adorned with stuccoes... one comes to some rooms filled with such a variety of fantastic inventions that the mind reels. For Giulio, who was full of capricious inventions and was highly ingenious, in order to show what he could do, designed a room with its structures adapted to the painted decoration, so as to deceive as much as possible anyone who saw it... It is not possible to see, far less imagine, a more beautiful fantasy in painting...'

Other work by Giulio in Mantua is in a similar vein. The court in the Palazzo Ducale, with extraordinary twisted columns deriving, via Raphael, from those in Old St. Peter's, is another and more complex example of his interest in surface textures (Plate 284). His work in the cathedral (Plate 285) shows him in a more severely classical mood, and his own house (Plates 286,287), built just before his death, is a reworking of the theme stated by Bramante in the House of Raphael. The variations are interesting and informative: where Bramante separated the upper and lower storeys by the use of rustication on the ground floor and a smooth surface articulated with coupled columns on the *piano nobile*, Giulio assimilates the two storeys to one another by rusticating both and doing away with the Order. The rustication on the ground floor is comparatively rough, but has a series of stripes of smooth stone which, on closer examination, turn out to be a string-course interrupted by the keystones of the windows. Immediately above this string-course is another, which becomes a pediment over the entrance arch, so that not only are the two string-courses difficult to distinguish but the upper one is a mixture of two architecturally separate elements. In the same way, the triangular pediments of the windows merge into the window-jambs, and the whole unit is placed inside a blind arch in a way which is the direct opposite of Bramante's careful separation of the elements of his composition. Where Bramante stated his theme

clearly and weightily, repeating each element without variation, Giulio produces a touch of fantasy which gives the building a quality of wit in the eyes of any spectator able to compare it with the House of Raphael. It is important to remember that Giulio was working for such a spectator, but his type of 'fantastical' architecture was repeatedly taken over by builders and patrons in northern Europe who had never heard of the House of Raphael.

Vasari makes it clear that, to contemporaries, one of the most important aspects of Giulio's work was his sheer technical skill, and this feeling of being able to do anything (and therefore looking for fresh things to do) can be seen at its highest in the work of Michelangelo in Florence. Here again we are able to rely on the contemporary testimony of Vasari, since he was himself responsible for finishing some of the work left incomplete when Michelangelo finally left Florence for Rome in 1534.

Michelangelo had been recalled to Florence to work for the Medici family in 1516, and after some four years the project for a façade for San Lorenzo was finally abandoned. Several sketches for this façade are known, as well as a wooden model (Plate 288) which, although not now accepted as Michelangelo's final design, certainly expresses his intentions at an earlier stage. The façade would have been a frontispiece containing a great deal of sculpture, and the idea of a building in which architecture and sculpture were to merge into an indivisible whole came to partial realization in the mortuary chapel built for the Medici family in the New Sacristy of San Lorenzo. This was begun in 1520 and worked on until 1527; after a break, while the Medici were expelled from Florence and Michelangelo was working for the Republican Government, the chapel was recommenced in 1530-31 and continued until Michelangelo's departure for Rome in 1534. During most of this time he was also building the Laurenziana Library in the courtyard on the other side of the church. This, too, was left incomplete in 1534, but its most important feature, the extraordinary staircase linking the vestibule and the reading-room, was completed in the 1550s by Vasari and Ammanati. Vasari's testimony is therefore crucial, since he had every reason to know what Michelangelo's intentions were. He says of the Sacristy and the Library (Plates 289-99): 'Michelangelo wanted to execute the work in imitation of the Old Sacristy made by Filippo Brunelleschi but with different decorative features; and so he did the ornamentation in a composite order, in a style more varied and more original than any other master, ancient or modern, has ever been able to achieve. For the beautiful cornices, capitals, bases, doors, tabernacles, and tombs were extremely novel, and in them he departed a great deal from the kind of architecture regulated by proportion, order, and rule which other artists did according to common usage

288. *Michelangelo, Florence, San Lorenzo, wooden model of façade (Florence, Casa Buonarroti).*
289. *Michelangelo, Florence, San Lorenzo, Medici Chapel.*

290. *Florence, San Lorenzo, Medici Chapel, section and plan.*
291. *Michelangelo, Florence, San Lorenzo, Medici Chapel, detail of door and niche.* ▷

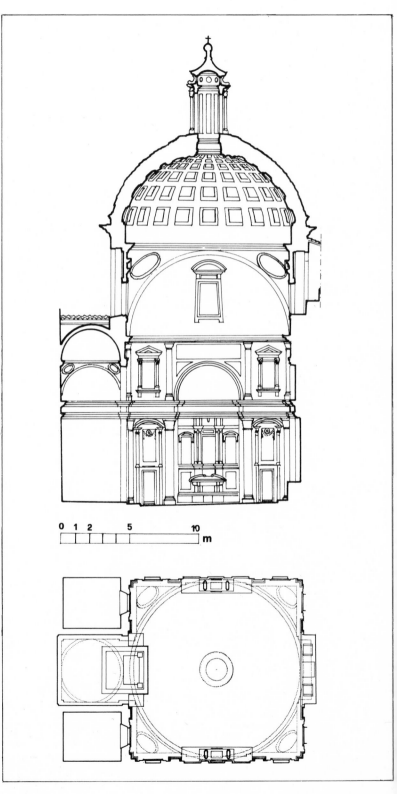

294. *Florence, Biblioteca Laurenziana, section and plan.*
295. *Florence, Biblioteca Laurenziana, axonometric drawing.*
296. *Michelangelo, Florence, Biblioteca Laurenziana, vestibule stairs.*

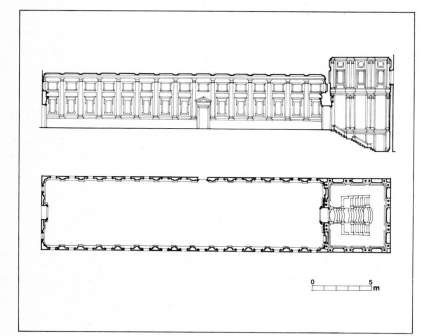

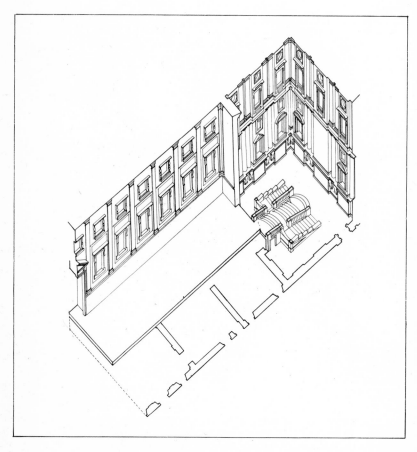

297. *Michelangelo, Florence, Biblioteca Laurenziana, vestibule stairs, detail.*
298. *Michelangelo, Florence, Biblioteca Laurenziana, interior.*
299. *Michelangelo, Florence, Biblioteca Laurenziana, wall of vestibule.*

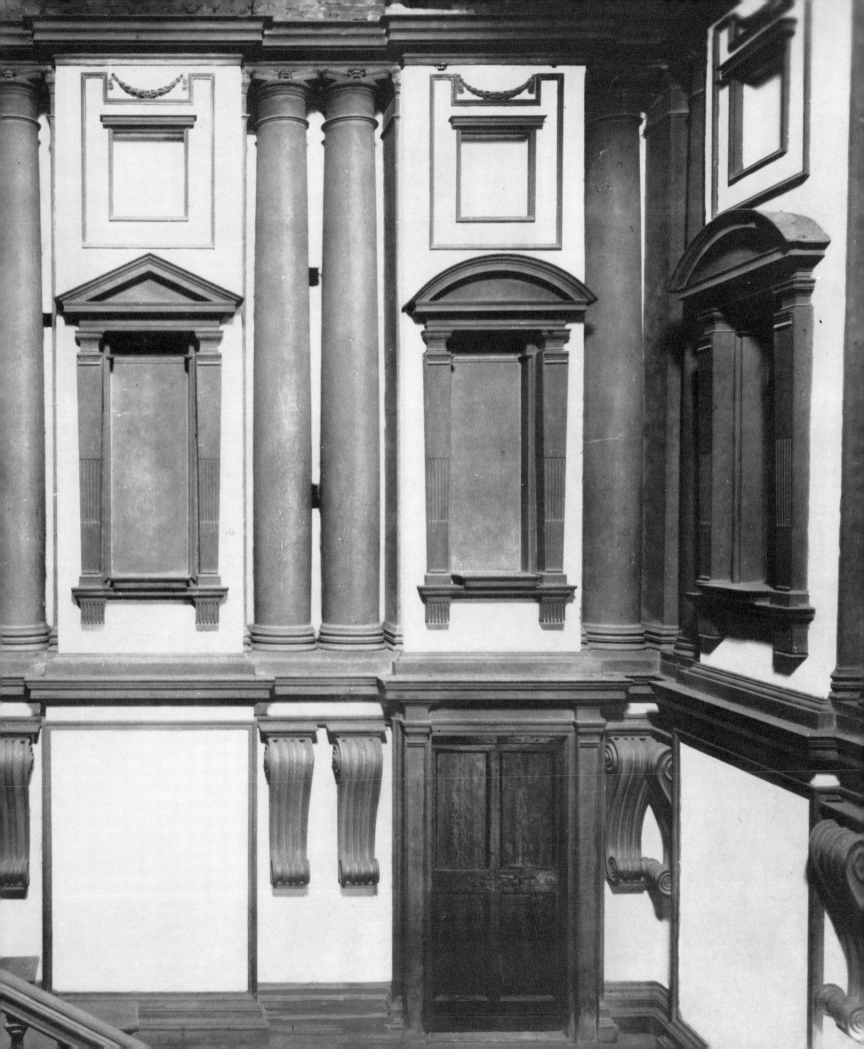

300. *Baldassare Peruzzi, Rome, St. Peter's, plan (from Serlio).*
301. *Raphael, Rome, St. Peter's, plan (from Serlio).*

302. *Antonio da Sangallo the Younger, Rome, Palazzo Farnese, elevation A 627 (Florence, Uffizi, Gabinetto dei Disegni e Stampe).*
303. *Antonio da Sangallo the Younger, Rome, St. Peter's, plan (Florence, Uffizi, Gabinetto dei Disegni e Stampe).*

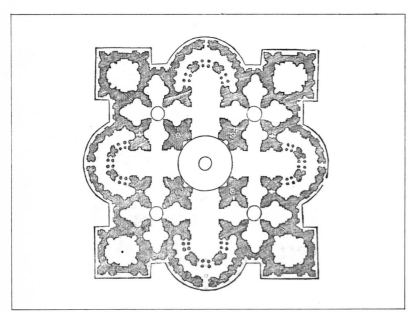

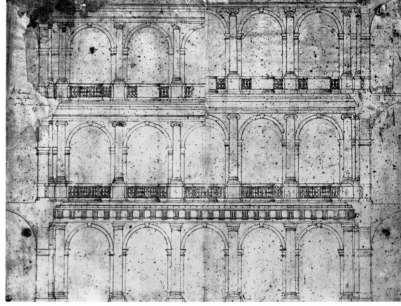

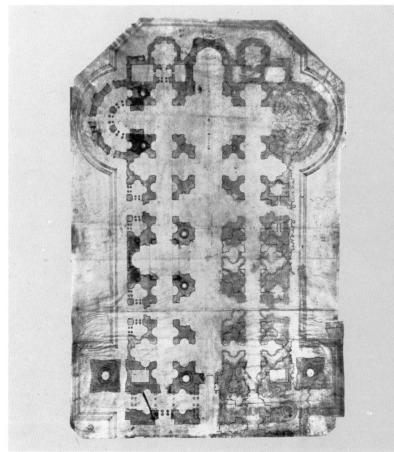

204. *Étienne Dupérac, Rome, St. Peter's, drawing of section (after Michelangelo's project).*

and following Vitruvius and the works of antiquity, but from which Michelangelo wanted to break away... Thus all artists are under a great and permanent obligation to Michelangelo, seeing that he broke the bonds and chains that had previously confined them to the creation of traditional forms.

'Later, Michelangelo sought to make known and to demonstrate his new ideas to even better effect in the Library of San Lorenzo: namely, in the beautiful distribution of the windows, the pattern of the ceiling, and the marvellous entrance of the vestibule... And in this staircase, he made such strange breaks in the design of the steps, and he departed in so many details and so widely from normal practice that everyone was amazed.'

This detailed account shows that, for contemporaries, Michelangelo's work in Florence in the 1520s marked a decisive break with the Vitruvian classicism established only a few years earlier by Bramante and his immediate circle in Rome. Vasari was writing some thirty years later, when the Vitruvian tradition had apparently petered out in the work of Sangallo, but, even so, he felt himself in a difficult position. He saw clearly enough that it was one thing for Michelangelo to invent new forms for cornices, capitals, or bases, but it was another matter when a lesser artist took the same liberty — 'and this licence greatly encouraged those who saw his works to imitate him, and their ornaments have subsequently shown more of the grotesque than of reason or rule...' He knew, too, that there was still great vitality in the Bramantesque tradition, as exemplified in the works, familiar to him, of a Sansovino or a Vignola.

In the Medici Chapel, Michelangelo made a free variation on the form of the Old Sacristy, but he employed the full Roman classicism of a Pantheon-type dome over his square plan. The walls, however, differ from Brunelleschi's simple harmony in that they are articulated by means of two Orders of pilasters, not obviously proportioned to one another, where Brunelleschi had used one great entablature to divide the rectangular parts of the composition from those based on half-circles. What is even more noticeable is the way in which Michelangelo deliberately picks up the rather clumsy treatment of the doors in the Old Sacristy, framed by heavy columns and pediments, the tips of which appear to cut into the frames of the large round-headed reliefs over the doors. Michelangelo's composition has the same heaviness of doorway and upper part in relation to the enframing bay, and it can hardly be a coincidence that he also exploits the effect of uniting the door with the zone above it. Brunelleschi may not have done this entirely deliberately, and, in any case, he employed normal classical forms for the component parts. As Vasari said, Michelangelo 'departed a great deal from the kind of architecture regulated by proportion, order, and rule'. The

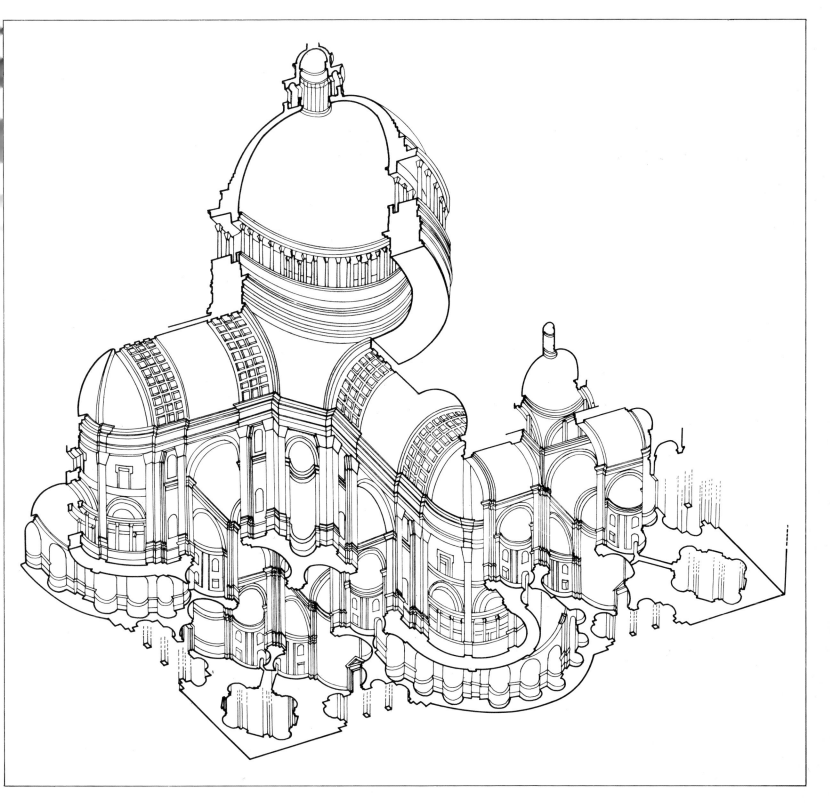

◁ 308. Rome, St. Peter's, exterior of apse.
309. Michelangelo, Rome, St. Peter's, detail of window.

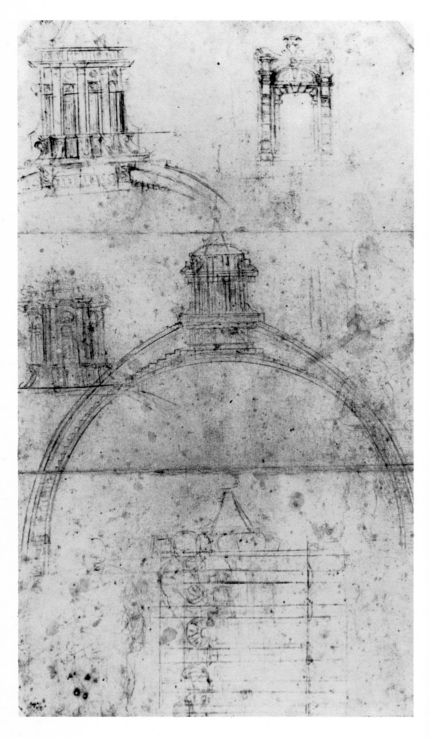

310. *Michelangelo, Rome, St. Peter's, drawing of dome (Haarlem, Teylers Museum).*

311. *Michelangelo, Rome, St. Peter's, model of dome (Rome, Musei Vaticani).*

312. *Michelangelo, Rome, St. Peter's, vertical section of model of dome (Rome, Musei Vaticani).* ▷

313. *Étienne Dupérac, Rome, Capitol, engraving (after Michelangelo's layout).*
314. *Michelangelo, Rome, Capitol, plan (engraving by Étienne Dupérac).*
315. *Giacomo della Porta, Rome, Capitol, general view.*

316. Rome, Capitol, Palazzo Senatorio (engraving by Falda).
317. Rome, Capitol, Palazzo Capitolino.
318. Rome, Capitol, Palazzo Capitolino, detail of central window.

doorway itself is a simple rectangle with a straight entablature supported on giant consoles, but above the door and almost dwarfing it, is a large niche-form, which might have been intended to hold a statue. Closer inspection reveals that it could not possibly contain a statue, nor was it ever intended to do so. The structure consists of a niche enframed by two pilasters carrying a pediment — the type of tabernacle window known from many ancient buildings. The difference is that the pilasters are not of any known Order and have sunk panels on their faces, the segmental pediment has lost the greater part of its lower border and compensates for this by doubling the central part of the upper arc, while the niche has broken into the pedimental zone at the top and has been distorted laterally at the bottom by the great block of marble that made one think of the plinth of a statue in the first place. Finally, the back of the niche has had a rectangular panel sunk into it, containing a very classical *patera* and swag, as if to make up for the absence of the statue. These are indeed in 'a style more varied and more original than any other master, ancient or modern, has ever been able to achieve'. If we look at the walls with the tombs of the Medici Dukes, we shall see (Plate 289) that a similar inversion of normal functions takes place, not in details, but between the component parts of the whole design. The statues of the dead men are placed in niches, but there are blind niches at either side of them, and these niches, not the 'important' central one, have pediments supported on consoles, and swags and decorations.

It may be argued that the Medici Chapel was conceived as an architectural framework for sculpture, and, had it been completed with the great central tomb which is the missing climax of the vista from the ideal viewpoint at the altar, we would not have paid so much attention to the architectural decoration. This argument — not in itself very convincing — can be disposed of by looking at the 'marvellous entrance of the vestibule' (of the Laurenziana Library), where, in the staircase, 'he made such strange breaks in the design of the steps, and he departed in so many details and so widely from normal practice that everyone was amazed' (Plates 296-99).

The Laurenziana Library exploits the pre-existing conditions of the site to make an extraordinary spatial effect. The entrance vestibule is very small in area but extremely high, and the greater part of the floor-space is taken up by the staircase, which seems to have flowed sluggishly, like lava, down from the level of the Library and congealed on the floor of the vestibule. The claustrophobic effect is increased by the walls, which are, in effect, palace façades turned inwards, with the coupled columns sunk into the walls and blind niches instead of windows. Inside the Library the

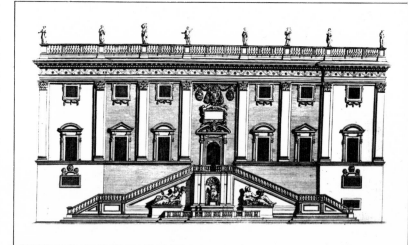

319. *Michelangelo, Rome, Porta Pia (engraving by Étienne Dupérac).*
320. *Michelangelo, Rome, Porta Pia.*

spatial effect is abruptly reversed, for the long wide room now has a low ceiling, richly coffered, and the light enters through real windows separated only by elongated pilasters. In short, both the New Sacristy and the Laurenziana are works of conscious art, in which the classical elements are used as a vocabulary to be arranged at will to suit the design, just as a contemporary poet like Sannazaro used Latin to convey non-classical sentiments. His *De partu virginis* was published in 1526.

After Michelangelo returned to Rome he immediately became involved in the painting of the *Last Judgement*, and his work as a painter and on the various revisions of the Julius Tomb kept him fully occupied until, at the end of 1546, he found himself once more undertaking large-scale architectural commissions. The years following the Sack had been lean ones for architects in Rome, and Antonio da Sangallo had had most of the available work. In particular, the headship of the Fabbrica of St. Peter's and the only major domestic commissions of the period, the Farnese and Massimo palaces, had gone to him and to his colleague in the Fabbrica, Baldassare Peruzzi.

Michelangelo did not like what was happening at St. Peter's, but there was no reason for him to interfere, occupied as he was with the *Last Judgement*. After the death of Raphael there had been a period of uncertainty, when everyone seemed to want to execute Bramante's plan, without being sure what it had been. The money was slow in coming in, and, although the old idea that the rebuilding of St. Peter's 'caused' the Reformation was never more than a myth, it is none the less true that the state of the Church in Germany and elsewhere was not conducive to the vast expenditures necessary to carry out the majestic design of Bramante and Julius. The Sack of Rome brought everything to a standstill, and the plans preserved by Serlio (Plates 300, 301) with the names of Peruzzi and Raphael attached to them, show that there was great uncertainty about the whole project. The 'Peruzzi' plan is a reworking of the original Bramante design — and indeed may well be by Bramante — but the 'Raphael' plan reverts to the design of Old St. Peter's, with a basilica attached to a tribune over the Tomb of the Apostle — the same idea as that used by Bramante for Santa Maria delle Grazie in Milan, which was in all probability intended as a Sforza memorial. This was already implicit in Leonardo's drawings (Plates 185-89), which may date from *c.* 1514 and therefore look back to San Lorenzo in Milan and forward to Raphael (if indeed they are not actually based on Raphael as well). The uncertainty which hung over the whole project can be gauged from the famous Heemskerck drawings (Plates 208-11), which treat the building on exactly the same terms as

any other Roman ruin. In the thirties, however, Antonio da Sangallo (who had been one of the architects in charge since 1520, after the death of Raphael) began to make an attempt to resume building and to find a definitive solution for the two main problems still outstanding — how to redesign the dome so that it would be statically viable (since it was evident that Bramante's original designs were quite impracticable), and how to meet the liturgical need for more space without losing the symbolism of the central plan. Antonio constructed a large wooden model in 1539-46 (Plates 235, 236), which was very expensive and must be judged an aesthetic failure; but it is important to notice that he tried, within the limits imposed by practical problems, to retain as much as possible of Bramante's forms. The great weakness of the model is the lack of that sense of the stupendous, of more-than-Roman grandeur, which marked Julius and Bramante. In intention, the Benediction Loggia, which became necessary when the Latin cross plan was adopted, was a great and solemn arch to enframe the Pope as he gave the blessing *Urbi et orbi*; in effect, it would have been so gigantic — when projected to the scale of Bramante's foundations — that the figure of the Pope would have appeared totally incongruous. In the same way, Antonio's solution to the treatment of the walls was simply to multiply Orders and to add attics to fill up gaps.

In fact, Antonio had a considerable sense of scale and a real feeling for simple Roman grandeur, as may be seen from his designs for the Palazzo Farnese in Rome (Plate 263). The palace in its present form is about 100 feet high, but St. Peter's was so much bigger still that Antonio's sense of scale no longer served to visualize effects. Probably no other architect of the time was any better equipped — except Michelangelo, which is why he criticized Sangallo's model as 'a pasture for oxen'.

The newly-rich Farnese had begun to build their great Roman palace in 1517, but the election of Cardinal Alessandro as Paul III in 1534 meant that the ambitious family at once began an enlargement of the palace, still employing Sangallo. The drawing by him (Uffizi A 627: Plate 302) shows that he was following the ancient precedent of the Theatre of Marcellus, already used by his uncle in the *cortile* of the Palazzo Venezia (Plate 125). According to Vasari, the Pope accepted a design by Michelangelo for the crowning cornice, to be executed by Sangallo, but it seems more likely that this design was prepared after Sangallo's death in October 1546. In any case, Michelangelo took over the unfinished palace and modified the rather dull correctitude of the Sangallo design in three important respects. First, he redesigned the main window of the *piano nobile* (Plate 264), in a sense rather like that of the New Sacristy, where the important elements are given a negative

323. *Michelangelo, Rome, San Giovanni dei Fiorentini, plan (Florence, Casa Buonarroti).*
324. *Giacomo della Porta, Rome, Sant'Atanasio, façade (engraving by Falda).*

325. *Giacomo del Duca, Rome, Santa Maria in Trivio, façade.* ▷
326. *Giacomo della Porta, Rome, San Luigi dei Francesi, façade.* ▷

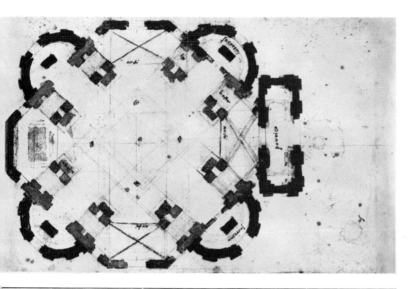

emphasis; next, he enlarged the cornice to a scale greater than that projected by Sangallo, and which also employs a mixture of decorative motifs — Farnese lilies and acanthus leaves used as a sort of metope and triglyph frieze — which was criticized on Vitruvian grounds. And thirdly, he redesigned the court (Plate 266). It is not certain that Sangallo intended to treat all three floors as open loggie, but it seems likely that Michelangelo filled the arches of the middle floor, since the windows are rather tightly fitted and have shapes closer to his formal language than to Sangallo's; similarly, he probably designed the unorthodox Ionic entablature. There can be no doubt that the upper storey, with its idiosyncratic Order and window frames, must be entirely his, and it demonstrates the development of his style since the New Sacristy as well as the way in which he varies his treatment to suit the building materials used.

When Sangallo died, the question of a successor at St. Peter's became urgent, since there was a new wave of activity there. It seems that Giulio Romano was chosen, but he died in November, only a few weeks after Sangallo. Michelangelo found himself *Capomaestro*. He was certainly the greatest living architect, but he was also in his seventy-second year, and presumably did not want the task. He accepted it in a spirit of resignation, saying that he was working for the glory of God, and for the rest of his very long life he worked on it with a dedication and energy that brought it almost to completion. In a letter written at the time of his appointment (January 1547), he makes it clear that his old enemy Bramante had made a design which ought as far as possible to be adhered to: 'One cannot deny that Bramante was as skilled in architecture as anyone since ancient times. He laid down the first plan of St. Peter's, not full of confusion, but clear, simple, and luminous, and detached in a way that did no damage to any part of the palace. It was held to be a beautiful design, and manifestly still is, so that anyone who has departed from Bramante's order, as Sangallo has done, has departed from the truth...' Michelangelo pointed to the contrast with Sangallo by preparing a model (now lost) very quickly and cheaply. The engraved plan (Plate 207), which probably represents his intentions accurately, shows that he redesigned the whole building as a central plan very similar to Bramante's (except for the very Mannerist idea of placing the main entrance on an angle instead of in the centre of one side). He solved the constructional problems with the simplicity of genius, by reducing the whole area and concentrating the outer bearing walls much closer to the enormously enlarged piers. The proportion between the solid supporting members and the open spaces was almost completely reversed — so that the present building can give no idea of Bramante's spatial sequences, and very little even of Michelangelo's — but the reduction of the

whole area in this drastic way (which involved pulling down some of Sangallo's work) meant that construction was both quicker and cheaper. Above all, Bramante now had a successor who could conceive on his own imaginative scale and who was even less bound by precedent simply as precedent. Bramante treated the ancient architects as equals, where Michelangelo seems to have regarded them more as a source of ideas.

The speed with which Michelangelo went to work meant that he transformed the whole building of the basilica, so that not only were the supports radically modified, but the dome itself was almost reached by 1564, the date of his death (Plate 306). The engravings by Dupérac, coupled with the extant western parts of the church (Plates 304, 305), give us an idea of Michelangelo's conception of the whole design, with the exception of the dome itself. The apse shows many traces of his personal and inimitable treatment of details such as windows (Plate 309), even though the seventeenth-century alterations have changed the front of the building almost beyond recognition.

The great problem is whether Michelangelo designed a hemispherical dome — as shown by Dupérac — in the Bramante tradition, or whether his drawing showing a slightly pointed profile (Plate 310) represents the final version. In the event, the dome and lantern were built between 1586 and 1593 by Giacomo della Porta and Domenico Fontana, using the pointed silhouette. Fontana was the best engineer of his day, so he must have felt that the pointed form, like Brunelleschi's dome in Florence, was the safest, since it was demonstrably better from the point of view of statics. What is not clear is whether Michelangelo himself would have agreed. On balance, the Dupérac engravings show a profile closer to the spirit of Michelangelo's other late works, but it may well be that he would have been forced to adopt the same solution as Fontana. The large model preserved in the Vatican (Plate 311) shows the internal dome as hemispherical and the external one with the shape actually built, but it is arguable that the model merely follows the executed work.

During this period Michelangelo was also concerned with several other major architectural undertakings. The Farnese and Capitol designs both date from 1546 and were followed by the Porta Pia, the transformation of the Baths of Diocletian into the church of Santa Maria degli Angeli, two sets of designs for the Florentine national church in Rome, San Giovanni dei Fiorentini, the design of a chapel for Cardinal Sforza in Santa Maria Maggiore, and various other commissions, of which the most important may have been the design he made for the mother-church of the new Society of Jesus, Il Gesù, actually built by Vignola and Giacomo della Porta.

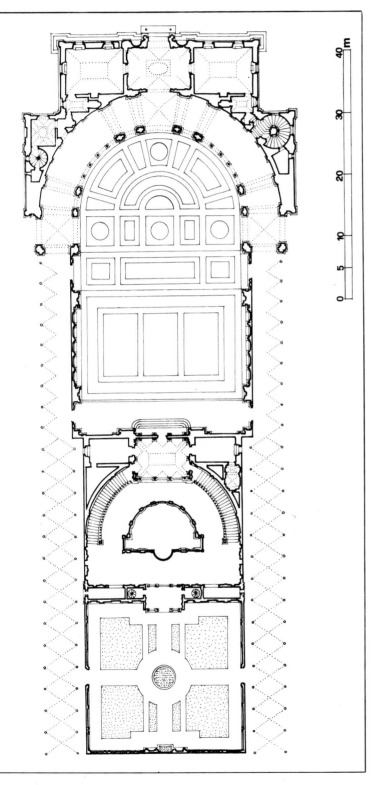

At the Capitol Michelangelo was able to undertake a large-scale town-planning design of a type not seen in Rome since the projected rebuilding of the Borgo under Nicholas V. The Capitol was and is the centre of Rome. In ancient times it was the seat of the government, and in Papal Rome it was — and still is — the seat of the secular administration. In the sixteenth century its importance was to be restored, for political reasons, and the first step was taken in 1538 when the statue of the Emperor Marcus Aurelius was moved there. He had long been misidentified as Constantine, the first Christian Emperor, and this great (and unique) equestrian statue of a Roman Emperor was a symbol of the continuity of Rome itself. Michelangelo had to adapt himself to an awkward site, with partially existing buildings, especially the Palazzo dei Senatori. His ideas can be seen in two engravings by Dupérac made a few years after his death (Plates 313, 314), but the execution by Giacomo della Porta varies in several significant ways (Plate 315), principally in the pavement with four (instead of three) small accents and the introduction of a massive window-feature into the centre bay of each of the side palaces. In addition, the *baldacchino* at the top of the steps up to the Palazzo dei Senatori, which was the 'ideal' viewpoint for the whole, was never built. Some thirty years ago, the pavement was relaid according to the Dupérac engraving, but retaining della Porta's four openings. Apart from the importance of the design as a piece of scenic planning, the two side palaces also introduced the new motif of a Giant Order of pilasters running through both storeys and binding them into a single unit. The exact origin of this motif is very obscure, since a single Order with one storey and an attic can be found much earlier (e.g. at the Palazzo del Te), and the occurrence of a Giant Order in France perhaps in the 1540s, and in England (Kirby, Northants.) by 1570, makes it seem likely that the idea originated in Italy much earlier. Michelangelo also introduced a ground floor with columns carrying a straight entablature, in the proper Roman manner, instead of an arcade, and a comparison with Brunelleschi's Innocenti (Plate 5), about 125 years earlier, shows how total was the change in the whole conception of ancient architecture and its modern interpretation.

The Porta Pia was one of Michelangelo's last works, begun in 1562. He made several drawings, and there is again an engraving by Dupérac (Plate 319). The complexity of the forms employed can be seen by comparing them with the Medici Chapel, designed some forty years earlier, and it was from details like these that many Mannerist architects drew their inspiration. At the same time as the Porta Pia, Michelangelo was also designing an elaborate chapel in Santa Maria Maggiore for Cardinal Sforza (Plates 321, 322), with

331. Giacomo da Vignola, Rome, Villa Giulia, façade.
332, 333. Bartolomeo Ammanati, Rome, Villa Giulia, views of portico.
334, 335. Bartolomeo Ammanati, Rome, Villa Giulia, views of Nymphaeum. ▷

an extremely sophisticated vaulting system, giving a series of internal shapes which merge in the centre, as if unfolding from a core. The same spatial complexities can be seen in his designs, never executed, for San Giovanni dei Fiorentini, for which he made some projects in 1550 and then, in 1559, submitted five designs (Plate 323). Here the central plan was obviously a reflection of his preoccupation with St. Peter's, but, in fact, all his later architectural work gives the impression that it was designed with the intention of learning something which could be put to use in St. Peter's. In his transformation of the Baths of Diocletian (altered in the eighteenth century) he was working with an actual Roman vault and its supports. These vaulting experiments were repeated in the Sforza Chapel, and, had he lived, he would no doubt have profited from them in covering St. Peter's.

When Michelangelo died, his personal and dynamic style very rapidly passed out of favour. This was partly because the prevailing taste — guided by men like Vignola and Giacomo della Porta — was largely against it, but also partly because Michelangelo had few direct followers. Tiberio Calcagni, who had been his assistant at San Giovanni dei Fiorentini, died in 1565; Giacomo della Porta, who designed the very 'Michelangelesque' central window of the Capitol palaces, changed his style; Vasari, although he became an architect of note, did no major work in Rome, so that the only real Michelangelo follower in the seventies and eighties was Giacomo del Duca. In 1588 he returned to his native Sicily, where his works have perished in earthquakes, but he built one church in Rome and radically altered another. The first is the tiny Santa Maria in Trivio (Plate 325), which bears the date 1575 on the façade; the other, even stranger, is Santa Maria di Loreto, begun by Antonio da Sangallo the Younger in the first years of the century. Giacomo took the substructure and added a grossly disproportionate dome, almost as though he were deliberately crushing Antonio's modest building. The lantern must be one of the most surprising pieces of Mannerist virtuosity of the time, but it is dated 1592 and was therefore executed after Giacomo's return to Sicily.

By the middle of the century, there was a marked recovery in building activity in Rome, which had been greatly reduced by the Sack and the ensuing political and economic difficulties. The Council of Trent, which began its eighteen-year sittings in 1545, marked the revival of confidence as well as a fresh religious impulse. The second half of the sixteenth century saw a wave of church-building in Rome, with many churches for 'national' communities, such as the Neapolitans, Lombards, or Florentines, as well as for the French, Dalmatians, and the Uniate Greeks. Several of these churches

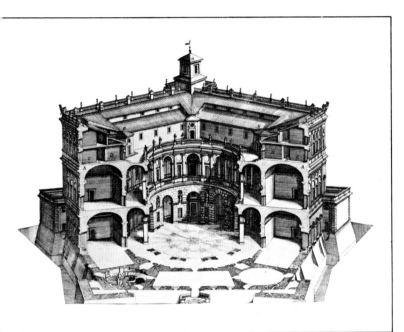

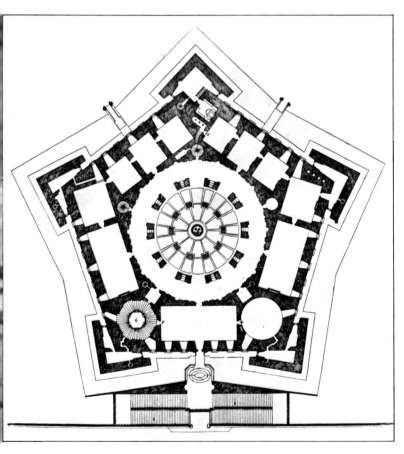

are of architectural importance — San Luigi dei Francesi (Plate 326), the projects for San Giovanni dei Fiorentini, the oval project for Santo Spirito dei Napolitani, Sant'Atanasio dei Greci — but very few are in any way elaborate. The new type of Counter-Reformation church, which was most completely expressed by Vignola's design for the Gesù, was originally executed in a rather dry, academically Mannerist style at the opposite pole from Michelangelo's inventive richness. The characteristic architect, and one of the most busy and successful of this period, was Giacomo della Porta, although he was inferior to Vignola as an artist.

The typical façade of these churches derives from Alberti's Santa Maria Novella in Florence, or from its derivatives such as Sant'Agostino in Rome (Plate 127): that is, the façade is divided into two storeys, each with an Order, and capped by a pediment the width of the nave. The ends of the aisles are masked by scrolls which help to preserve the pyramidal composition. One of the earliest of the sixteenth-century Roman versions is Santo Spirito in Sassia, which Antonio da Sangallo the Younger designed in the 1530s (the façade was built by Ottavio Mascherino during the course of the century), and something very similar can be seen in a plate in Serlio's Book IV, of 1537, which gave the design a wide currency (Plate 328).

Giacomo della Porta, 'Architect to the Roman People', used this formula for several of his churches; but he also employed another form with two storeys running the full width of the building and a tower at each end, which derives from Michelangelo's San Lorenzo model (Plate 288) and may be seen in San Luigi dei Francesi, or in Sant'Atanasio dei Greci with the addition of twin campanili (Plates 324, 326). Both these churches were designed in the eighties, and the French church was probably in collaboration with Domenico Fontana, with whom he worked on the dome of St. Peter's. Fontana was best known for his engineering feat of moving the Vatican Obelisk to its present position (1586), but he has a greater claim on posterity in that he was the executant of Sixtus V's grand plan for the layout of the main streets of Rome, especially what is now via delle Quattro Fontane, originally called the Strada Felice after Sixtus (Felice Peretti, 1585-90). By comparison, Fontana's huge palaces — Vatican, Lateran, and Quirinal — pale into insignificance. They are, in any case, no more than variants of the Palazzo Farnese (Plate 263).

The most sensitive and original architect working in Rome in the third quarter of the sixteenth century was the Bolognese Vignola, but most of his career was overshadowed by Michelangelo. Nevertheless, many people felt that Michelangelo's conception of architecture was too personal and too capricious, and Vignola was able to secure commissions and exert a great influence on the next gen-

eration, especially through his churches. He began his career by drawing the antiquities of Rome in the 1530s, went to France and worked at Fontainebleau for a period in 1541-43, and then came back to Bologna to build the Sangallesque Palazzo Bocchi and the Palazzo dei Banchi. The Palazzo Bocchi was apparently designed in accordance with the ideas of the owner and is certainly heavier than the elegant and idiosyncratic Palazzo dei Banchi, which was probably designed about 1548, although the execution is later. The elaborate window-heads on the upper floor are very characteristic of Vignola, and may be found equally in the Villa Giulia and at Caprarola. By 1550 he was back in Rome and working on the Villa Giulia with Vasari and Ammanati. The villa proper is Vignola's and is an interesting variation on the *villa suburbana* theme of the Villa Madama, with a certain amount of influence from Bramante's Belvedere and from the style of Peruzzi: in short, Vignola was inaugurating a Bramante revival at the moment when Michelangelo was returning to Bramante's plan for St. Peter's, but was executing it in a very different spirit. Vignola later wrote one of the most influential of all treatises on the Orders, and his whole style seems to be an effort to achieve a truly academic set of principles — derived from Bramante and the antique — which could be applied to all architectural problems.

At the Villa Giulia he designed a severe external façade, composed of advancing planes, divided vertically and horizontally and enlivened by touches of heavy rustication *alla Giulio Romano* (Plate 336). This, however, is done with deliberation for textural effect, and not with any dramatic intention. Vignola's skill in setting heavily textured rustication against flat, sharply-cut, smooth planes is well seen in the gateway to the Farnese Gardens; but at the Villa Giulia the real contrast is between the rectilinear front and the deep re-entrant curve of the garden façade, which is almost as much of a surprise as the garden front of the Palazzo del Te. Originally, the plain wall above the straight entablature of the smaller Order — a reminiscence of Michelangelo's new Capitol — was decorated with frescoes, traces of which can still be seen in early nineteenth-century engravings. The garden buildings (Plates 332-35) are attributed to Ammanati, but they breathe the same spirit of sophisticated elegance. By comparison with their much larger model, the Cortile del Belvedere, they seem almost precious, but this is a characteristic of the best Mannerist art of the mid-sixteenth century.

Vignola's other great villa, the huge Farnese castle at Caprarola, near Viterbo, is an undertaking on the scale of the Belvedere, but rather different in intention. The building was originally a genuine fortress, since it lies at the heart of the vast Farnese estates, and the pentagonal plan, established early in the century by Antonio

la Sangallo and Peruzzi, was in accordance with current practice in fortification. The drawing by Vignola (Plate 337), dated 1559, shows that he took over an established plan, and his share was largely confined to the construction of the upper part above the bastions, and the building of the circular inner court. The loggia of the *piano nobile* and the floor above are treated in Peruzzian terms, deriving from the Villa Farnesina, while the circular court is a revised version of the alternating rhythms of the Belvedere, placed over a rusticated podium, recalling the House of Raphael design. The flat, sharply-cut panels are intentionally austere and Bramantesque, but in the interior, decorated with stucco and frescoes, there is a much greater richness, as in the spiral staircase derived from the Belvedere (Plates 343, 344).

The great villas of the next century at Frascati and Tivoli owe nothing to Caprarola, any more than they do to Palladio's villas, but Vignola's churches have had a profound effect all over the world, right up to the present century. This was principally due to the fact that he designed the Gesù, the mother-church of the Jesuits, and their missionary activities involved the building of similar churches all over the globe. Nevertheless, Vignola's other church designs were also of considerable importance, so that the four churches attributed to him — two of Latin cross shape and two ovals — had a great influence on later generations. Santa Maria dell'Orto, which is attributed on stylistic grounds to Vignola rather than to Martino Lunghi the Elder, to whom it is attributed in the old guidebooks, has a particularly interesting façade design (Plate 345). It resembles the plate in Serlio's Fourth Book very closely (Plate 328), so that it belongs to the same group as Sangallo's Santo Spirito in Sassia (Plate 327) and its descendant, Guido Guidetti's Santa Caterina dei Funari of 1564 (Plate 346), but the differences are significant. In the first place, Santa Maria dell'Orto has a long façade, relative to its height, and the length is emphasized by the flatness of the pilasters and panels. The central doorway, by contrast, has fully rounded columns and a strongly projecting segmental pediment. In the upper storey, the curved forms masking the aisle roofs are deliberately kept flat and simple, unlike the rich scrolls of Santa Caterina and similar churches. This flatness and sharpness is maintained in Vignola's first design for the façade of Il Gesù (Plate 348), which also has the obelisks and the same 3:2 proportion between the width and the height. In his final design, engraved by Cartaro in 1570, Vignola altered the proportion to one more nearly approximating to a square, with a more dominant triangular pediment, but he retained the importance of the central door and the window above it. The executed façade (Plate 349) is by Giacomo della Porta, finished in 1577, four years after Vignola's death, and marks a return to the over-

347. Rome, Il Gesù, section (engraving).
348. Giacomo da Vignola, Rome, Il Gesù, project for façade (engraving by Cartaro).

349. Giacomo della Porta, Rome, Il Gesù, façade. ▷

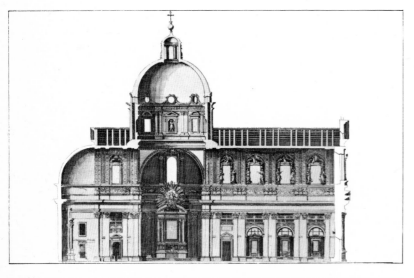

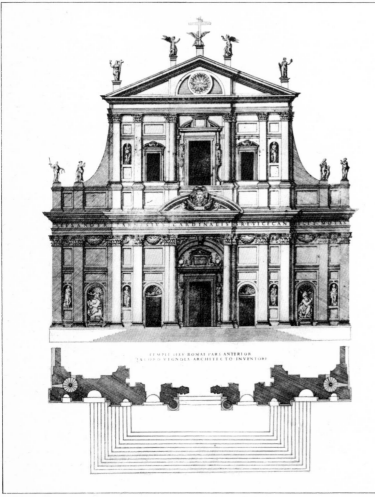

loaded type of two-storey church front, with heavy scrolls and profusion of columns and pilasters, not very clearly separated o ordered in planes. It is often said that the confusion of element in della Porta's design makes it 'more Mannerist', but it may b no more than confusion in della Porta's mind by comparison wit the economy of statement in Vignola's project.

The plan of the Gesù, which is Vignola's, was fixed about 156 by the architect in consultation with the patron, Cardinal Farnese and the Jesuits themselves. The Cardinal, who was paying for th church, made his own wishes quite clear in a famous letter, writ ten in August 1568, after the foundation stone had been laid. H is naturally anxious to keep the costs down, but his ideas on th subject of a church suitable for preaching are made explicit: 'Th church is not to have a nave and two aisles, but is to consist of on nave only, with chapels down each side... The nave is to be vault ed [Plate 347], and is not to be roofed in any other way, in spite o any objections they [i.e. the Jesuits] may raise, saying that the voic of the preacher will be lost because of the echo. They think tha this vault will cause the echo to resound, more than is the case wit an open timber roof, but I do not believe this, since there are plent of churches with vaults... well adapted to the voice.'

In practice, this meant that Vignola reworked the ancient barrel vault type which Alberti before him had used for his Sant'Andre at Mantua (Plates 84, 85), but, in order to meet the demand — unimportant in Alberti's day — for frequent preaching to larg congregations, which was the direct result of the Council of Trent Vignola made his nave relatively shorter and wider, so that th whole church is more compact and better 'adapted to the voice'

So successful was this design that the Gesù is probably the mo del for more churches than any other, but it should be remembered that it was originally decorated inside with Counter-Reformatio austerity. The rich illusionistic decoration of the present church i partly by Baciccia and partly nineteenth century, and would un doubtedly have been distasteful to Vignola himself, whose own in terior is known from a contemporary engraving as well as a paint ing by Andrea Sacchi and Jan Miel.

In addition to providing the most influential model for Lati cross churches, Vignola designed two centrally-planned churche which, though comparatively unimportant in themselves, played considerable part in the evolution of a characteristically Baroqu form. These churches, Sant'Andrea in via Flaminia and Sant'Ann dei Palafrenieri, both in Rome, come at the beginning and end o his career.

Sant'Andrea was built while Vignola was working on the nearb Villa Giulia and was finished in 1554. The plan is rectangular, wit

350. *Rome, Sant' Andrea in via Flaminia, axonometric section.*
351. *Giacomo da Vignola, Rome, Sant' Andrea in via Flaminia.*

352. *Giacomo della Porta, Rome, Santa Maria dei Monti, façade (engraving).*
353. *Rome, San Giacomo degli Incurabili, plan.*

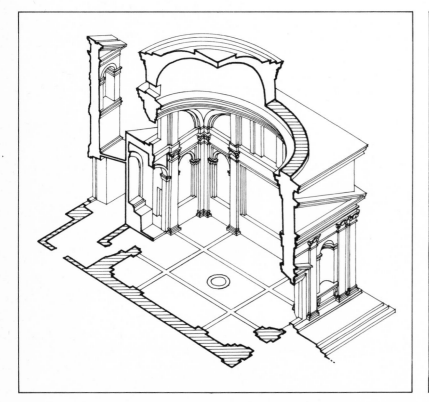

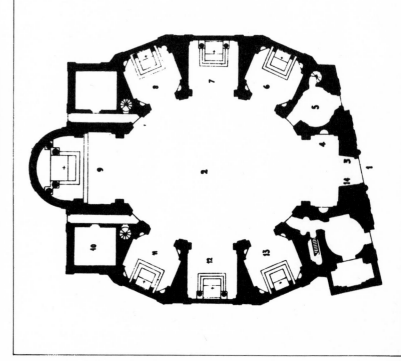

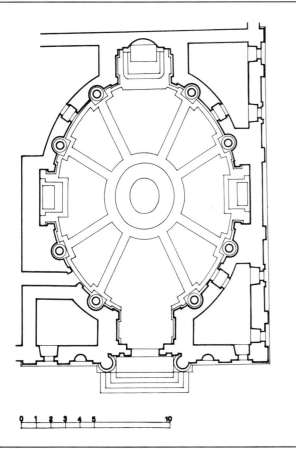

a simple temple-front façade, three bays wide, but above the pediment there is a high attic, reminiscent of the Pantheon, and above that again there rises an oval drum with a shallow roof. Internally, this is an oval drum rising to an oval dome, so that the whole church has the appearance of a square central plan with a circular drum and hemispherical dome which has been stretched along one axis (Plates 350, 351). In fact, the idea is derived from ancient tombs, of the kind which line the great roads leading out of Rome, and the Tomb of Cecilia Metella (Plate 354) is usually quoted as a prototype.

Nearly twenty years later, Vignola took the logical step of extending the oval to the ground-plan as well as the upper level of the church. His Sant'Anna, in the Vatican (Plate 355), built as the chapel of the Papal grooms, was begun in 1572-73 and has an oval plan, with the door and High Altar on the long axis and two side altars on the shorter one. The outside of the church, however, is still rectangular, with a flat façade (probably by Vignola's son), and the next step — curving the façade — was not to come for nearly a century, when Baroque architects took up the oval plan and exploited it beyond anything previously attempted. One other oval church built in the sixteenth century is interesting in this connection: San Giacomo degli Incurabili (San Giacomo in Augusta, via del Corso). This was rebuilt between 1595 and 1600 by the little-known Francesco da Volterra on an oval plan with radiating chapels (Plate 353), of the greatest significance for Baroque developments. It seems that the idea was not Francesco's, and it may even ante-date Vignola's churches since there is a Peruzzi drawing which shows an oval plan for the church. There is also an oval plan in Serlio's Fifth Book (published 1547) which may be related to the project, but may also go back to an ancient Roman prototype, which would be common ground for all these designs. The façade, however, is a version of a Giacomo della Porta design. Porta's Santa Maria dei Monti (Plate 352) is dated 1580, and is itself a simplified version of his own façade for the Gesù.

By 1600 the oval plan had been established and the possible variations on the theme of the Gesù façade had been exhausted. Only della Porta's twin-tower design for Sant'Atanasio — which probably goes back to Bramante's first project for St. Peter's — had not been fully exploited, except by della Porta himself in his scenically splendid Trinità dei Monti (c. 1583-87: Plate 356). All these motifs were to be taken up in a new way by Maderno at Santa Susanna, and by Borromini and their successors.

The main centres of architectural progress in the sixteenth century were Rome and the Venetian Republic, but most Italian towns have at least one good building dating from the Cinquecento, usually the work of a local man who had trained in one of the great centres under an architect who had himself been influenced by the circle around Bramante, active in Rome and concerned with the building of St. Peter's during the first half of the century. Famous examples are the churches at Todi and Montepulciano (Plates 222, 228), but there are numerous less ambitious buildings. An exception to this general rule is Florence, where the three leading architects of the sixteenth century — Ammanati, Vasari, and Buontalenti — were all more influenced by Michelangelo than by any other architect; they were, perhaps, more directly influenced by his works in Florence than by those in Rome. In this sense, the Biblioteca Laurenziana and the Medici Chapel continued to exert the strongest influence on Tuscan architecture until well into the seventeenth century.

Ammanati and Vasari were both born in the same year, 1511, and they began their architectural careers together in 1550, along with Vignola at the Villa Giulia in Rome. Ammanati was a Florentine (Vasari was born in Arezzo), whose first impressions of modern architecture must have come from the Medici Chapel, built during his adolescence. Like Sansovino before him, he was a sculptor — he made the Neptune Fountain in the Piazza della Signoria — as well as an architect, and it was therefore fitting that he went to Venice to train under Sansovino. He worked on the Library and other Venetian undertakings before leaving, in 1550, for Loreto, where he married the poetess Laura Battiferri before going on to Rome. His work at the Villa Giulia is comparatively easy to distinguish from Vignola's (Plates 334, 335), in that it is fundamentally more decorative and has a greater feeling for sculptural richness than Vignola's austerely tectonic forms. In any case, Ammanati claimed to have built 'the loggia and its internal court'. The Villa Giulia was under the general supervision of Michelangelo himself, acting as artistic adviser to the Pope, and Vasari seems to have begun his own successful career as an organizer at the villa, rather than acting in a creative capacity. Certainly, there are only two clearly distinguishable styles in the villa, and they are recognizably those of Ammanati and Vignola. After this work, Ammanati returned to Florence, where he spent the rest of his long life in the service of the Medici. In fact, Ammanati, Vasari, and Buontalenti were all employed principally as Medici artists, and the sixteenth century in Florence is, architecturally speaking, largely a history of Medici patronage after Cosimo I became first Duke (1537) and then Grand Duke of Tuscany (1569).

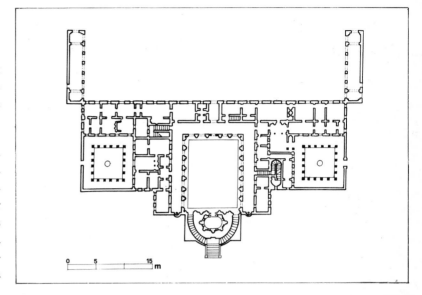

357. Florence, Palazzo Pitti, plan.
358. Bartolomeo Ammanati, Florence, Palazzo Pitti, court.
359. Bartolomeo Ammanati, Florence, Palazzo Pitti, façade towards the court.

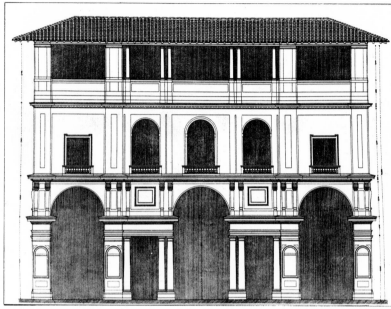

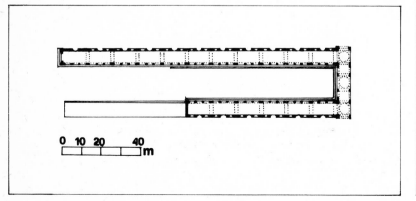

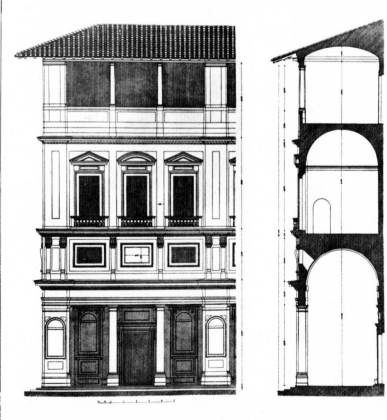

As part of the artistic policy consciously pursued by Cosimo to build up his dynasty after its re-establishment by force of arms in 1530, he began, as soon as he felt himself secure enough, like most other sixteenth-century despots, to build a series of palatial residences. Two of the biggest buildings in Florence, the Palazzo Pitti in its present form, and the Uffizi, owe their origin to this propaganda. In 1549, Cosimo used the dowry brought him by his Spanish wife Eleonora of Toledo to buy the Palazzo Pitti, and in the following year he began a campaign to increase its size and to lay out the gardens in a manner befitting the official residence of a ruling Prince. The original seven bays (Plate 360) were incorporated in the extensions made at either side of the palace, which is now twenty-three bays long on the *piano nobile* and thirteen bays on the top floor, but most of this was built between 1620-30 by Ammanati's follower, Alfonso Parigi. The very heavy rustication, which must have been overpowering in the original building, is well suited to this enormous cliff-like block, which is even larger than the Palazzo Farnese and was vastly increased by the addition of wings at the back (Plate 359). These are by Ammanati and were begun about 1558. He took over the heavy rustication of the street front and turned it into a rusticated Order which makes a particularly impressive central court (Plate 358). The effect is very similar to that of Sansovino's Mint, but, of course, without the justification Sansovino had for giving his building the air of a fortress. The Pitti extensions show Ammanati exploiting an almost theatrical sense of contrast — the ground floor has solid rings round the columns, the *piano nobile* has square blocks with spaces between them, and the top floor has rings with spaces. However, he was also capable of a more graceful style, almost Vignolesque in its flatness, as shown in the Palazzo del Governo at Lucca, begun in 1578 (Plate 361), and, in the best-known of his works, the Ponte Santa Trinita over the Arno (Plate 362) at Florence, which has very flat but beautifully proportioned arches, often popularly attributed to Michelangelo (who discussed the project with Vasari in Rome in 1560).

Ammanati began a treatise on architecture during the 1560s, a fragment of which is in the Uffizi, but his most important theoretical contribution was the open letter addressed in 1582 to the Accademici del Disegno (the Academy founded by Vasari in 1563) in Florence. This is a famous document of Counter-Reformation art theory, reflecting the ideas of the Jesuits. Ammanati had close links with the Society, for whom he built San Giovannino in Florence, to which he contributed money and where he is buried. He also designed the Collegio Romano for them, but it seems to have been executed by Giuseppe Valeriano S.J., who altered it considerably.

371. Bernardo Buontalenti, Florence, Santa Trinita.

372. Galeazzo Alessi, Genoa, Villa Cambiaso, façade.
373. Genoa, Santa Maria di Carignano, plan.

In the Letter, Ammanati repents publicly of some of his nude
statues as possible occasions of sin, and he claims that patrons
cannot be blamed for what is the responsibility of the artist: 'We
know that most of the people who give commissions do not
provide any inventions, but leave things to our judgement, saying,
"Here I want a garden, or a fountain..." and when we do meet
with a patron who asks for things which are shameful or obscene,
we ought not to obey him.' This is one of the few documents of
the Cinquecento which states specifically that the *invenzione* was
normally the province of the artist.

Giorgio Vasari is much better known as an author and painter
than as an architect, and as far as his *Lives* are concerned this is a
just estimate, but it is true to say that his buildings display a much
more sensitive appreciation of Michelangelo's works than do his
paintings, most of which are Michelangelesque to the point of ab-
surdity. The greater part of Vasari's active career, which took him all
over Italy, was spent as a painter, or as a kind of artistic impresario arranging temporary decorations for state ceremonies. These
festive decorations played a great part in the social and political
life of the sixteenth century, and their lath-and-plaster architecture
must have afforded opportunities for experiments that would hardly
have been possible in permanent materials. Although we know
little about the appearance of these triumphal arches and
similar decorations, there is enough evidence to be certain that
they encouraged a kind of capricious inventiveness, and also a
tendency to overload façades with inscriptions and allegorical reliefs, which sometimes found their way into solid architecture.

Vasari was responsible for many such decorations, and his masterpiece, the Uffizi in Florence, owes much to his experience in
these fields. A great part of the effectiveness of the design comes
from the skilful exploitation of the light patch at the end of a very
long perspective.

After his work at the Villa Giulia, according to his own account,
he made models and designs for Santa Maria Nuova at Cortona
in 1554. In many ways this church resembles Francesco di Giorgio's
Santa Maria del Calcinaio, built half a century earlier at Cortona
(Plates 116, 363). Vasari also worked on the Madonna dell'Umiltà
in Pistoia (begun in 1492 by Ventura Vitoni), which also shows
him as a comparatively restrained architect working within an established tradition.

As early as September 1555, Michelangelo wrote to him about
the completion of the staircase in the Biblioteca Laurenziana, saying that he was confident that Vasari and Ammanati would be able
to execute it, as he could no longer remember much about it. There
are several letters from the winter of 1558-59, concluding with

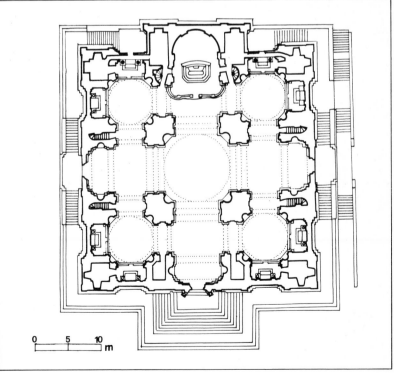

the news that Michelangelo had made a small model in clay and had sent it to Ammanati. The contact with Michelangelo is evident in the development of Vasari's architectural style during the sixties. In 1560 he began work on the Uffizi (i.e. the Offices), designed as the government offices of the new Tuscan state, since Cosimo was deliberately moving the centres of power away from the Palazzo della Signoria and its republican memories. The Uffizi must have been very large for its original purpose, since it now stretches for about four hundred feet on either side of a very long, narrow, street-like piazzetta (Plate 364), and the buildings are three storeys in height. The tall buildings are higher in relation to the width of the street than one would expect, so that a long tunnel-like effect is created, either from the Piazza della Signoria or from the Arno looking towards the Palazzo della Signoria and the cathedral, which appear bathed in light at the end of the long, dark perspective. The finest point of the design is the lovely, airy loggia overlooking the Arno, with its delicate pattern of vaulting supported on heavy coupled columns, in a variation of the Palladian motif that Palladio himself might have admired (Plate 369). The rest of the building is little more than a repetition of motifs invented by Michelangelo for the Biblioteca Laurenziana some forty years earlier.

When Vasari died in 1574, his work at the Uffizi was carried on by Bernardo Buontalenti, whose details — such as the celebrated Porta delle Suppliche (Plate 370) — are among the best-known examples of Mannerist decoration in the last quarter of the sixteenth century. This doorway takes a Mannerist segmental pediment breaks it in half, and reverses the two scrolls to create a curious wing-like effect which acts as a base for the bust of Duke Cosimo. The door is lit by a semicircular opening behind the bust which provides a dark, fan-shaped accent setting off the sculpture.

Buontalenti worked almost exclusively for the Medici, for whom he built the villa (now destroyed) at Pratolino, outside Florence, and the Casino Mediceo in Florence itself. He was also responsible for the façade of Santa Trinita (1593-94: Plate 371), which is over-decorated by comparison with the simple and elegant Fortezza di Belvedere, on a hill above Florence and commanding a superb view. His last work, the Loggia dei Banchi at Pisa, was begun about 1605, so that the influence of Michelangelo was continuous in Tuscany from the 1520s until the seventeenth century.

Galeazzo Alessi of Perugia and Pellegrino Tibaldi of Bologna (also known as Pellegrino Pellegrini) were the leading architects of the second half of the century in Genoa and, especially, in Lombardy. They both worked for St. Charles Borromeo, the Archbishop of Milan, whose book on church-building, *Instructiones Fabricae et Supellectilis Ecclesiasticae* (1577), was a direct reflection of the

concern for church design which arose from the Council of Trent and from the missionary activities of the new Orders, in particular the Jesuits. Both architects probably reflect Borromean ideas as well as share a background of Michelangelo-della Porta-Vignola, so it is not surprising that their works have been confused, but Alessi was the elder by some fifteen years and Tibaldi began his career as a painter, owing his architectural practice to St. Charles.

Alessi received his first training in Perugia from the architect Caporali, whose edition of Vitruvius (Perugia, 1536) is hardly more than a plagiary of the Como edition of 1521, edited by Cesariano, Bramante's pupil. Alessi seems to have gone to Rome, where he became a follower of Michelangelo, before returning to Perugia to begin his architectural career. According to Vasari, he went to Genoa at the request of the Republic and there designed elaborate fortifications for the great harbour. These no longer exist, and it is difficult to be sure how much of the layout of the Strada Nuova (now via Garibaldi) was due to him: the general supervision of the palaces along it was apparently his responsibility, but most of the actual building seems to have been executed by others. What is certain is that he was in Genoa by 1548, when he began the Villa Cambiaso, and, in the following year, the contract between him and the Sauli family was signed for the design of Santa Maria di Carignano. Alessi undertook to work for two years on the project, but the actual execution was delayed for many years.

The Villa Cambiaso (Plate 372) belongs to the type established by Peruzzi at the Farnesina and introduced to the north by Falconetto at the Loggia Cornaro (Plate 389), but there is a significant difference, in that the Villa Cambiaso has a much richer surface texture and has a Corinthian Order with tabernacle windows and mezzanines of the type invented by Peruzzi at the Palazzo Massimo. This combination can be found in the Palazzo dei Senatori, as executed by Giacomo della Porta — but it is not shown in the Dupérac engraving of Michelangelo's original design (Plate 313): it seems that the form used on the Senatorial palace dates from about 1570, which would make the Villa Cambiaso the earlier example, improbable as this seems. The overall effect of the Villa Cambiaso is like Sanmicheli's work in Verona — an enriched version of a Bramantesque prototype.

In 1549 Alessi signed the contract for Santa Maria di Carignano (Plates 374, 375), but the actual building was not finished until long after his death in 1572. The design is a reworking of the early Bramante project for St. Peter's (cf. Plates 206, 373), but it lacks the finesse of Bramante — the width of the church is disproportionate, the triangular pediment too high, and the towers have bases that are visually too narrow for them. The interior is more Braman-

378. *Pellegrino Tibaldi, Pavia, Collegio Borromeo, façade.*
379. *Pellegrino Tibaldi, Pavia, Collegio Borromeo, court.*

tesque, but there is a general feeling that the decoration is too rich, and, by comparison with his much simpler Umbrian works, almost vulgar.

The commission for the Palazzo Marino in Milan arose from the Genoese works, since Marino (who later became Duca di Terranova) was a Genoese merchant established in Milan. The palace is enormous, so that it was not wholly finished until the nineteenth century, but the façade towards Piazza San Fedele and the great court, with their Victorian exuberance of decoration and grand scale, are typical of Alessi (Plates 376, 377). Like the Palazzo Pallavicini-Cambiaso at Genoa, there is a certain amount of ill-digested Sansovinesque richness in the design, although the decoration of the court of the Palazzo Marino, designed about 1553, has much in common with the contemporary court of the Palazzo Spada in Rome. The alternation of straight entablatures and arches supported on pairs of columns, reminiscent of Giulio Romano at Mantua, as well as Serlio and Palladio, is, in this variation, characteristic of both Alessi and Tibaldi. It may be the source of Vasari's more graceful loggia at the Uffizi (Plate 369). Much of Alessi's work consists of a strange alternation between simple, Bramantesque classicism of form and an elaborate and tedious richness of decoration, evident in the masks, herms, and swags of the Palazzo Marino, and surprisingly close in spirit to the engraved pattern-books of Flemish and Dutch designers of the next generation. The basic simplicity of Alessian architecture can be seen in buildings like the Palazzo Viviano Atti at Todi, or from the fact that he made a model in 1568 for Santa Maria degli Angeli at Assisi (built from his design from 1569 onwards), for which a project had also been submitted by Vignola. In 1570, Cardinal Farnese asked him to submit a design for Il Gesù at a time when Vignola was actually working on it. Alessi was therefore regarded by contemporary experts as an architect rather similar to Vignola, and this can be confirmed by San Vittore Grande in Milan, although it has been much altered since it was designed — as Vasari tells us — by Alessi in about 1560.

The career of Pellegrino Tibaldi falls naturally into three parts, with all his architectural activity taking place in the middle period from about 1564 until about 1587. At about the age of twenty, Tibaldi went to Rome (c. 1547), where, like Alessi, he worked as a draughtsman and was influenced by Michelangelo. Up to about 1550 he worked as a painter, and, when he returned to Bologna his first major commission was for the frescoes in the Palazzo Poggi, which show his skill in foreshortening and Michelangelesque draughtsmanship. In 1560 he met St. Charles Borromeo, then the Papal Legate in Bologna, and went to work in Lombardy for him (St

Charles became Archbishop of Milan in 1564). Tibaldi devoted him-self to architecture, becoming architect to both the city and the cathedral of Milan. In 1585, he received an invitation from Philip II of Spain to supervize the Escorial works, but in fact Tibaldi left Milan only in 1587, and his work at the Escorial consists of a series of sixty-three frescoes, which greatly influenced later Spanish painters, for which he was rewarded with the title of Marchese di Valsolda in 1596. He returned to Milan and died there in the same year.

His first major undertaking for St. Charles was the Collegio Borromeo at Pavia, founded in 1564 (Plates 378, 379), where the court closely resembles Alessi's Palazzo Marino designed about ten years earlier. The façade, remotely descended from the Palazzo Farnese, has some of the wilfully picturesque Michelangelism that Alessi occasionally displays, but the deliberate awkwardness of the pedi-ment above two arched windows in each of the end blocks is remi-niscent of much earlier Venetian palaces. As a whole the building shows a painter's rather than an architect's feeling for forms dis-solved in light.

Tibaldi's most important church design was probably San Fe-dele in Milan, begun in 1569 for the Jesuits, but under the patron-age of St. Charles. This is exactly comparable with Vignola's Gesù in Rome (Plates 347, 348), built for the Society under the patron-age of Cardinal Farnese, but the two churches are quite different, both in plan and in the treatment of the façade. San Fedele is a single space, without aisles, and consists of two square nave bays, follow-ed by a typical Milanese *tiburio* — a high drum and dome, like Santa Maria delle Grazie — with a semicircular apse. This makes an even simpler preaching-box than the Gesù, while the two-storey side elevation, with the windows in the upper range, means that the façade is a two-storey block unlike the Gesù, but rather closer to della Porta's San Luigi dei Francesi. At San Fedele, however, the façade is square and has a well-proportioned triangular pedi-ment across the whole width (cf. Plates 380, 381). In detail, the façade is strikingly similar to Vignola's forms, and even the variations in width of the bays — a wide one in the centre, a narrow one next to it, and then another still narrower, but made to appear bigger because it has a statue in a niche surrounded by a heavy tabernacle frame — is a characteristically Mannerist and Vigno-esque feature.

In 1571, Tibaldi designed the great pilgrimage church at Cara-vaggio, now much altered, the original form of which is known from a model at Brescia, and, in the following year, the votive church of San Sebastiano in Milan. This was commissioned in 1576, follow-ing the cessation of the great plague, and is therefore comparable

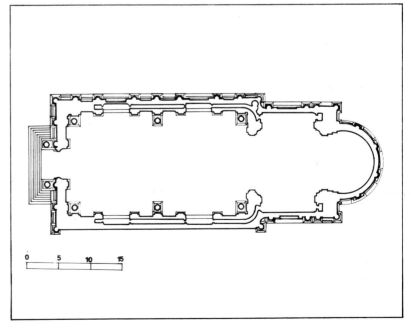

383. *Milan, San Sebastiano, engraving of façade.*
384. *Pellegrino Tibaldi, Saronno, Santuario della Madonna dei Miracoli, doorway.*
385. *Pellegrino Tibaldi, Saronno, Santuario della Madonna dei Miracoli, façade.* ▷

ith Palladio's Redentore in Venice, a votive church commemorat-
g that plague (Plate 461). San Sebastiano is a centrally-planned
artyrium, but it is unusual in that it has two concentric cylinders,
e inner being only very slightly smaller than the outer (Plate 383),
d supported by small flying buttresses. In addition, the upper
orey has a small order of pilasters corresponding to the large
oric pilasters on the ground floor, but the Ionic upper storey has
ind niches between the pilasters (very Michelangelesque in form,
d almost identical with those on San Fedele). The actual windows
e set in the attic between the pairs of buttresses. The whole design
far removed from the Doric *martyrium* of two concentric cylin-
ers that Bramante designed for San Pietro in Montorio.

Tibaldi worked on many other sanctuaries of the type popular
Lombardy and the foothills of the Alps — at Cannobio, Ver-
elli, Novara, and Saronno, where he designed a façade combining a
evere Palladian motif with a pair of huge herms (Plate 385). This
as in 1583, and within a few years Tibaldi had gone to Spain. He
eturned only to die; but the example he had given in the areas
round Como can hardly have failed to impress the architects from
ese sub-Alpine valleys who were to play so decisive a part in the
volution of Baroque architecture, even in Rome.

The architectural innovations made in Rome in the first quarter of the sixteenth century and developed there during the latter part of the century spread at varying speeds over the rest of Italy. The architecture of Tuscany and central Italy, which had been of primary importance in the fifteenth century, was relatively unimportant in the sixteenth, and the most significant developments of Bramante's ideas took place in the north. This was largely due to the economic and political difficulties of Florence and central Italy generally, so that many of the artists who fled from Rome as a result of the Sack went to the more stable northern states such as Venice or Genoa, or to places like Milan which were within the French sphere of influence. After 1527, some of the most interesting architecture in Italy was produced in Mantua, Genoa, or Milan; but above all in the Venetian Republic — in Venice itself, and in Padua, Verona, and Vicenza.

In the history of painting, the Venetian School proceeded majestically from Giorgione, through Titian and Tintoretto to Veronese, in a stylistic succession hardly affected by Mannerism, but fundamentally that of a great decorative tradition of restrained magnificence of colour and form. The sculpture of Vittorio or Jacopo Sansovino himself parallels the stylistic development of Titian, so that it is not surprising to find Sansovino as the most important architect working in the city and employing a similar, non-Mannerist, style. Almost all the architects working in the north at this time were either pupils of Bramante or were greatly influenced by him, and Sansovino and Sanmicheli, great artists in their own right, are important historically because they acted as carriers of his ideas. Sansovino, the most characteristically Venetian architect of the sixteenth century, was not a Venetian by birth, but a Florentine who had been trained as a sculptor under Andrea Sansovino, whose name he took. He worked in Rome in the early years of the century, at the same time as Sanmicheli, in contact with Bramante and the Sangallo circle. Although he was employed on San Giovanni dei Fiorentini and built the Palazzo Gaddi, his career as an architect really beings with his arrival in Venice in 1527. He was soon employed on miscellaneous small jobs and, even after he was made Chief Architect to the Republic, much of his time was spent on the ordinary administrative duties of a city architect. He was fortunate, however, in receiving several important commissions very early in his career, so that when he died, in 1570, most of his major buildings were complete or nearly so. The Venetian Republic, although already in political decline, was much less affected by the French and Spanish invasions than other Italian states and was, therefore, still able to undertake buildings of the size and cost of the Mint or the Library, and great families like the Cornaro were still able to afford a huge palace like the one on the Grand Canal they commissioned from Sansovino in 1533.

When Sansovino arrived in Venice, he must have been impressed by the great difference between the architectural traditions of the city and those of the mainland. Even cities like Padua, Verona, and Vicenza, profoundly Venetian as they were in all other respects, still differed from Venice itself in not being built on water. Venetian architecture, and particularly Venetian palaces, have always been conditioned by the extreme shortage of land and the consequent need to support buildings on very expensive piles driven into the shallow lagoon. The churches also retain a distinct flavour of Byzantium. Thus, when Sansovino arrived, he found palaces, most of which were built by Mauro Coducci or his relations, the Lombardi family, and churches such as Santa Maria dei Miracoli, or San Michele in Isola, which introduced Albertian ideas into Venice. Other churches, such as Spavento's San Salvatore, of c. 1507, though apparently closer in type to traditional Latin cross forms, also present features not to be found outside Venice.

The two great buildings of the city, the Doge's Palace and the Basilica of San Marco (which is technically the Doge's private chapel), provided models for most later secular and religious buildings. The Doge's Palace, with its unique arrangement of a mass of solid wall above a double arcade, was often imitated in detail, although its basic form with a great central court was far too extravagant of land to be followed by most palaces. The Ca' d'Oro (c. 1427 - c. 1436: Plate 386) provides an extraordinary contrast with such nearly contemporary buildings as the Spedale degli Innocenti or the Palazzo Rucellai in Florence (Plates 5, 67), and it shows the picturesque aspect of the Gothic style which lingered in Venice for many years after it had been banished from the rest of Italy. The Ca' d'Oro is obviously imitated from the Doge's Palace in its general arrangement, but it also demonstrates the essential constructional feature of the Venetian palace, which was to remain constant throughout the city's building history. The typical Venetian palace has three rather than two storeys, partly to economize on land and partly because the ground floor — at water level — is hardly habitable and must be used for storage. The *piano nobile* is therefore the main floor, but, because there is not usually a central court, the rooms are best lit by making one great room (the *gran salone*) in the centre, with very large windows at front and back. This gives the grouping of windows in the centre of the façade which is so typical of Venetian palaces, even when the architect has also attempted the symmetrical grouping of the House of Raphael type, the product of a totally different set of social conditions: thus, the Palazzo Vendramin-Calergi (Plate 388), begun about 1500 — earlier than the House of Raphael — shows an attempt to articulate the façade by means of columns, but the three great windows in the centre are still flanked on either side by symmetrically disposed single windows. Not until the advent of Sansovino and Sanmicheli was a satisfactory solution evolved to the problem of fitting a classical façade around this specifically Venetian window-grouping.

Sebastiano Serlio, the author of one of the most influential of all architectural treatises, was another refugee from the Bramante circle in Rome who also arrived in Venice in 1527. Unlike Sansovino, he did not settle there, and no building by him is known to have survived there, but he spent his time preparing the first parts of his treatise for publication (Book IV, Venice, 1537; Book III, Venice, 1540), before going to France to work for Francis I in 1541. Little survives even of the work he did in France (see p. 336), but he was enormously influential in transplanting Italian ideas. His own style, however, was by no means purely Bramantesque and the influence of Venetian art can be seen in some of his illustrations (Plate 387), which reflect the work being done in Venice by Sansovino and Sanmicheli.

In actual fact, Bramante's style probably first reached Venetian territory through the little-known painter and architect Giovanni Maria Falconetto, whose work in Padua in the 1520s is marked by Bramante's and Peruzzi's interpretations of Roman architecture. The first appearance in Padua of a new, more classical style provides an exact parallel with the introduction of Florentine Quattrocento ideas by Donatello eighty years earlier, which were taken up by Mantegna and developed in Venice by the Bellini. Falconetto, who was born in 1468 and died in 1534-35, was one of a family of Veronese painters who went to Padua about 1521 and worked on the Santo. His paintings were influenced by Mantegna, and, like him, he was a passionate archaeologist, visiting Rome more than once and making drawings of the antiquities. He was the friend of Alvise Cornaro, the author of a treatise on sobriety of life, for whom he designed the Loggia Cornaro (1524: Plate 389) and the Odeon next to it. This was designed on a central plan, part of which is an almost exact copy of the Baptistery type used by Bramante in the sacristy of Santa Maria presso San Satiro in Milan. The loggia proper is a two-storey, five-bay building rather like the Villa Farnesina, but it has Bramantesque elements, particularly on the upper storey. The heavy richness of the Doric on the ground floor, especially the triumphal arch treatment of the projecting centre bay with winged Victories in the spandrels, foreshadows the ornate yet simple classicism which was to be characteristic of Sansovino and of Venetian Cinquecento art in general. It is quite different from

389. *Giovanni Falconetto, Padua, Loggia Cornaro.*
390. *Padua, Loggia Cornaro, plan.*
391. *Jacopo Sansovino, Venice, San Marco, Libreria Sansoviniana, general view.* ▷

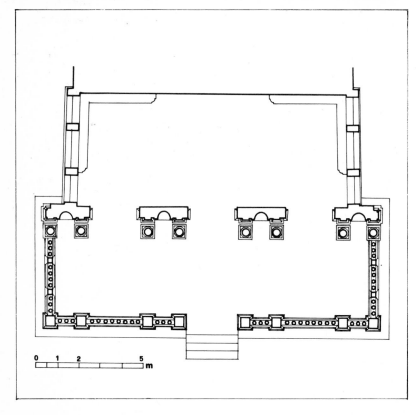

258

392. *Venice, San Marco, Libreria Sansoviniana, plan.*
393. *Jacopo Sansovino, Venice, San Marco, Libreria Sansoviniana, detail of angle.*

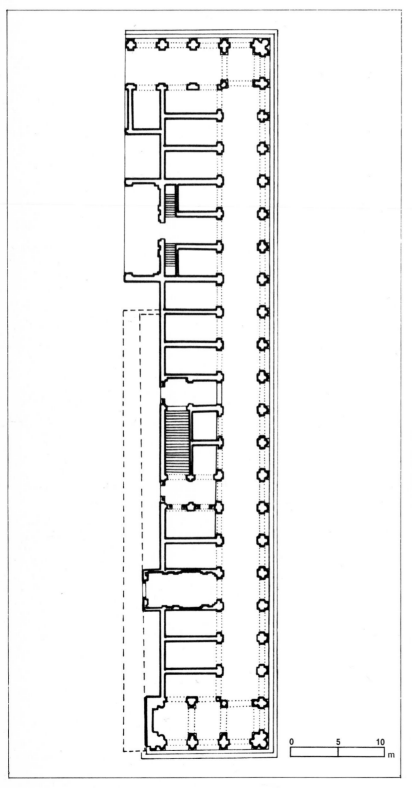

the sophisticated architecture of Giulio Romano, whose Palazzo del Te was begun at about the same time, but Falconetto has only recently been recognized as the man who introduced these forms into the Veneto, before the arrival of the two men who were to lift Venetian architecture onto an entirely new plane.

For most people, the quintessence of Venice would be a view from the Piazzetta including the Doge's Palace, the Library, and, impossibly, both San Marco and Santa Maria della Salute. Sansovino's masterpiece, the Library, built to house the books bequeathed to the Republic by the great Greek scholar, Cardinal Bessarione, fits so naturally into this complex, and is so obviously a classical successor to the palace, as well as the ancestor of the Salute, that it is difficult to imagine the Piazzetta without it (Plate 391). Put another way, it is a perfect expression of the grand-scale civic loggia *all'antica,* first adumbrated in the north by Falconetto hardly more than a dozen years earlier, but which goes back at least as far as the Benediction Loggia in Rome (Plate 123). The great civic loggie in North Italy — at Padua, Vicenza, and elsewhere — were all Gothic, but are obvious forerunners of Sansovino's design, as of Palladio's.

The primary purpose of the building was to house the books safely and provide a reading room, and Sansovino decided to do this on the first floor of his building (perhaps on the model of the Laurenziana), thus securing a very long arcade which could be used as a public amenity, for shade and recreation, and which could also be used for small shops of the type familiar to Sansovino from Roman palaces like the House of Raphael. This resulted in a forum for Sansovino's adopted city, the grandest to be built since classical times, although something similar — but much less ambitious — had been carried out for the Sforzas at Vigevano by Bramante (Plate 394).

When he began work in 1537, Sansovino had found the solution to two main problems — the siting, and the basic outline of the building, the latter being in part dependent on the former. A sixteenth-century woodcut shows the Piazzetta when the construction had only just begun (Plate 395), and another, earlier woodcut from Breydenbach's *Sanctae Peregrinationes* (Mainz, 1486) confirms the general appearance of the Piazzetta. Sansovino decided to use the Campanile and the Column of St. Theodore as the boundaries of his perspective composition, more or less following the existing houses, but with the important consequence that his large building would now appear to compete with the Doge's Palace, since the two were converging in fact as well as in perspective. He was thus faced with the problem of making a monumental, ornate building which, because of its classical form, was necessarily supe-

395. 'Il Volo del Turco', woodcut (Venice, Museo Correr).
396. Jacopo Sansovino, Venice, San Marco, Libreria Sansoviniana, view from pier.
397. Jacopo Sansovino, Venice, San Marco, Libreria Sansoviniana, view from lagoon.

rior to the Gothic Palace — yet, for reasons of tact, must not seem to diminish the seat of government. His solution is brilliantly simple. First, the site demanded a very long, but very narrow, building (the whole Library is twenty-one bays long, sixteen of them built in Sansovino's lifetime); second, the Doge's Palace consists of a double arcade, which, when translated into classical Roman terms, gives something like the Theatre of Marcellus or the Colosseum. Sansovino therefore decided on a double arcade, the total height of which is considerably less than the total height of the palace, though somewhat greater than that of the arcades alone. This meant that he kept his skyline below that of the palace, and therefore did not compete with it; he then added the statues and obelisks to increase the height, while at the same time dissolving the silhouette, since the deep entablature would otherwise have been oppressively heavy. What he lacked in colour, he made up in richly carved stone.

Once the decision had been taken to use a classical *porticus*, it was easy to design the lower range as a public forum and to decide to use the upper range, anachronistically, as a *piano nobile*. The choice almost automatically involved the Doric and Ionic Orders, and here Sansovino had several difficulties to overcome. To begin with, there was the problem of the Doric angle. According to Vitruvius, the Doric Order needs a half-metope at the angle, when an Order is being taken right round a building. This is not easy to arrange and was the subject of discussion during the sixteenth century. It had been solved quite satisfactorily in practice, by Sanmicheli and others, but Sansovino's more ambitious solution — according to the account by his son — was the result of much study and was arrived at after making a wooden model which won the approval of architects and connoisseurs. It was to provide a wide pier at the actual angle, to which he added an applied pilaster, adjusting the width of the pier to accord with the frieze of metopes and triglyphs; certainly this gave a very satisfactory strength to the angles, which otherwise would have seemed too slender for the apparent weight.

Unfortunately, by transforming the upper arcade into a *piano nobile*, Sansovino had to introduce windows and had also to stress the fact that it, and not the ground floor, was the public building. His solution to the problem of the windows was to use the so-called 'Palladian motive' (called *serliana* in Italian, but in fact a Bramante discovery), which meant that he had to use two small, fluted, Ionic columns to frame the windows, setting the whole inside the main arcade. He left less space between the columns and the wall than is usual with the Palladian motif, but there are two columns set in depth to give visual weight and richness. His bay-design can be

01. Jacopo Sansovino, Venice, La Zecca, detail of second Order.
02. Venice, Palazzo Corner della Ca' Grande, axonometric drawing.

403. Jacopo Sansovino, Venice, Palazzo Corner della Ca' Grande. ▷
404. Jacopo Sansovino, Venice, Palazzo Corner della Ca' Grande, detail of façade. ▷

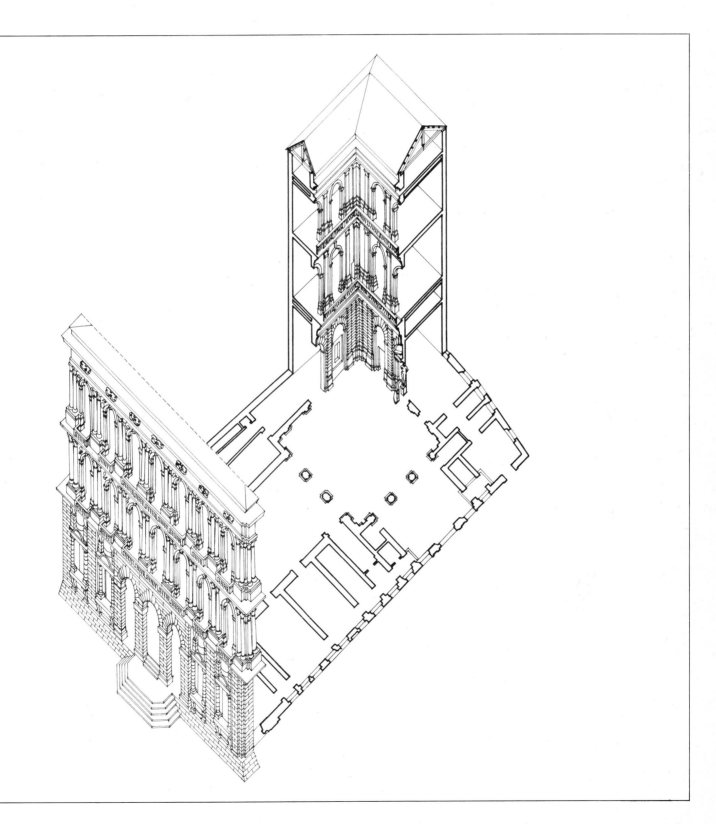

405-407. Jacopo Sansovino, Venice, Palazzo Corner della Ca' Grande, views of court.

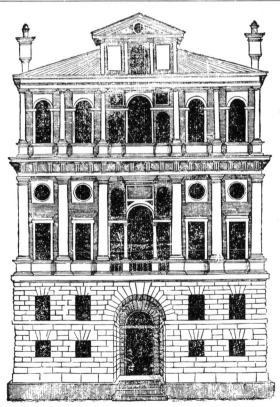

compared with the form illustrated by Serlio in his Fourth Book, published in 1537, and with the form adapted from Sansovino by Palladio, who described the Libreria Sansoviniana as 'perhaps the richest and most ornate building erected since the time of the Ancients' — and it is important to remember that 'ornate' was, at this date, a term of eulogy.

The very deep frieze of the Ionic Order contains mezzanine windows as well as sculpture, so that the effects of light and shade in this part are rich and varied, from the spandrel figures, the masks on the keystones, the swags and putti, right up to the balustrade and the crowning figures and obelisks.

Sansovino's concern for texture and painterly effects of chiaroscuro can be seen even more clearly in his buildings at either end of the Library. The Loggetta at the base of the Campanile (Plates 398, 399) is an elaborate piece of architectural sculpture to mask the otherwise too sharp contrast between the horizontal lines of the Library and the vertical shaft of the Campanile itself. The triumphal arch motive, with its freestanding columns, is exactly right a sa way of unifying the two buildings while maintaining visual diversity. The Mint — La Zecca — (Plates 400, 401), at the other end, is a different problem. In fact, it was built before the Library, and originally there would have been no clash between the two, but the visual effect is made worse for us by the fact that the Zecca was designed to be only two storeys high. It is built entirely of rusticated stonework, very similar in effect to Giulio Romano's exploitation of textures, but this was because the Zecca was the bullion-store of the Republic, and the fortress appearance was therefore deliberate, like the fortified gates by Sanmicheli. It was probably Sansovino's first work as Chief Architect, and Vasari says that it was the first time the 'Rustic Order' had been seen in Venice.

Sansovino's official duties did not leave him much time for private commissions, but he was given the opportunity to impose a classical form on the Venetian palace when the Cornaro family employed him to design their huge palace on the Grand Canal — Palazzo Corner della Ca' Grande (Plates 402-7). The foundations were laid in 1533, but work was very slow — it was still unfinished in 1556 — and it has also been altered. For a Venetian palace, it has a large court, but the plan (Plate 402) shows that the main front of the building is very deep, and the *gran salone* has only three windows in spite of its great depth. The façade has been regularized by the use of paired columns in a sequence not unlike that of the Library (Plate 391), but the three central windows are still noticeably closer together than the outer ones. The triple entrance is very similar to Michele Sanmicheli's Palazzo Canossa, which is exactly contemporary, and the two provide an instructive comparison between the types in

277

411. Giovanni Falconetto, Luvigliano, Villa dei Vescovi.

412. Pontecasale, Villa Garzoni, plan.
413. Jacopo Sansovino, Pontecasale, Villa Garzoni, façade.
414. Jacopo Sansovino, Pontecasale, Villa Garzoni, detail of façade. ▷

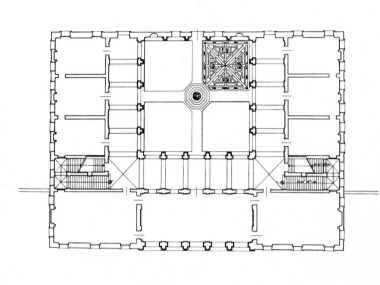

415, 416. Jacopo Sansovino, Pontecasale, Villa Garzoni, views of court.
417. Michele Sanmicheli, Treville di Castelfranco Veneto, Villa Soranza, elevation (from Ronzani e Luciolli).

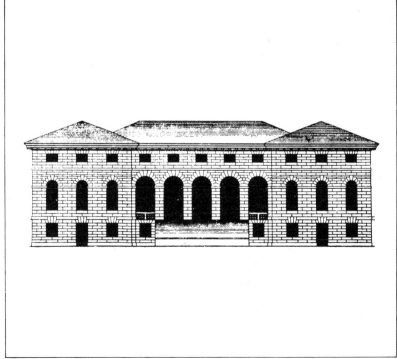

use in Venice and Verona (Plates 426, 427). The same comparison can be made between Palazzo Corner and Sanmicheli's Palazzo Grimani in Venice (Plate 408), designed at the end of his life, in 1559. The Palazzo Grimani was originally of two storeys only (as is evident even now), but the Palazzo Corner-Mocenigo a San Polo, also by Sanmicheli (Plate 409), had two main storeys and two mezzanines in an attempt to compromise between the House of Raphael type and the higher shape normal in Venice. In both the Palazzo Grimani and the Palazzo Corner-Mocenigo, the *gran salone* window problem is met by the use of the Palladian motive, and it is likely that the inspiration came from Serlio (Book IV: Plate 387). By comparison, the Sansovino palace is classical in inspiration and simple in its decoration.

Another direct comparison between Sansovino and Sanmicheli can be made in their treatment of the villa. The classical villa, as described by Pliny the Younger, had been a subject of architectural interest at least since Giuliano da Sangallo's designs for Poggio a Caiano and Poggio Imperiale. The Roman villas — Villa Farnesina and, above all, Villa Madama — had been more classical, perhaps because of Bramante's Belvedere, and were succeeded by the Palazzo del Te. After 1550, Palladio was to provide a series of definitive solutions which remained valid for the whole of Europe for more than two centuries, but the earliest of his villa designs date from about 1538, and it was during the forties that both Sansovino and Sanmicheli each designed a villa to meet the new demand for them in the Veneto. In point of fact, it may have been Falconetto, once again, who was the first to design a formal villa in the Venetian countryside, the Villa dei Vescovi at Luvigliano, near Padua (*c.* 1529-35: Plate 411). However, there were many fifteenth- and even fourteenth-century predecessors (such as the Villa Colleoni or Ca' Brusa), which served as starting points for the sixteenth-century architects.

Sansovino's Villa Garzoni at Pontecasale, near Padua, was probably designed as early as 1540 (Plates 413-16), and the Villa Soranza, also near Padua, was designed by Sanmicheli about 1540-50, but is now lost (Plate 417): both are examples of the loggia with wings, which makes them perhaps closer to the Villa Farnesina (known to both architects) than to the Palladian type, in which the farm buildings are usually integrated into the whole design. The plan of the Villa Garzoni is identical to that of the Farnesina (Plates 257, 412), but at the Villa Garzoni the wings also contain loggie and there is a closing wall at the end of the composition (Plate 415). The size and grandeur of the Villa Garzoni, and especially the central court (Plates 415, 416), give it rather the appearance of a palace planted in the countryside and make it difficult to think of it as a working farm,

as most of Palladio's clearly are. As far as we can reconstruct La Soranza, the central block was linked by straight walls to the *bar-chesse* (farm buildings), and the central block of the villa (unlike the Villa Garzoni) had a loggia with short projecting wings on the entrance side. This is very close to the type used by Palladio's patron Trissino and by Palladio himself (Plate 450).

Michele Sanmicheli of Verona was an architect and nothing else. Unlike Falconetto, who was a painter, or Sansovino, who was a sculptor, and indeed unlike almost all his contemporaries and pre-decessors — even Bramante — he was never anything but a builder. True, he was the most distinguished military engineer of his time, but no one would have thought of that as a profession distinct from architecture.

He was born in 1484, the son of an architect and sculptor, and, according to his own account, he went to Rome at the age of sixteen — i.e. about 1500, the year of Bramante's arrival from the north. We know that he became Surveyor of Orvieto Cathedral in 1509 and held the post for nearly twenty years before returning, about the time of the Sack of Rome, to his native Verona, where he worked for the rest of his life as an official of the Venetian Republic, like Sansovino.

His formative years must therefore have been spent in Rome during the decade when, in Serlio's phrase, 'Bramante resuscitated architec-ture from the dead.' The years between 1500 and 1509 saw the build-ing of the Pace cloister, the Tempietto, the apse of Santa Maria del Popolo, the Belvedere, the first projects for St. Peter's, and, pro-bably, the House of Raphael. In fact, it might be argued that San-micheli's knowledge of this design is evidence for dating it before 1509, but we also know that he returned to Rome in 1513, sent by the *operai* of Orvieto to take counsel with Antonio da Sangallo the Younger over the cathedral façade. In 1526, he was employed by Clement VII, somewhat tardily, to accompany Antonio da Sangallo on a tour of inspection of fortresses in the Papal States.

Sanmicheli's Roman years were those of the High Renaissance, although he seems to have left before the completion of the Sistine Ceiling or the Vatican Stanze. He had probably reached the same stage of development as his contemporary, the Sienese Baldassare Peruzzi (*b.* 1481), whose first work, the Villa Farnesina, was begun in the year Sanmicheli left Rome. Michele had almost certainly been a pupil or assistant of Sangallo, who was himself a draughtsman and assistant to Bramante, and from him he would have received a sound training in draughtsmanship and construction, and, above all, an almost Chinese reverence for the ancients. He could hardly have escaped — even if he wanted to — the influence of Bramante, by far the greatest mind then grappling with the problems of archi-

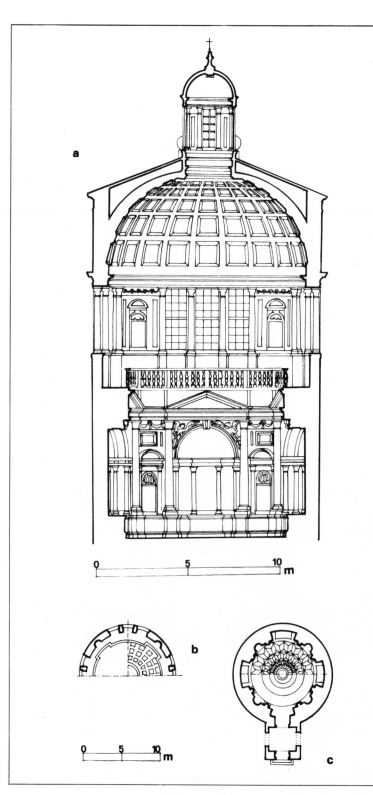

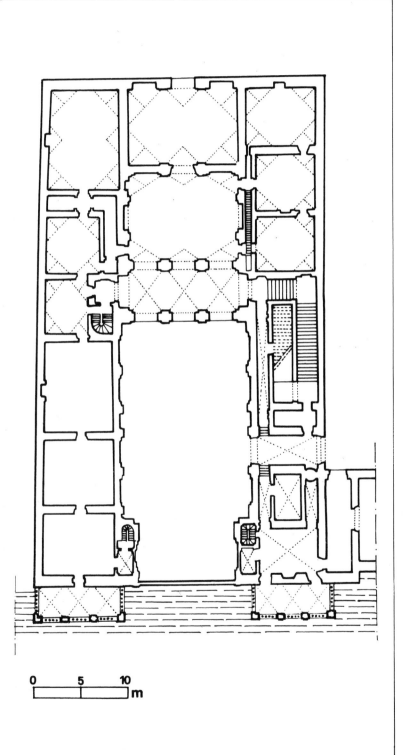

0   5   10
m

tecture — 'in our own times architecture has arisen from sleep and we see it now very closely resembling the style of the Ancients, as is evident in many of Bramante's beautiful works...' (Letter to Leo X).

These were the ideas he took to the north of Italy, following in the footsteps of Giulio Romano (who went to Mantua in 1524) and Sansovino and Serlio (who went to Venice at about the same time as Sanmicheli himself), but he was certainly closer in spirit to Bramante than was Giulio Romano — although Giulio's Palazzo del Te influenced him greatly. His style can be seen most clearly by contrast with Bramante, Sangallo, and Roman austerity on the one hand, and with the rich decoration and sculptural feeling of Sansovino on the other. His relationship to Giulio Romano — and to Mannerism — is more difficult to define and can be interpreted in more than one way.

First of all, there is the problem of the evolution of his style. The cathedral at Montefiascone (Plate 418), about twenty miles south of Orvieto, was taken over by him probably before 1519, but his dome was burnt and a new one built in the seventeenth century. The façade, with its two campanili, derives from the Foundation Medal of St. Peter's, like the contemporary San Biagio at Montepulciano (Plate 222). His work at Orvieto, though apparently extensive, was not important; so we find him working in Verona by about 1527, when he was in his middle forties, with no clear picture of his development to prepare us for such complex works as the Cappella Pellegrini in San Bernardino, which seems to represent a later stylistic phase than, say, the Bramantesque Palazzo Pompei (Plates 419, 425). A partial explanation is to be found in his military activities. In the early sixteenth century, the Venetian State was gravely threatened, not only by the Turks, who had dominated the eastern Mediterranean since their capture of Constantinople, but also by the various and shifting alliances between the Papacy, ehe Empire, France, Spain, and the other Italian states, all of which tyed Venetian opulence with envy. Because of this, Sanmicheli was sent all over the Terra firma and to Dalmatia, Crete, and Corfu to inspect and build or strengthen fortresses. For the Republic, and presumably for him as well, this was the greatest service he could render his country. We may regard it as a waste of a great artist's time, but it left its mark on his architecture.

The development of artillery led to changes in the design of fortresses — many older ones were no longer defensible — but Sanmicheli had grasped a basic principle: a fortress must not only *be* strong, it must *look* impregnable. The fortified gateways he built in Verona and elsewhere, such as the Porta Nuova (Plate 423) or the Porta Palio (Plates 421, 422), are admirable examples of his technique of giving rich decoration, which serves a functional purpose,

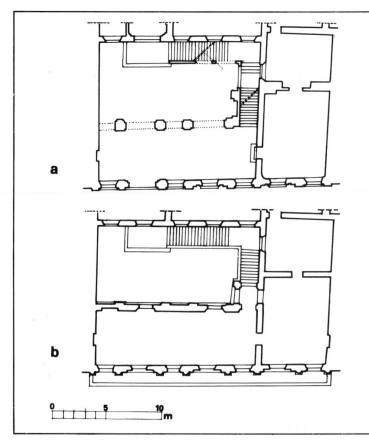

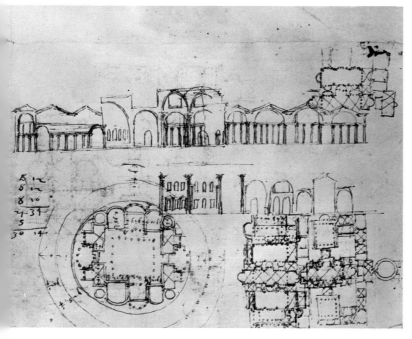

to a building intended as an embellishment of the city as well as a protection to it. Sanmicheli's principal artistic aim was to observe the classic harmony of proportion he had learned in Rome, while at the same time enriching and varying it in conformity with north Italian taste, and also perhaps in accordance with a general trend of taste towards those monuments of antiquity that were richly decorated and slightly exotic in style. This tendency is to be seen in the later works of Raphael as well as in Giulio Romano, and, from the point of view of 'correctness', the architects could justify themselves by reference to such impeccable antiquities as the Porta Maggiore in Rome or the Porta de' Borsari in Verona (Plate 424). The latter was used as well as admired by Sanmicheli, and the type of ornate Roman decoration which it represents was the more acceptable to him because it fitted in so well with the style of his own gateways.

The Porta Nuova was begun about 1533, only a few years later than the Palazzo del Te, but the influence of Giulio Romano is plain to see in the rustication, the heavy keystones, and the triumphal arch rhythms. Nevertheless, it is probably true that both men were imitating a particular form of ancient building, such as the Porta Maggiore in Rome, and therefore achieved similar results.

The Porta Palio, completed c. 1557, is still more complex, or, to put it another way, Mannerist. The top layer of the rustication is apparently cut back to reveal yet further rustication (Plate 421) on the outer side of the gate, giving an impression of rugged solidity that contrasts with the more open treatment of the town side, rusticated though it still is (Plate 422). The detailing of the outer side, exposed as it was to cannon-balls, is nevertheless treated with the maximum richness permissible to the Doric Order. On 6 November 1557, the Venetian Senate decided that, for reasons of economy, no further rusticated masonry was to be used in the works at Verona, with the sole exception of the Porta Palio. Their reward came in 1568, when Vasari, in the *Life* of his friend Sanmicheli, described the Porta Nuova and Porta Palio, saying: 'In these two gates it may truly be seen that the Venetian Senate, by making full use of the architect's powers, has indeed equalled the buildings and constructions of the Ancient Romans.'

Apart from his military work, Sanmicheli built four major palaces, three in Verona and one in Venice, and several churches and chapels, one of which, the Cappella Pellegrini, seems to be datable from the beginning of his activity in Verona, about 1526-27, since the building was certainly under construction in 1529; yet a will of 1557 of Donna Margherita Pellegrini, who commissioned the chapel, specifically states that it is not yet finished, and Vasari says this: 'It was left unfinished, for what reason I do not know, by

432. *Andrea Palladio, Maser, Villa Barbaro-Volpi, plan and elevation.*
433. *Andrea Palladio, Maser, Villa Barbaro-Volpi.*

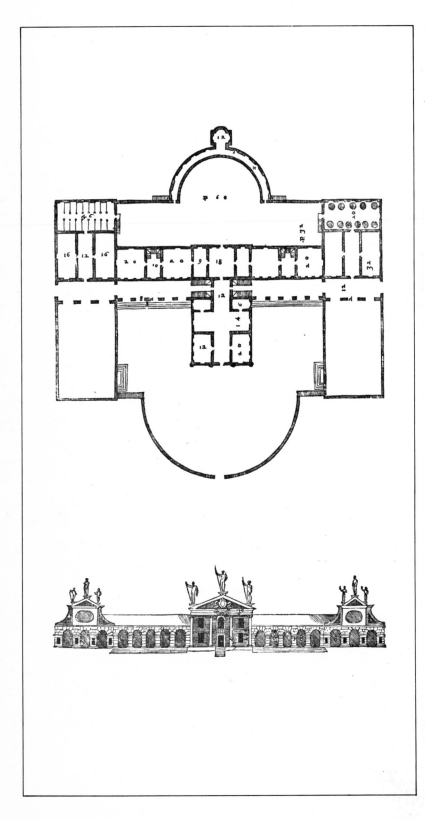

Michele and was given, either from avarice or lack of judgement, to others to be finished, who spoiled it... Michele, in his own lifetime, saw it ruined before his very eyes...' The most notable thing about the chapel, as we have it, is its likeness to the Pantheon. The plan (Plate 425) is almost a copy, and the coffered dome is a further reminder, but the introduction of an intermediate storey may be due to the example of Michelangelo's New Sacristy, also a mortuary chapel. The windows are in the upper part, the whole of the lower part being taken up by three deep niches containing altars, with smaller niches between them. The articulation is based on a triumphal arch rhythm, with columns supporting the shallow curved pediments above the altars, and a smaller pilaster system running round the walls and supporting the segmental pediments above the niches. A particularly striking feature, borrowed from the Porta Palio, is the use of columns with twisted fluting, the left-hand column of each altar-bay being twisted to the left, and the right-hand column in the opposite direction. This unusual feature recurs in the façade of the Palazzo Bevilacqua and might be evidence for dating the palace to the same period. This, however, is by no means certain, since there are two other Sanmicheli palaces in Verona, both datable in the thirties, which seem to be stylistically earlier than the Bevilacqua. The Palazzo Pompei (Plate 419) is undated, but is often regarded as his earliest palace, largely because of its close dependence upon the House of Raphael (Plate 244). The design is reduced to the simplest elements – a rusticated ground floor serving as a podium for the single columns articulating the *piano nobile*, with an equal number of bays disposed symmetrically about the entrance. The differences between it and the House of Raphael are few and simple, for Sanmicheli has given to centre and ends an importance denied them by Bramante, whose bays repeat identically. Sanmicheli has made his single door-bay wider in order to match its height (he does not provide shops); and as a result of this emphasis, the bay above is wider than its fellows. To compensate, Sanmicheli has given a slight stress to the ends by closing them with a square pier in addition to the normal column.

The Palazzo Canossa (Plates 426, 427) was probably begun about 1533 and was in building in 1537, so it may help to date the Palazzo Pompei, which seems to be stylistically slightly earlier. Here, the rhythm of the ground floor with its triple arched openings differs from the evenly articulated bays of the *piano nobile*, which originally had a single, central, emphasis in the form of a coat of arms. The sources of the design include Bramante, but the triple arches must surely come from Giulio's Palazzo del Te, while the treatment of the paired pilasters with sharply cut panelling behind is a reminiscence of Bramante's Belvedere. The court repeats the motif in a different way, this time with an even clearer reference to the Belvedere (Plates 238, 239). It is unusual in being three-sided, with long side-arms reaching down to the River Adige, which acts as a boundary.

The problem presented by the Palazzo Bevilacqua is, therefore, to explain how it seems to fit into a stylistic sequence which must make it later than the mid-thirties, when it employs motifs already used in the Cappella Pellegrini. The façade of the Bevilacqua Palace (Plate 429) is different from the other two principally in its greater richness and in its apparent asymmetry. As with Raphael's Palazzo Branconio dell'Aquila (Plate 247), the basic form is that of the House of Raphael, and indeed Sanmicheli's building retains the rusticated podium and the *piano nobile* distinguished by an Order, but the articulation of the whole is far more sophisticated, having no less than three separate rhythms. This 'illegibility' has caused it to be taken as evidence of Sanmicheli's adhesion to Mannerism, at about the same time as Giulio was building the Palazzo del Te. There can be little doubt about the importance of the Te in Sanmicheli's style, but it is worth considering how far the Bevilacqua can truly be called a Mannerist work. To take the asymmetry first, it is clear that either the main entrance is off-centre or the façade is incomplete and needs four more bays on the left-hand side. The plan (Plate 428) is ambiguous, but there are several arguments against this hypothetical enlargement of the palace, proposed in some recent studies. In the first place, if we disregard the off-centre entrance, we find that the basement is really symmetrical, since the wide door-bay is balanced by an equally wide bay in the centre and at the right, each corresponding to the big windows of the *piano nobile*, so that the rhythm of the basement is: a.A.a.A.a.A.a. The cornice of the building does in fact continue round the angle, as though the façade were complete, which gives a 2:3 proportion of height to width, where the addition of extra bays would make an awkward — and extravagantly large — design.

The basement is, therefore, basically simple, though rich in its decoration, with the very unusual and Mannerist feature of banded rustication on the pilasters themselves. The *piano nobile* is even more complex in its decoration, but it, too, has a fundamental simplicity of rhythm. Taken as a whole, it consists of a series of triumphal arches, each having one bay in common with its neighbour; thus, the façade is a.A.a.A.a.A.a., the same as the ground floor. This, however, is only the simple articulation, and there are two further rhythms in what can best be described as counterpoint. If we take the elements of the triumphal arches themselves, it becomes clear that they consist of three arches articulated by four columns, the arches being a small one, with a triangular pediment

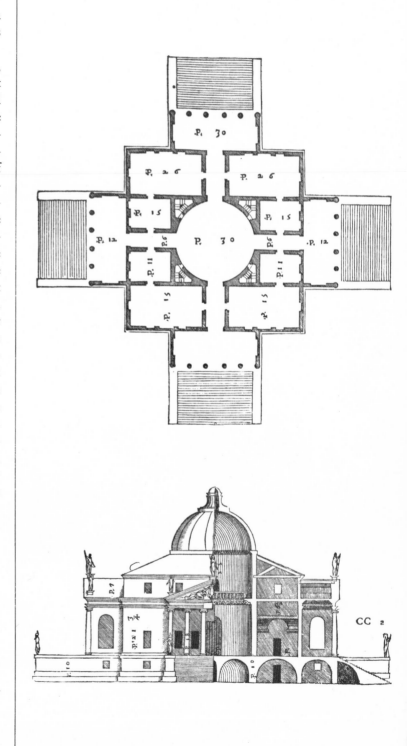

set over it; a large one; a second small one, this time with a segmental pediment. Thus, the simple a.A.a. rhythm is really a.A.*a...* and the façade as a whole now reads: a.A.*a.*A.*a.*A.a. which is still symmetrical. The next complication comes from the fluted columns. These are evidently inspired by the Porta de' Borsari (Plate 424) and have, therefore, a respectable classical ancestry, like every other feature of the palace. Here, the rhythm is: I\/II\/I which is again symmetrical, but could be expressed as: a.b.c.a.a.b.c.a. In other words, all three systems make sense when the façade *as a whole* is considered — like a fugue, they reach a *stretto,* and this is obviously more sophisticated than the simple repetitions of Bramante, whose palace fronts can be extended almost indefinitely, provided only that the extensions balance.

In his ecclesiastical architecture Sanmicheli seems, on the whole, to have remained more faithful to Bramante's ideals, perhaps because he designed several centrally-planned churches, most of them austere and simple in their forms — much more so than in the case of the Cappella Pellegrini — and he may have felt that this was suitable, since *decorum* in these matters was a cardinal point in the architectural theory of Vitruvius, Alberti, and, later, Palladio. At San Giorgio in Braida, Verona, he built a simple drum and dome, but his designs for the Madonna di Campagna (Plate 430) and for the chapel of the Lazzaretto are interesting variations on the theme of Bramante's Tempietto.

The Lazzaretto was an isolation hospital, designed about 1548, which consisted of an enormous court containing 152 cells, so arranged that each had a view of the central chapel, exactly like the arrangement of Filarete's hospital a century earlier. The chapel itself, now ruined, was designed on the lines of Bramante's Tempietto (Plate 196), but was an open screen of columns arranged in concentric peristyles, without walls, so that all the inmates could see Mass celebrated without leaving their cells. The actual proportions are not happy, but Sanmicheli was probably not responsible for the execution.

This is also the case with the very similar disposition of the Madonna di Campagna in a suburb of Verona (Plate 430), designed in 1559 following the report of a miracle in April of that year. Sanmicheli died in the autumn, so Vasari's indignant account of the way in which his design was being ruined is entirely plausible, especially as the Tuscan peristyle is obviously much too low. Because it is a *martyrium* it has a central plan, but there are really two interlocked central plans — one an octagon contained in a circle and the other a modified Greek cross, one arm of which is merged with the octagon, which thus becomes a kind of nave, although from the outside it is the dominant feature. This seems to be a

439. *Andrea Palladio, Vicenza, Basilica Palladiana.*

distant reminiscence of Bramante's problem at St. Peter's, although the Tempietto was the formal model.

Andrea Palladio of Vicenza belonged to a different generation from Sansovino and Sanmicheli, since he was not only younger (he was born in 1508), but even more because he had no direct contact with the Bramante circle in Rome. He was the son of a Paduan miller and was a stonemason and sculptor until his gifts were discovered by the humanist Giangiorgio Trissino, who educated him and took him to Rome, probably in 1541 for the first time, and for a long stay in 1545-47. Palladio was brought up on Vitruvian principles and first saw the antiquities of Rome soon after Vignola drew them for the Vitruvian Academy: he also made many superb drawings of the ruins, most of which are now in the collection of the Royal Institute of British Architects in London (Plate 431). During later visits to Rome, he was temporarily influenced by the works of Michelangelo, but this phase soon passed, and his most characteristic works are based on Vitruvian and mathematical theories of proportion and harmony, expressed in terms of the Orders and of Bramantesque decoration. Palladio's theoretical principles are known to us from his treatise — *I Quattro Libri dell' Architettura* — published in 1570, the four Books of which contain woodcuts, much better executed and finer in detail than those in Serlio's earlier treatise, showing the setting-out and details of the classical Orders; a series of selected antiquities, mostly, but not exclusively, from Rome; illustrations of Bramante's Tempietto, on the grounds that he was 'the first to bring back to the light of day the good and beautiful architecture, which had been hidden from the time of the Ancients until his own', as well as a series of Palladio's own works, including the Basilica at Vicenza and many villas and palaces. Because the treatise was published in 1570, it could not include the masterpieces of the last decade of his life, San Giorgio Maggiore and the Redentore in Venice, and several others.

The *Quattro Libri* is a lucid statement of the aims of a classical architect, who based himself partly on antiquity and partly on his own interpretation of the rules laid down by Vitruvius. Palladio's knowledge of Vitruvius was at least equal to that possessed by any of his contemporaries, since he was responsible for the illustrations in the edition published by his patron Daniele Barbaro in 1556, which soon became the standard text. He had accompanied Barbaro to Rome in 1554, and was later to build one of his finest villas for him at Maser (Plate 433). Palladio's theory of proportion, though based on Vitruvius, was more subtle, since he advocated a complex series of harmonic relationships, based on musical scales, which were to govern the proportions, not merely of one room, but of each of the rooms in a sequence. In addition to this, he retained a strictly

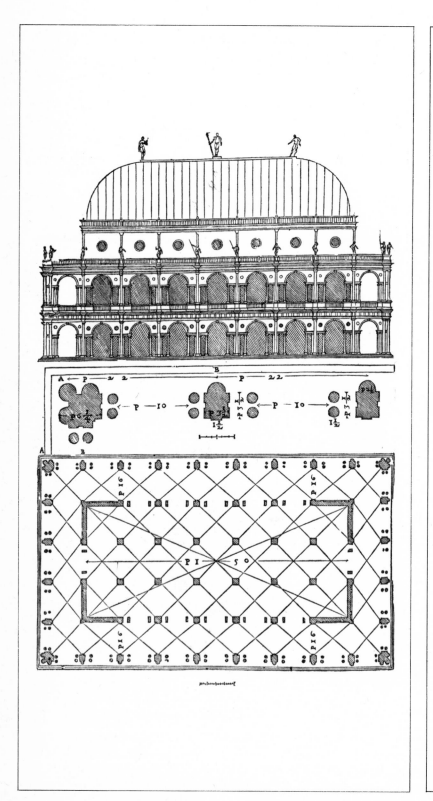

symmetrical disposition of rooms, sometimes extended as far as a complete bi-axial symmetry, as in the Villa Rotonda (Plates 435, 436). His archaeological scholarship places him firmly in the Bramante-Sangallo-Vignola tradition, and only rarely does he betray any interest in Mannerist ideas; when he does — as in the Palazzo Valmarana of 1565-66 (Plate 437) — his inspiration seems to be Michelangelesque, but there is also evidence that he studied the work of Giulio Romano, and the Palazzo Thiene (of *c*. 1545-50) has a sophisticated handling of textures (Plate 438) derived from Giulio's treatment of rustication. The connection between Giulio and Palladio dates back to Palladio's first great success, the reconstruction of the medieval town hall of Vicenza.

Like many other north Italian cities, Vicenza had a large Palazzo del Comune ('Palazzo della Ragione'), dating from the thirteenth century, but rebuilt in the fifteenth, which served as a law-court, meeting-place for the Council of Four Hundred, and general administrative offices — i.e. it was the modern equivalent of a classical basilica, whence its name. In his Third Book, Palladio specifically makes a distinction between the basilicas of the ancients and those of our own times, citing his own at Vicenza and giving illustrations (Plate 439).

By the middle of the sixteenth century, the old building needed repair, and in particular the walls needed support against the thrust of the massive roof. In 1538 Sansovino, in 1539 Serlio, and in 1541 Sanmicheli were all consulted. Finally, in the early 1540s, Giulio Romano prepared a project, which would almost certainly have been executed had he not died in 1546. Palladio, who had also prepared a design, was commissioned by his fellow-citizens to proceed, but the actual construction was to last throughout his lifetime and beyond. The design was formally approved in 1549 and Palladio was at once established as a major architect.

In effect, he proposed to shore up the earlier building by constructing a great stone arcade round the outside of it, to support it by a series of linked buttresses. Since the palazzo was already two storeys high, Palladio was not free to design entirely in the void, and the obvious solution was to provide two arcades, the lower corresponding with the height of the ground floor, while the upper would be conditioned by the height of the arcade below it and by the need to rise high enough to contain the thrust exerted by the roof. To a man of Palladio's training, a double arcade of this type would immediately suggest the Theatre of Marcellus in Rome, which had so recently served as the prototype for Sansovino's Library in Venice, and it was probably a tactful move on Palladio's part to design something similar but less elaborate.

The Basilica Palladiana is a combination of Sansovino's Library with two plates from Serlio's treatise (Plates 439-41); but this does not explain the extraordinary subtlety and delicacy of the design as a whole, in which the contrasts of light and shade and of carefully calculated masses produce an effect as satisfying aesthetically as Sansovino's without elaborate and expensive sculpture. In some ways, Palladio's forms are superior, since he has an even finer solution to the problem of the Doric angle. The basilica consists of a series of identical Palladian motives, separated by attached columns which face the great pier-buttresses. The pattern is, however, varied at the ends, where the Palladian motive is reduced in width (it is more like the form used by Sansovino), but, at the same time, the whole bay projects slightly and is given additional visual weight by coupled columns at the actual angle. By this means the angle-bay not only looks but is more solid than its neighbours and therefore gives extra support to the corners of the building. Where Sansovino increased the depth of the friezes and filled them with decorative sculpture, Palladio retained a strictly classical form and obtained a decorative effect by simply piercing the spandrels of the arches with circular *oculi*. The classic simplicity of this design is best seen by contrast with the Loggia del Capitanio of 1571-72, another, much smaller public building by Palladio opposite the basilica (Plate 442). This shows what is probably the highest degree of Mannerist influence in his work, especially in the side façade, with the relief commemorating the victory of Lepanto (7 October 1571), which caused a considerable modification to the design.

Palladio's other works in Vicenza were for private patrons, although the Palazzo Chiericati of 1550 was a semi-public building in so far as it was designed as part of a great 'Forum', intended to run round all four sides of the piazza, one end of which is formed by the palace itself. This scheme would have provided a covered loggia as a public amenity, but as it was never completed, the façade has a rather strange appearance (Plate 443), with what is apparently a great waste of space on the ground floor and a single central projection on the *piano nobile* instead of the more usual loggia. Unlike the basilica or Sansovino's Library, this forum would have been correctly Roman in that it had straight entablatures over the columns, instead of the arches carried on piers or columns of the normal Italian city-loggia type. This may be a reflection of the straight entablatures introduced by Michelangelo in his design for the Capitol, although this was still hardly begun. It is noteworthy that there is no reflection of Michelangelo's influence in other respects, and Palladio adopted the Giant Order only in 1565, at the Palazzo Valmarana.

Another early work, the Palazzo Iseppo-Porto, designed before

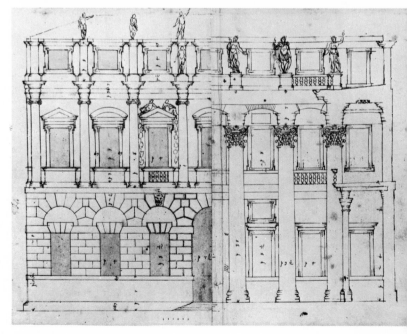

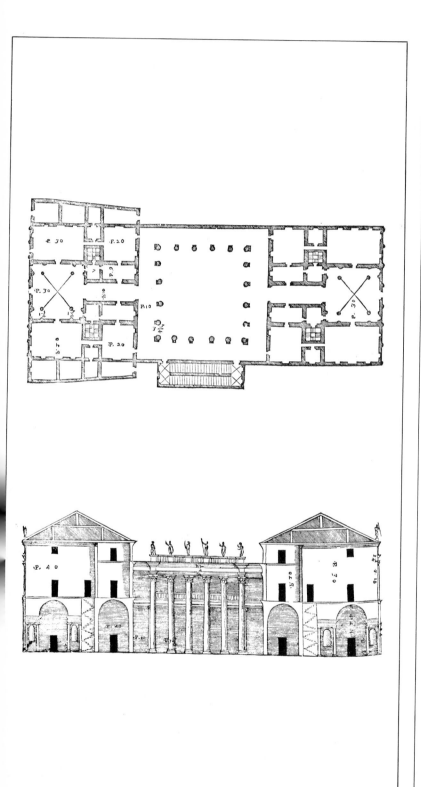

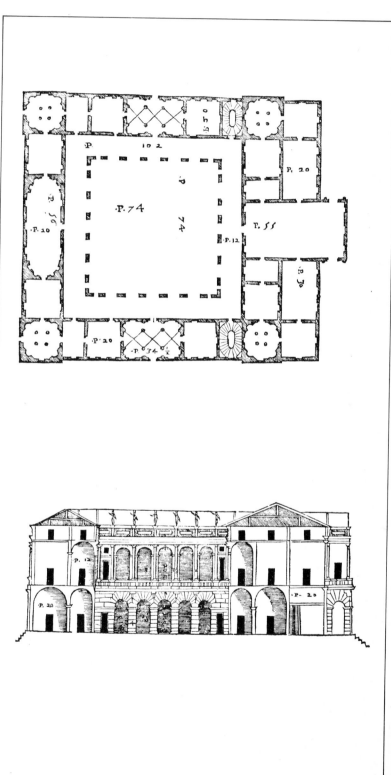

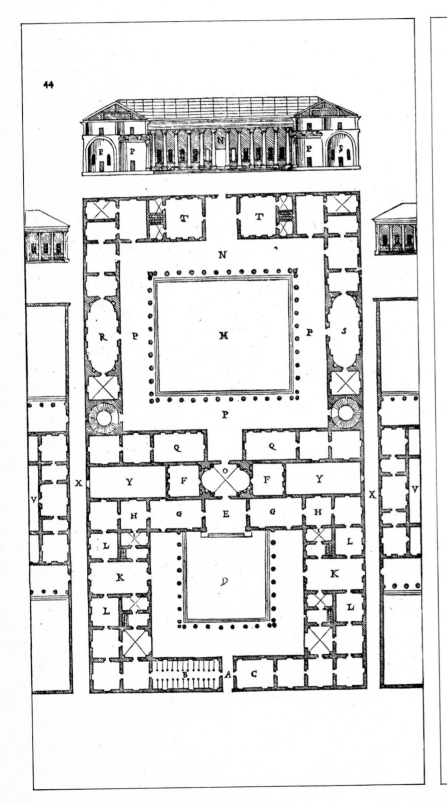

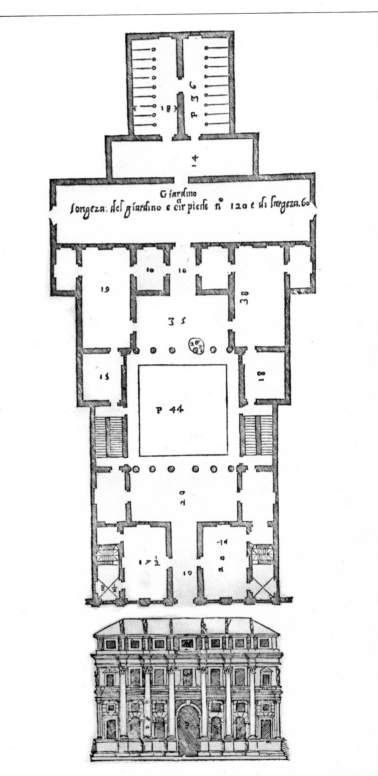

1552, is based on the House of Raphael. A drawing for it, in the Royal Institute of British Architects, London, and the façade itself (Plate 444) show close analogies with Sanmicheli's Palazzo Pompei (Plate 419) of some twenty years earlier. The interior layout, however, shows that Palladio was more ambitious, for he attempted a full-scale reconstruction of an ancient house with its atrium: both the London drawing and the woodcut in the *Quattro Libri* (Plates 445, 446) show that he designed a Giant Order of Corinthian columns to run the whole height of the building in the central court, with a symmetrical disposition of the rooms on either side of it. In the accompanying text Palladio says: 'This court divides the whole house into two parts: the one in front is for the use of the owner and his family; the one at the back will act as quarters for strangers, so that the household and the strangers are each entirely free to go about their business, a thing which was regarded as most important by the ancients, especially the Greeks. In addition to this, the division of the house will be useful if the children of the owner wish to have apartments of their own...' (*I Quattro Libri*, II).

In other Vicentine palaces, he was less programmatically archaeological, but a new element can be found in his planning which must be due to his firsthand knowledge of Roman antiquities, especially the Baths, of which he made many drawings. The Palazzo Thiene, in the illustration in the *Quattro Libri* (Plate 447), shows a more traditional central court, with a double arcade corresponding to the two main storeys, but the disposition of the rooms is new. There is not only a symmetrical arrangement, but the actual shapes are varied and are planned in careful sequences. For example, the four-columned hall in the centre of each side is succeeded by a square room, which is followed by one of the same depth but only half the width, and this is followed by a circular room, the diameter of which is equal to the side of the square. The main *salone*, opposite the entrance hall, is a long rectangle with apsidal ends, very like those of Roman Baths — or, indeed, Palladio's own reconstruction of the ancient Greek House (Plate 448).

By contrast, the façade of the Palazzo Thiene is so similar to Giulio Romano's versions of the House of Raphael that it has been suggested (partly on the evidence of a note by Inigo Jones in 1613) that the design is really Giulio's 'but adjusted by Palladio'. Certainly the type is close to the House of Raphael with the textural interest of a Giulio design, rather like his house in Mantua, but it is even closer to a drawing by him for a palace in Rome. The Palazzo Thiene probably dates from the 1540s, and it is known that Giulio was in Vicenza to advise on the basilica in 1542.

The façade of the Palazzo Valmarana, equally richly textured (but in a different way), derives from entirely different sources. It

DEO VTRIVSQ TEMPLI AEDIFICATORI AC REPA
AC CEDE AD HOC
NON SINE IVGI EXTERI ORI

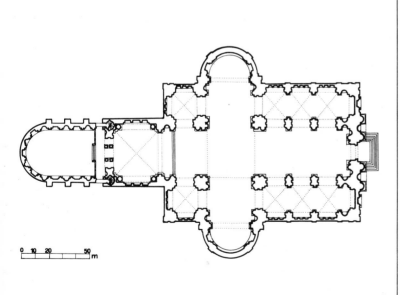

is much later — it is datable 1565-66 — and clearly shows the influence of Michelangelo (Plate 437), especially in the use of a Giant Order to articulate the façade. The most unusual feature of the design is the 'weak' ending, since the extremities have no Composite column, but a smaller Corinthian one on the ground floor and an Atlas figure above it. That this was Palladio's intention is proved by a drawing in London and the woodcut in the *Quattro Libri* (Plate 449). From this elevation, it can be seen that the end bays were quite different from the others, having a vertical arrangement of two small windows and two mezzanines, and the most likely explanation for this *decrescendo* is that it exploits the internal arrangements to obtain an effect of binding the palace into the texture of the narrow street in which it stands — in fact the street is so narrow that it is hardly possible to see the façade except in steep foreshortening. In the same year, Palladio was working on San Giorgio Maggiore in Venice, in which there is no trace of Mannerist fantasy, so the Palazzo Valmarana must be, to some extent, a freak. The unfinished fragment of the Palazzo Porto-Breganze, of the 1570s, has the same sense of grand scale but is simpler in general effect than its contemporary, the Loggia del Capitanio (Plate 442).

Palladio's feeling for noble simplicity is better seen, perhaps, in his villas. Here, the problem was basically that of a reconstruction of the ancient villa, as described by Pliny the Younger and others, and the simultaneous creation of a type of useful building. Ackerman has shown that economic conditions were propitious for a development of large-scale farming in the Veneto with capital withdrawn from trading enterprises in the now Turkish-dominated Mediterranean, so that Palladio's noble clients could combine profitable farming with ancient-style country life. As a result, his versions of the *villa rustica* and *villa suburbana* were not only closer to their prototypes, but were far more influential than their Cinquecento predecessors or their Baroque successors at Frascati or Tivoli. Their simple elegance made them ideal models for the Whig aristocracy of England or Colonial America, so that they are probably the most influential small buildings ever erected. Even Palladio's mistaken archaeology — he believed that ancient villas must have had porticoes and pediments — gave his works a dignity they might otherwise have lacked. Yet he did not invent the type: earlier examples, such as the fifteenth-century Ca' Brusa, or, specifically, the villa at Cricoli designed for himself by Trissino (about 1538) were evident sources for him, and his own first essay, the Villa Godi at Lonedo (*c.* 1540: Plates 450, 451), is not by any means superior to the Villa Trissino. Soon, however, he developed his theories of symmetry and harmonious proportion, which can be seen in the illustrations to the *Quattro Libri* more clearly than in some of the buildings. The actual

degree of luxury varied, and few are as splendid as the villa at Maser (Plates 433, 434), built for Daniele Barbaro and his brother about the time of Barbaro's Vitruvius edition (1556). However, the most splendid of all, and the only true *villa suburbana*, is the Villa Rotonda (Plate 436). This, like the Palazzo del Te, is just outside a city (in this case Vicenza) and was not intended to be a residence for a family. It was built for a retired prelate as a place for entertainment. For this reason, it is strictly in accord with Palladio's basic theories — absolute symmetry of disposition, even to four identical porticoes which are themselves the principal decorations, external simplicity of line and block-line massing, with the riches reserved to the interior. In so far as the Rotonda was thought of as a sort of Belvedere, it shows how different Palladio's conception of the villa was from, say, Ammanati and Vasari at the Villa Giulia, Sansovino and Sanmicheli at the Villa Garzoni or La Soranza, or Giulio at the Palazzo del Te.

Late in his life, Palladio designed two major churches in Venice — San Giorgio Maggiore and Il Redentore — as well as a façade for San Francesco della Vigna and the church (later altered) of Le Zitelle. At Maser he also built a small chapel for the villa, based on the Pantheon, which resembles Sanmicheli's version of the same prototype in its plan, and to some extent in its rich interior.

San Francesco della Vigna was originally designed by Sansovino, but the façade was built by Palladio about 1565, thirty years after the writing of a famous Memorandum on the proportions to be observed in the building of the church. This, written by Fra Francesco Giorgi, dated 1 April 1535, and countersigned by Sansovino, Titian, and Serlio, contains statements on the theory of proportion which accord precisely with the ideas of Palladio and other Renaissance architects. It is, as Wittkower recognized, a key document of sixteenth-century architectural theory. Giorgi says: 'In order to build the fabric of the church with those fitting and very harmonious proportions... without altering anything that has been done, I should proceed in the following manner. I should like the width of the nave to be nine paces, which is the square of three, the first and divine number. The length of the nave, which will be twenty-seven, will have a triple proportion which makes a diapason and a diapente... We, being desirous of building the church, have thought it necessary, and most appropriate, to follow that order of which God, the greatest architect, is the master and author... To this perfect and complete body we shall now give the head, which is the *cappella grande*. As for the length, it should be of the same proportion, or rather symmetry which one finds in each of the three squares of the nave, that is nine paces. I consider it advisable that it should

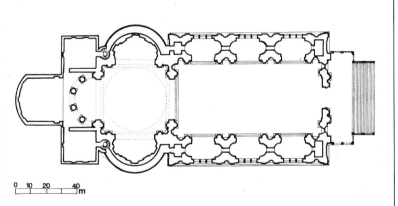

be of the same width as the nave (which as we have said should not be longer than twenty-seven); but I prefer that its width be six paces, like a head, joined to the body proportionately and well balanced. And to the width of the nave it will be in the ratio of 2:3... Turning now to the height, I commend the same as that which M. Giacomo Sansovino has given to his model, namely twelve paces, in the sesquitertial proportion to the width, which results in a diatessaron, a celebrated and melodious harmony... Similarly, I recommend the orders of the columns and pilasters to be designed according to the rules of the Doric, of which I approve in this building as being proper to the Saint to whom the church is dedicated... Lastly it remains to speak of the front, which I wish should be in no way a square, but it should correspond to the inside of the building, and from it one should be able to grasp the form of the building and all its proportions. So that inside and outside, all should be proportionate...'

The façade of San Francesco della Vigna (Plate 455) fulfils these conditions, and, like those of San Giorgio Maggiore and the Redentore (Plates 456, 461), it is based on the idea of a pair of ancient temples, each with its own pediment, interlocked to form a tall narrow temple-front for the nave of the church, and a wide low one for the aisles. The problem facing architects who wanted to equate the temple form with the façade of a Christian church had always been that the earliest Christian churches took their form from the ancient basilica, and deliberately avoided any connection with pagan temples and their associations. In the age of Theodosius, this had been a serious consideration, but, more than a thousand years after the end of paganism, the associations mattered much less than the re-assertion of the antiquity of the Church. The other great Counter-Reformation churches, such as Vignola's Gesù or Tibaldi's San Fedele, avoided the problem by modifying the interior, eliminating aisles in favour of chapels opening at right angles (like Alberti's Sant'Andrea at Mantua), or a single internal space.

The interiors of San Giorgio and the Redentore are much more interesting than either Vignola's or Tibaldi's, and are virtually unique. The plans show that the internal arrangements are basically those of a basilican nave-and-aisles church at San Giorgio, and a Gesù-type nave-with-side-chapels at the Redentore (Plates 347,348,380,381, 455-63). The actual interiors, however, are quite different from these norms and the two churches have a common feature in the strong emphasis on the altar, with its screen of columns behind, partly opened to allow a glimpse into a brilliantly lit choir beyond. The precedent for this idea was probably the columnar screens in ancient baths — e.g. Palladio's own drawings of the Baths of Agrippa — but light as an emotional overtone can hardly have been a Roman idea, unless the

464. *Andrea Palladio, Vicenza, Teatro Olimpico, plan.*
465, 466. *Andrea Palladio, Vicenza, Teatro Olimpico, section.*
467. *Andrea Palladio, Vicenza, Teatro Olimpico, detail.*

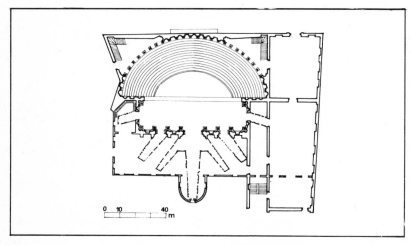

disc of the sun moving round the Pantheon inspired Palladio. At the Gesù, Vignola had irradiated the dome and crossing with a flood of light, but it seems slightly obvious by comparison with Palladio, just as Bernini's *Santa Teresa*, almost a century later, is made to look theatrical. The purity of the effect is far closer to Sant'Eligio in Rome or San Biagio at Montepulciano. Palladio thus remained true to the ideals of the High Renaissance.

The plan shows that the dome of San Giorgio is much nearer the door than one might expect, and the curious shape of the plan needs explanation, especially since the two churches were hardly ever copied. The reason is probably that they arose from peculiarly Venetian needs and circumstances: both churches were visited annually by the Doge in a solemn *andata*, accompanied by large crowds and with the choir of San Marco in attendance. The Benedictine monastery of San Giorgio had existed since the tenth century and was visited on St. Stephen's Day (26 December), but the Redentore was founded as a votive-offering by the Venetian Senate after the cessation of the great plague of 1576 (cf. San Sebastiano in Milan), and a new *andata*, on the third Sunday of July, was created for it. In both cases, the choir of San Marco accompanied the Doge and joined forces with the normal choir. During the sixteenth century — and particularly under Willaerts and the two Gabrieli — this choir had become the finest in the world and had developed a technique of multi-choral singing (*cori spezzati*) designed to exploit the resonances of San Marco.

The strange squat shape of the plan of San Giorgio is thus explained by the need to house a small, monastic choir and congregation for most of the time, and a huge crowd and multiple choirs once a year: in fact, the sound of the monks' choir singing in the space beyond the High Altar is extraordinarily impressive, and matches the effect of the light filtering through the columns. Palladio himself had decided views on the planning and decoration of churches: 'Of all the colours, there is none more suited to churches than white, considering that the purity of the colour, like that of life, is most pleasing to God. If there are to be paintings, there should be no place for any which by their subject-matter, distract the mind from the contemplation of divine things...' (*I Quattro Libri*, IV, 2).

Even more important is his maintenance of the opinion — as against Borromeo — that the central plan is more suitable for churches than the Latin cross. A long passage in Book IV deals with the significance of plans: 'Temples are made round, rectangular, of six, eight or more sides, all of which partake of the nature of a circle; in the shape of a Cross; and of many other shapes and figures, according to the invention of men. When they are beautiful, and of proper proportion, and adorned with elegant and ornamented architecture, then they deserve praise. But the finest and most regular

rms, from which all others take their measure, are the circle and
he rectangle; and it is for this reason that Vitruvius speaks only of
hese two... The Ancients had regard, when they erected temples,
ot only to the selection of sites, but also to the choice of shape;
o that for the Sun or Moon they chose the circular...

'Thus, we read that the Ancients, in building their Temples, strove
o observe Decorum, which is a most beautiful part of Architecture.
And therefore we, who do not serve false gods, in order to observe
ecorum in the building of temples, should choose the most perfect
nd most excellent — which is to say, the round; for only it, of all
hapes, is simple, uniform, equal, strong and capacious. So let us
nake our temples round... most suitable to demonstrate the Unity,
ne infinite Essence, the Uniformity, and the Justice of God...
Those churches are also praiseworthy which are made in the form
f a Cross... because, being in the shape of a cross, they present
o the eyes of the spectator that Wood from which depended our
alvation. And of this form, I made the church of San Giorgio
Maggiore in Venice.' Palladio's preference for a central plan for a
otive church such as the Redentore was shared by many Senators,
or in a letter of 1577 to his friend Conte Giulio Capra, he tells us
hat his design was for a Latin cross, 'and because the church will
e served by the Capuchins, and I was instructed to make it *divota*,
have arranged for the choir at the end, which forms the head of
ne cross, to have a simple and humble shape (*sia di umile struttura*)...'
We also know that Palladio submitted two models, one centrally-
lanned and the other of a Latin cross shape. The latter was chosen
y a majority, and it is likely that Palladio himself agreed with the
ecision, given the conditioning factors and the site available.

In his churches, Palladio emerges as a great Tridentine artist,
oncerned with iconography as well as shape, so that his churches
re as much a liturgical as an aesthetic experience. In this he shared
ne outlook of a Titian or a Tintoretto, but he was also a more
rchaeological artist than either of them, as may be seen in his last
vork, the Teatro Olimpico at Vicenza (Plates 467-70), built for
ne Accademia Olimpica, of which he was himself a member. This
s a three-dimensional reconstruction of the ancient theatre, as de-
cribed by Vitruvius and illustrated by Palladio in the Barbaro edi-
ion. There were also several ancient theatres, drawn by him, in
ome, Verona, Pola, and Vicenza itself, where the ruins of the
eatro Berga still exist. Construction of the theatre was well ad-
anced at the time of Palladio's death in August 1580, and he de-
igned the strikingly illusionist perspective scenes, although (accord-
ng to his own account) they were executed by Vincenzo Scamozzi,
alladio's *epigone*. The fully classical intentions and shape of the
eatro Olimpico did not accord with the new ideas on stage-design

which were to lead to the modern type of theatre, but it had at least three successors: Scamozzi's theatre for Vespasiano Gonzaga's new city of Sabbioneta (1588: Plate 471), Aleotti's Teatro Farnese at Parma (1619), and a design by Inigo Jones.

Scamozzi built the Procuratie Nuove in Venice, travelled widely in France and Germany, and also designed the cathedral at Salzburg. He was the last of the Renaissance architects, both on account of his ponderous *Dell'Idea dell'Architettura universale...* of 1615, incomplete but enormous, and on account of his ideal city, founded in 1593, at Palmanova in the Veneto (Plate 472), which looks back to Filarete and Sforzinda. Inigo Jones, who knew him, had a low opinion of him as Palladio's successor: 'this secret Scamozio being purblind under stoode nott.' By 1614 it was possible for a non-Italian to speak so disparagingly, but until then the rest of Europe was scarcely conscious of the real meaning of Renaissance architecture.

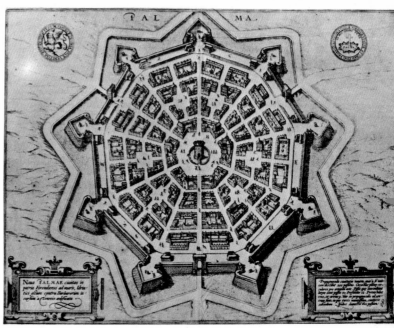

PART THREE

The history of the spread of Italian architectural ideas has yet to be written in detail, but the main outlines are easily established. During the fifteenth century, almost the whole of Europe was still so Gothic that Italian, or, rather, classical ideas made no impression. It is an odd fact that the most noticeable Italian influences in the fifteenth century occur in Hungary, in the time of Matthias Corvinus, who ruled from 1458 to 1490, or even in Russia, where the so-called Facetted Palace was copied from the Palazzo dei Diamanti in Ferrara and was begun in about 1487. Nevertheless, by the early sixteenth century, the revival of classical forms became an object to be pursued in humanist circles in the greater part of Europe. This was partly due to the spread of Latin letters, so that the educated classes took their cue from Italy in all the arts. Equally, by their influence on the higher nobility and in courts, the humanists promoted an anti-Gothic feeling in the arts which expressed itself naturally in the copying of Italianate fashions.

It is important to distinguish between the two main aspects of Renaissance architecture, as practised outside Italy in the earlier years of the sixteenth century. The forms of ancient and modern classical architecture were always much more easily imitated than the ideas behind them, and the imitation of the superficies of classical design — columns, swags, pedestals — was so deceptively easy that the old Gothic spirit could come back in the form of a jungle of decoration. Pilasters were soon overgrown with a thicket of scrolls, nominally based on the newly-discovered *grotteschi* employed by the followers of Raphael, and from this it was a short step to the monstrous growth of the so-called 'strapwork', which, though characteristic of Flemish or German Mannerism, can be found as early as the 1530s on the façade of the Palazzo Massimo in Rome. The term 'Flemish Mannerism' is misleading, in so far as it seems to equate Flemish sixteenth–century architecture with the style of artists like Giulio Romano: this is quite wrong, if only because almost all Northern architects managed to pass from exuberantly decorative Late Gothic to equally flamboyant pseudo-classical, without passing through a truly classic stage at all. In this they differed very markedly from highly sophisticated Italian architects who had been brought up in a tradition established several generations earlier.

The basic distinction, in fact, is that between the assimilation of ideas and forms. The superficial imitation of forms was quite a simple matter for any skilled craftsman, especially as the task was much simplified (by far-seeing Italian architects and engravers) by the provision of several convenient models. These were either single plates of ornament, such as those by Nicoletto da Modena and various followers of Mantegna — or even Bramante himself

(the engraving of 1481 and the stage settings) — or the much more ambitious and important treatises, headed by Serlio's, which were such a feature of architectural thought in the sixteenth and seventeenth centuries. These engravings all have in common the fact that they are simplified diagrams, intended to be used by unsophisticated craftsmen or naïve nobles following the latest fashion. They are therefore always easy to read, even at the expense of artistic content (many of Serlio's plates, for example, are aesthetically a disgrace to a man who used Peruzzi's drawings), but their effectiveness is proved beyond doubt by the huge success of the book.

Nowhere, however, does Serlio discuss the rationale of classical architecture, as Alberti had done and as Palladio was to do some thirty years later. For this reason, it was necessary to employ Italian artists to secure truly Italian results, and this accounts for the competitive spirit among monarchs such as Francis I of France in obtaining the services of artists. The spread of Italian-classic ideas in Europe falls into two separate categories, namely the early buildings and tombs by Italians (usually of the second rank) specially employed for the purpose, and the beginnings of a national classic architecture, the creation of men like Philibert de l'Orme, Herrera, Holl, or Inigo Jones, who had been to Italy and read the treatises for themselves. Their work lies in the later years of the sixteenth century, or even the early seventeenth, and it is therefore only just within the period covered by this book.

Nevertheless, there is the great gulf of the Reformation. Italian ideas can be found in the Fugger Chapel in Augsburg; Landshut; King's College, Cambridge; Poland; Prague; Granada; and even Fontainebleau — but the French and Spaniards were fighting for the control of Italy and, therefore, for the first claim on emigrant artists. The Gesù type of Counter-Reformation church is therefore more common in France or Spain than, say, the north Netherlands. The Netherlands and Germany were split by religious wars and England, where Italy was highly fashionable, was deeply suspicious of Rome, so that most of the Italian ideas before the time of Inigo Jones were due to immigrant Italian artists like Torrigiano or to natives like John Shute, who seems to have had no influence at all. It is in France, with its military hegemony in Lombardy, that the ideals of Renaissance architecture first took root outside Italy, and first became transmuted into a national version of the classical style.

In France during the sixteenth century several new building types were evolved, and the novelty of the types lent itself to experiment with Italian ideas. There was, for example, very little church building, and such churches as were built were usually survivals

473. *Château de Gaillon, entrance.*
474. *Château d'Azay-le-Rideau, exterior staircase.*
475. *Château d'Azay-le-Rideau, general view.*

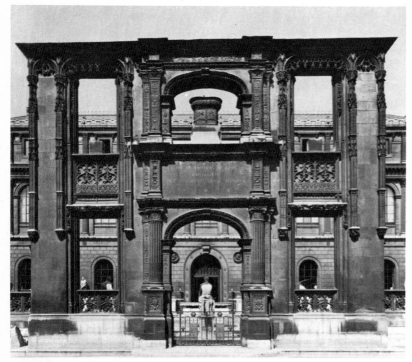

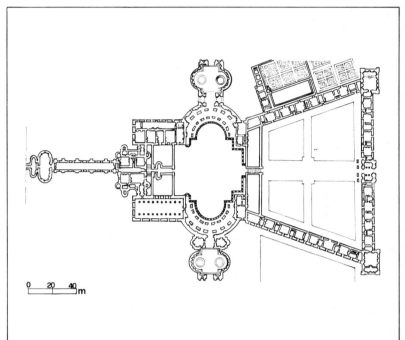

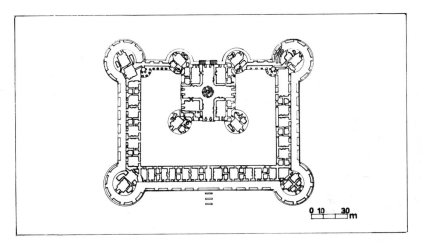

from an earlier age, like Saint Eustache in Paris, built in 1532, but which, for all its date, is no more than a slightly modernised Late Gothic structure of an entirely traditional type. On the other hand, there was a great upsurge of secular building, and the old castle type evolved into the château, the fortress into the palace, and, in the towns, the characteristic hôtel made its appearance as a town house. Civic buildings, such as town halls, were also built with less attention to fortification than formerly. While these new types were being developed there was obviously a chance for new formal ideas to be adopted, but, nevertheless, the initial impact of Italian architecture largely took the form of the introduction of decorative details, while the structural principles remained those derived from Gothic practice. Gothic decoration, however, is evolved directly from construction, and many French sixteenth-century buildings consequently lack the harmony of Gothic work, just as they lack the harmony between structure and decoration of classical architecture.

At the beginning, the actual sources of Italian ideas were almost exclusively Lombard, since the Italian wars of Charles VIII, Louis XII, and Francis I had all turned on the possession of the Duchy of Milan. Francis I, who reigned from 1515 to 1547, began by occupying a large part of northern Italy, but was defeated and captured by the Spaniards at the Battle of Pavia in 1525. Francis himself was an enthusiast for Italian art and tried to lure several major artists to his court. He succeeded spectacularly with Leonardo da Vinci, who went to France in 1516 and died there three years later. Leonardo conferred great prestige on his royal patron, but it is not clear that he was particularly active as an artist in France. He did, however, make a drawing for a royal château at Romorantin, work on which was actually begun immediately after his death, but it was abandoned in favour of Chambord. Probably, too, it was Leonardo who inspired the complicated spiral staircases which are a feature of several sixteenth-century châteaux. Leonardo's drawings, many of them done in Milan thirty years earlier, show that he had worked out the principles of interlocking spiral staircases, which allowed for one flight to be used by people going up and another flight, twisted round it, by those coming down. Other Italian artists who visited France included Andrea del Sarto in 1518 and Benvenuto Cellini in the 1540s, but neither was successful or felt at home there.

Three others, who stayed until their deaths, exerted a profound influence on French art and architecture, and, through it, on the rest of Europe. They were Rosso Fiorentino, who went in 1530 and stayed until his sudden and premature death in 1540, Primaticcio, who stayed from 1532 until 1570, and Serlio. The first two,

482. Château de Chambord, staircase, interior view.
483. Palais de Fontainebleau, plan.

484. Gilles Le Breton, Palais de Fontainebleau. Porte Dorée. ▷

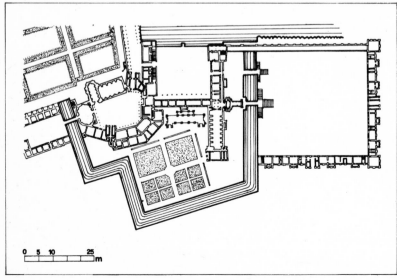

and especially Primaticcio, invented the elaborately Mannerist decorative style which is always associated with the palace at Fontainebleau. Primaticcio had worked with Giulio Romano on the decoration of the Palazzo del Te at Mantua, and he imported Giulio's sophisticated Mannerism into France, where it became essentially a court style. The third Italian, Serlio, who came in 1541, also exerted a great influence on French architecture, but it is rather more difficult to trace, partly because his ideas reached the whole of northern Europe through his treatise.

The influence of these three men dates from the middle of the century and is quite different from the Lombard influence of the earlier years, summed up in the judgement of Philippe de Commines, that the Certosa at Pavia was 'the finest church I ever saw and all of fine marble'. As the Certosa is one of the least classical buildings in Italy and follows the combination of Gothic and Antique that we find in Filarete, it is easy to see why it should have appealed to French taste.

There is a certain amount of ancient Roman architecture surviving in France — the Maison Carrée at Nîmes, the amphitheatre at Orange, the Alyscamps at Aix, the gateways at Autun or Saintes — but they are nearly all in the South, and the total is very small compared with Italy, so that the idea of a continuous classical past merging into the present is virtually unknown. Nevertheless, by the middle of the century, when modern Roman, Mantuan, and Florentine Mannerist ideas were imported, the general climate of taste was both more receptive and more knowledgeable than was the case elsewhere in Europe. French Mannerism of the type practised at Fontainebleau was essentially elegant and fashionable, and the understanding of classical precedent, which was so important an element in a building like the Palazzo del Te, was necessarily less significant. This very sophisticated Mannerism was confined to court circles, and even the earlier importation of classical details was largely restricted to the Loire valley, the main seat of the courts of Charles VIII, Louis XII, and Francis I, or occurred on the estates of people like the Cardinal d'Amboise, principal minister to Louis XII, who were acquainted with Italy.

The Château de Gaillon, near Rouen, was built by Cardinal Georges d'Amboise in the first years of the sixteenth century. The only part to survive, the great gateway of about 1508 (Plate 473), shows the use of classical pilasters on an alien structure, without regard for their proper proportion, and merely as a decorative edging. The scroll motif over the windows in the two towers is very similar to the scrolls at Urbino and Naples, and probably derives from Alfonso's triumphal arch (Plate 98). Another example of reckless borrowing can be seen in Rouen Cathedral, in the tomb

486, 487. *Palais de Fontainebleau, details of stucco decorations.*
488. *Palais de Fontainebleau, Gallery Francis I.*

of two Amboise Cardinals, made by French workmen about 1515: this has an agglomeration of Orders, shell niches, arabesques, coffering, and friezes of putti, all jumbled together in that mixture characteristic of all imitation Italian work of this date anywhere in northern Europe.

Contemporary with Gaillon, but in the Loire district, is the Hôtel d'Alluye at Blois, with a galleried court, built before 1508 by Florimond Robertet, later Minister of Finance to Francis I. Robertet also built, between 1511 and 1524, the Château de Bury, perhaps the earliest example of the form which later became characteristic — a main block of living-quarters, known as the *corps-de-logis*, with projecting wings at right angles forming three sides of a square, the fourth side of which was closed by a screen. This was the basic shape adapted by Serlio, and it was to become equally characteristic of town and country houses. Some of the earlier forms survived for a long time, side by side with the new ideas, and three of the most important châteaux of the Loire district — Azay-le-Rideau, Chenonceaux, and Chambord (Plates 475, 476, 481) — all preserve the moats and angle towers of medieval fortified manors and castles, along with the open courts, indefensible windows and doors, and the great staircases of the new type. To some extent, this is due to non-architectural circumstances, for several of these châteaux were built by newly-rich financiers, who may well have felt that the older forms gave them an air of settled respectability.

Azay-le-Rideau (Plates 474, 475), built between 1518 and 1527, is a curious L-shape in plan, with part of the house jutting out into the river, so that it appears to be moated on two sides. The splendid staircase (Plate 474) rises through three storeys of the *corps-de-logis* in straight flights in the Italian manner, and this must be — with the contemporary staircases in Spain — one of the earliest examples of a staircase as a major architectural feature. The staircase at Azay was originally open, and the ceiling is a very flattened barrel-vault decorated with coffering. The fluted pilasters of the ground floor change into candelabra as the staircase progresses and most of the details have an exuberance which has nothing in common with Italian work.

Chenonceaux was begun before Azay (1515) and completed in 1524. The builder was Thomas Bohier, whose brother had almost certainly been to Italy and who employed Italian craftsmen on his own buildings. Chenonceaux, like Azay, has an extraordinary setting: it stands in the River Cher, where the corner turrets and the high gables give it the air of a Gothic fairy castle (Plate 476). Much of the detail is now nineteenth century, and it is hard to say how much of the original has survived; but, again like Azay, the form of the staircase, in straight flights with coffered ceiling, is

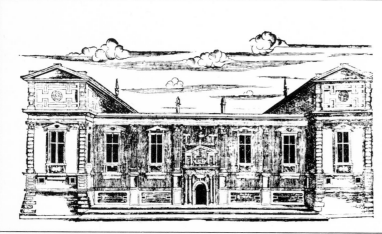

Italian in inspiration rather than French. It differs from the one at Azay, however, in that it does not run from front to back, splitting the house in two: Chenonceaux is divided into two blocks by a long central-vaulted corridor with the staircase at one side.

The châteaux at Blois and Chambord were royal works, which explains their much greater scale. Immediately after his accession Francis I started rebuilding the north wing at Blois on the foundations of a medieval castle, the surviving wall of which is used as a sort of spine with a double *enfilade* of rooms, one on each side of it. The great outside staircase in the courtyard replaces an earlier tower (Plate 479). All of the four storeys, from the plain ground floor up to the highly ornamental gables of the roof and the elaborate chimneys, are decorated with pilasters of a variegated Ionic type (it is notable that the Ionic is used consistently throughout the period to the exclusion of the other Orders), which frame the windows and the panels on the wall-surface. No attempt is made to establish proportional relationships between the storeys or the different areas of the same storey. The staircase has everything — pilasters, capitals, pedestals, balustrades, armorial emblems, and the salamander (Francis's personal device). On the outer side of the wing, above the town, there has been an attempt to create the effect of an open loggia, but the French builders understood their model so little that they made a series of windows, each separated from the next, so that there is no communication from one to another. At the top there is a rather more successful loggia *all'italiana*.

Chambord was begun as a hunting-lodge in 1519 and, like Blois, it was interrupted by the disaster of Pavia. Resumed in 1526, it was never finished. The medieval character of the plan is clear, since it consists of a square central block with great *donjons* at the corners, and wings ending in bastions (Plate 480, 481). The real problem at Chambord is to estimate the share of the Italian, Domenico da Cortona (known in France as le Boccador), since he had been a pupil of Giuliano da Sangallo and Sangallo's Villa Medici at Poggio a Caiano (Plates 135, 136) was the source for the most important feature of Chambord, the division of the rooms into suites, which developed into the characteristically French *appartement* system. Many of the decorative features of Chambord are Lombard in origin, but the majestic central staircase (Plates 481, 482), which replaces the normal central court and the proper use of loggie are novel in France. The staircase at Chambord must be due to the direct influence of Leonardo da Vinci, but the rest probably goes back to earlier Italian forms. When Cardinal della Rovere, the future Julius II, was in France in 1495, he was accompanied by his architect Giuliano da Sangallo and his pupil, Domenico da Cortona, who stayed on in France when the others returned to Italy.

Félibien, in the seventeenth century, made drawings of a wooden model for Chambord, apparently by Domenico, who was paid in 1531 for work done 'at Chambord and other places over the last fifteen years', which suggests that the design might go back to Leonardo's lifetime, since he died at the neighbouring château of Amboise in 1519. The great stair at Chambord stands at the intersection of four huge barrel-vaulted halls, originally open to the winds, though at a later date the mullions were filled with glass windows, and the halls were divided by floors into two storeys. The great *donjons* at the angles each contain three *appartements*, one above the other, all with huge and elaborate fireplaces of the kind already known from Azay, Chenonceaux, and Blois.

Francis built other palaces, but they were mostly in the Île-de-France, since residence in or near Paris became essential for reasons of state after his return from captivity in Spain in 1526. It was in these years that the centralized monarchy began to acquire real power. Nothing now remains of the châteaux de Challuau, La Muette de Saint-Germain, and Madrid, though du Cerceau's engravings give us a picture of the Château de Madrid, and Evelyn described it in 1650: he comments on its 'open manner of architecture, being much of terraces and galleries one over another to the very roofe', and on its materials 'which are most of Earth painted like Porcelain or Chinaware, whose colours appeare very fresh, but is very fragile. There are whole statues and rilievos of this potterie, chimney-pieces and columns both within and without', doubtless referring to the work of Girolamo della Robbia, who was employed on the decoration and probably also had a share in the design. The house consisted of two main blocks, containing four *appartements* on each floor, both the blocks being symmetrically planned and having square elements at the corners, joined by a narrower bridge which served as a main entrance *salle*. True Italian loggie ran round the house on ground and first floors. The high-pitched roof was pierced by attic windows and had simple chimneys, unlike the fantastic skyline of Chambord.

The most important of Francis's palaces was, however, Fontainebleau. A medieval castle, which served as a small hunting-lodge, was transformed from 1528 under Gilles Le Breton, who built the Porte Dorée (Plate 484) and a long gallery joining the old *donjon* to a new range of buildings at the head of the Cour du Cheval Blanc (Plate 485). Le Breton's style shows the expected mixture of older forms and new details, but the Porte Dorée is, in some ways, less classical even than Gaillon — the superposed loggie are flanked by bays with pilasters, but there are two windows in a vertical strip, one above the other, in each bay, so that the pediment of one window is the base of the one above it. Such a device in Italy about

494. *Château d' Anet, Chapel, section.*
495. *Château d' Anet, Chapel, plan of dome.*
496. *Philibert de l' Orme, Château d' Anet, Chapel, interior of dome.* ▷

1530-40 would be called Mannerist. Here, each pilaster runs through two storeys — that is, it is technically a Giant Order, and must be one of the earliest examples — but no one could believe that it is due to anything but ignorance. In the same way, the comparatively restrained decoration is probably due to the hardness of the local stone (*grès*) rather than to classical discipline. The arrangement of the blocks round the Cour du Cheval Blanc is symmetrical, though the disposition of the windows and some of the arcading is haphazard, so that if one calls this a 'Renaissance' building, it is not so much because of its derivation from Italian precedents as because it is markedly different from its predecessors in France. When Rosso arrived in Fontainebleau, followed two years later by Primaticcio, French decoration changed radically. The long gallery (Plates 485-88) is itself a form of uncertain origin, perhaps derived from Bramante's project for the Belvedere. It was later very popular in England, where it was introduced by Cardinal Wolsey in his Hampton Court a few years earlier than Fontainebleau, although the original gallery there was part of Le Breton's design and was taken over by the Italians and decorated by them in a completely novel style.

At Fontainebleau, we find the first use of the stucco frame round decorative paintings (Plates 486, 487) with figures in such high relief as to be almost detached from the wall, so that they, and not the paintings, are the important elements in the decoration. The precedents are, of course, Italian, and can be found in Giulio Romano's Sala di Costantino at the Vatican or his Palazzo del Te, where the Sala degli Stucchi is by him and Primaticcio; but in the Sala di Costantino, the paintings are separated by painted, not modelled, figures, and even in the Sala degli Stucchi there are friezes of small stucco figures, but no paintings. A possible source for these figures may be the huge and elaborately decorated fireplaces which, from about 1515, were a feature of the new French châteaux — Azay, Chenonceaux, Blois, or Chambord. The gallery at Fontainebleau is far more graceful than any of these, exploiting the contrast between the elegantly slim nude figures and the convoluted forms of the thick frames surrounding the paintings, the so-called 'strapwork' based on curled leather which was the most popular decorative feature in Europe for more than a century. Each of the paintings has a salamander above it, the attitude of the beast subtly reflecting the mood of the picture, and the rich vocabulary of Italian Mannerist art — garlands, sphinxes, masks, satyrs' and rams' heads — at the height of its inventiveness and complexity is introduced into French art at one blow.

In 1541 Primaticcio returned to Fontainebleau from Italy, where he had been buying casts of the most famous antique statues and

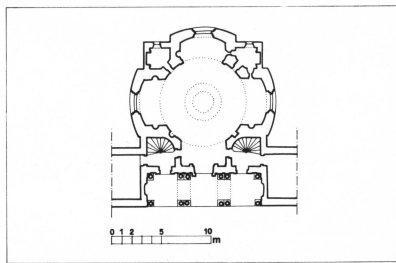

other works of art for Francis I. He brought the young Vignola back with him to help with the casting of these antiques in bronze. In the same year, Serlio succeeded in getting an invitation from Francis to leave Venice and come to take charge of the building at Fontainebleau. Nothing remains of his work there, and of the house he built for the Cardinal of Ferrara only one gateway survives (Plate 490).

About this time, Philibert de l'Orme returned from Italy and settled in Paris. Rosso died in 1540, and Primaticcio's work at Fontainebleau was more that of a decorative impresario than an architect, except for the Michelangelesque Grotto and the much later Aile de la Belle Cheminée (1569: Plate 489), where the forms are simpler and in keeping with the purely French developments elsewhere. Primaticcio also made a design, never executed, for a circular mausoleum for the Valois dynasty, to be added to the burial place of the French kings at Saint Denis. This project was a centrally-planned domical structure, derived from Bramante and Michelangelo, but it is more important in the tradition of French centrally-planned chapels, which stemmed from Philibert de l'Orme.

Serlio's impact was far more through his treatise than through his actual buildings — from 1542 his books began to appear in French as well as Italian, and the first Flemish translation appeared in Antwerp in 1553, to be followed by German and English versions early in the seventeenth century. This treatise was the main vehicle of watered-down Italian ideas in northern Europe and it was so profusely illustrated with crude woodcuts that the reader obtained a vague impression of many of the great buildings of ancient and modern Rome, but so inaccurately that his imagination was not hampered by any pedantic adherence to rules, even though Serlio gives the outline of a theory of the Orders. Other books deal with geometry, planning, churches, and, most popular of all, there exists an 'Extraordinary Book' of fantastic gateways (Plate 490) which provided exactly what was wanted by French, German, Flemish, and English master-masons trying to keep up with the new fashions.

His only important surviving building is Ancy-le-Franc (Yonne), designed about 1546, which is an interesting compromise between his Italian training and the French type of house with high-pitched roofs and projecting corner blocks (Plate 498). Serlio designed it round a central court, the main motif of which is derived from his own woodcut of Bramante's Belvedere, perhaps the first example of the way in which one of his woodcuts was used as a starting-point for a design which ended by having little in common with its nominal prototype.

Exactly contemporary with Ancy-le-Franc is a building of far greater importance in the history of French architecture — the rebuilding of the Louvre, one of the biggest undertakings of royal patronage, and destined to last for centuries. In 1527, Francis decided to begin by demolishing the central *donjon* and replacing it with a range of buildings round a square court, but work was not started on this until 1546. This was under the direction of Pierre Lescot, who had studied mathematics, painting, and architecture and came from a successful legal family, so that his background was quite different from that of the normal French master-mason, born to his craft. Lescot apparently did not visit Italy until his architectural career was over, so that he must be the first modern French architect without Italian training. He was nevertheless able to use classical forms with correctness and distinction, and with an individuality of style that makes him outstanding for his time. He built the southwest corner of the Cour Carrée of the Louvre (Plate 492), the rest of the court being built later to conform with his work. Originally, the project was for a two-storey block, and the rather small attic was added during building, as were the two projecting wings at the sides, built when the staircase was moved from the centre to the side, to enable grander rooms to be made on both floors. The proportions and treatment of the Orders, the skilfully arranged alternating pediments, the feeling for movement, and the fine detailing make this the first truly Renaissance building in France. With Lescot, French Renaissance architecture appears in its own right, for, despite the use of features which are classical by origin and Italian in the modern context of their use, Lescot's Louvre could not be confused with an Italian building.

With Philibert de l'Orme, French architecture reaches complete independence, despite the fact that Philibert was partly trained in Italy. He was in Rome for about three years from 1533, and he seems even to have had access to the projects for St. Peter's while Peruzzi and Sangallo were in charge. He settled in Paris about 1540, when his Roman patron, Cardinal du Bellay, commissioned him to build a house at Saint-Maur-lès-Fossés, just outside Paris. Nothing survives of it except the architect's description, the plan and elevations included in his own treatise, and a few other engravings, some of them projects by du Cerceau for later alterations. It is therefore difficult to be certain what the house looked like, although it seems to have been a single-storey structure built round a square court, rather like the Palazzo del Te, the resemblance to which was strengthened by the use of pilasters. Outside, it was raised on a rusticated basement which probably had a moat round it, and inside there were arcades all round the court. Corner pavilions projected on two sides, the façade had single, rusticated pilasters and the court coupled pilasters, while the main entrance was

adapted from a triumphal arch, and the door from the court was set in a large pedimented feature reached by a flight of steps (Plate 491). On the garden front, Philibert designed the first horseshoe staircase in France, to reach up to the main suite of rooms. Some of the ideas were Italian, such as the single-storey elevation, the articulation by a consistently used Order, and the flat roof; others, such as the plain mullion windows and the entrance side of the court made lower than the *corps-de-logis*, were traditionally French.

Anet, near Dreux in Normandy, was begun in 1547 for Diane de Poitiers, mistress of Henry II. The château itself was destroyed after the Revolution, and only the entrance gateway and the chapel survive on the site, together with some of the garden construction, but the entrance front of the house itself is preserved in the courtyard of the École des Beaux-Arts in Paris. Fragmentary as it is, this strikes a totally different note from the compromises of Serlio or the decorative fluency of Lescot's Louvre, with which it is contemporary. It was designed as a tower of the Orders, with a projecting element on either side rising the full height of the frontispiece, with a pair of coupled columns (Doric, Ionic, and Corinthian) one above the other on each of the projecting sides. This is a new form of the conventional towered gateway, and it probably derives ultimately from the towers Bramante planned for St. Peter's, reflected in the paired columns of San Biagio at Montepulciano (Plate 222).

The gateway at Anet (Plate 493) is even more unusual, for it is the first instance of a French architect considering the various elements of his building as masses to be grouped effectively. The lower part of the gate is similar to the fragment in Paris — paired columns on either side of a large opening, Italian in inspiration — but the detail of the balustrading of intertwined scrolls has precedents in Late Gothic forms, like the balustrading in Saint-Pierre, Caen, made between 1515 and 1545. An entirely novel element is introduced by the four chimneys in the form of sarcophagi on tall pedestals, used at the ends of the gateway to balance the high central block with the clock and the group of hounds baying at the stag. In the lunette over the main door was placed the bronze relief of Diana as a huntress (now in the Louvre), which, despite Cellini's account of it as one of the works he produced for Francis I's Fontainebleau, does not appear to have been erected there before the King's death in 1547, when Diane de Poitiers probably obtained it from Henry II. One characteristic feature of the gateway is the contrast between the massive blocks of the architecture and the delicate detailing, such as the inlays of coloured stone and marble, the pattern in the vaulting of the entrance, and the contrast of brick and stone at the sides.

The glory of Anet is the chapel. Originally, there was a gallery over the colonnaded portico, so that the mistress of the house might attend Mass from a private pew, where the round-headed window in the façade is now to be found. This flat façade was to be flanked by two towers with high spires, the whole forming a vestibule to the centrally-planned circular chapel, reminiscent of Palladio's Maser or Sanmicheli's Cappella Pellegrini. The swirling pattern of the inlaid marble floor is echoed in the complex pattern of the dome itself (Plate 496), based on the Temple of Venus and Rome. The very high lantern crowning the hemispherical dome is based on Lombard *tiburi* and may derive from Bramante's use of coupled columns at Santa Maria delle Grazie, Milan.

Few other works by Philibert de l'Orme survive. He was responsible for the architecture of Francis I's tomb in Saint Denis and for the bridge added to Chenonceaux for Diane de Poitiers, between 1556 and 1559, to carry a long gallery and reach across to the other side of the river. He built only the first five bays and the rest was built by his successor, Bullant. After Anet, he was employed by the Queen, Catherine de' Medici, on the Tuileries and on the enlargement of Saint-Maur. But on the death of Henry II in 1559, he was dismissed from all his offices. His last years — he died in 1570 — were spent in working on his treatises, the *Nouvelles Inventions pour bien bastir et à petits frais* (1561), which deals with practical problems of construction, and his *Architecture* (1567), a larger work inspired by Vitruvius and Alberti, concerned not only with practical matters but with the training of the architect, the problems of planning, and the theory of the Orders and their application, including the invention of a new 'French' Order, better adapted to the stone available in France than the ancient Orders, primarily designed as marble monoliths.

The only other important French architect of the century was Jean Bullant, a slightly younger contemporary of de l'Orme. He is first recorded in the service of the Connétable de Montmorency at Écouen, where, in the mid-1550s, he built the north wing, which once contained a frontispiece (known from du Cerceau's engravings) which was a cross between the open arcades of the Porte Dorée and the tower of the Orders at Anet. He also built an entrance portico on the south side, probably in the 1560s, which is often said to be the earliest surviving example of the Giant Order in France. It does not range very well with the windows on either side, and, in spite of the Order itself being copied from that of the Pantheon portico, it gives the impression of being a purely decorative feature applied to the wall (Plate 493). At Chantilly, Bullant built the *petit château* for Montmorency about 1560 with a frontispiece (Plate 500), perhaps derived from Bramante's Abbiategrasso, a great arch sup-

ported on paired columns. There are also typically French Mannerist features, such as the dormer windows which are incorporated into the pediments carried on great brackets over the main windows. After Philibert's dismissal, Bullant succeeded to all his offices and worked for Catherine de' Medici on buildings which are known to us only from du Cerceau's engravings. He also wrote two books, the more important of which is the *Reigle générale d'Architecture des cinq Manières de Colonnes* of 1563, containing the results of his studies in Italy, probably during the 1540s.

Although no buildings are known to survive by him, the importance of du Cerceau is capital. Like Bullant, he was probably in Italy in the 1540s, and his engravings, made from 1549 onwards, document the dissemination in France of classical and Italian forms, often treated with licence and fantasy. From 1559 he published designs for town houses and châteaux as models for prospective builders and patrons and, in 1576 and 1579, he published *Les plus excellents Bastiments de France*, an invaluable compendium which is often our only source of knowledge about houses that have been destroyed or radically altered. Without these engravings, we should know much less about the reception of Renaissance ideas in France.

The introduction of Italian Renaissance ideas and forms into Spain was effected in much the same way as in France: the Spaniards ruled in Naples and the politics of Italy depended very largely upon Charles V and Philip II, so it is not surprising that several Italian artists went to Spain (especially in the second half of the century) and that many Spaniards spent some time in Italy.

The 'Plateresque' style, so called from its affinity with silversmith's work, is rooted in the ornamental forms, mainly Lombard in origin, that could be added as a sort of decorative skin to tombs, whence they found their way on to the surfaces of buildings. These Lombard elements, not usually architectonic in themselves, were completely transformed, but the result has little to do with architecture. There are, however, a few buildings which really reflect Italian practice and can be dated surprisingly early — around 1500, or even earlier — and it is usual to include these in a first phase of Renaissance influence, which gave way about 1526 to a second, more classical style that lasted almost to the end of the century. Finally, the austere 'Herreran' style, beginning about 1560, lasted into the early seventeenth century. A few buildings from each of these stylistic phases will serve as examples.

The court made up of two arcades, one above the other, is an obvious vehicle for Italian influence, and the court of San Gregorio at Valladolid, built by the Breton Juan Guas (who had trained in Flanders) between 1487 and 1496, is sometimes quoted as an

343

08. *Diego de Siloe, Granada, Cathedral, interior.*

509. *Enrique de Egas, Granada, Cathedral, plan of choir.*
510. *Granada, Alhambra, Palace of Charles V, plan.*
511. *Pedro and Luís Machuca, Granada, Alhambra, Palace of Charles V, façade.*

example, since the double arcades of the upper floor have a distant similarity to, for example, the contemporary *cortile* by Bramante at Sant'Ambrogio; on the other hand, it seems at least equally like the type represented by the Court of Lions at Guadalajara of 1483. What is probably the earliest example of an indisputably Italian type is the Medinaceli Palace at Cogolludo, built by Lorenzo Vázquez between 1492 and 1495 for the Duke of Medinaceli, who died in 1501. This is clearly modelled on Florentine Quattrocento prototypes, but the overall effect is quite remarkably like Filarete's drawing of the Medici Bank in Milan (Plate 154), and one may well assume that a Lombard rather than a Tuscan example was being followed. It has been suggested, on purely stylistic grounds, that Vázquez may have been trained in Italy, perhaps in Bologna.

Another very early example of a pure Italian taste is the Royal Hospital at Santiago de Compostela, built for the pilgrims by the Catholic sovereigns from 1501, at the same moment as they were also commissioning Bramante to build the Tempietto. The architect of the hospital was Enrique de Egas, who must have been aware of Italian models, since Filarete is again recalled by the plan of his hospital with its cruciform arrangement (like Filarete's design for the Ospedale Maggiore in Milan). The courts, too, closely resemble Milanese prototypes, even Bramante's Doric cloister at Sant'Ambrogio being called to mind. Another hospital of similar design, the Hospital of Santa Cruz at Toledo, built between 1504-14 and therefore contemporary with the Santiago one, is also attributed to Egas. However, the contemporary staircase at San Juan de los Reyes in Toledo is an even more important attribution to Egas, for Pevsner has shown that it and the staircase in the hospital (Plate 502) are the first datable open-well staircases in Europe. The old attribution to unspecified Genoese architects is improbable, since the great Genoese examples are all of a later date, and it seems that the only real Italian precedents are drawings of unexecuted buildings by Francesco di Giorgio and Leonardo da Vinci. Certainly, the great examples by Diego de Siloe in Burgos Cathedral and by Villalpando or Herrera in the Escorial, where the 'Imperial' type appears for the first time, were destined to become one of the most important features of any ambitious building.

Enrique de Egas also began another major building, Granada Cathedral, in 1523, but was dismissed and replaced by Diego de Siloe in 1528. Egas died in 1534.

Santa Cruz at Toledo has also been attributed to Alonso de Covarrubias, Egas's son-in-law and a sculptor in the Italian style, but it seems that he did not practise architecture until 1534, thirty years

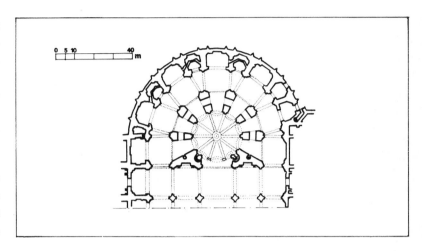

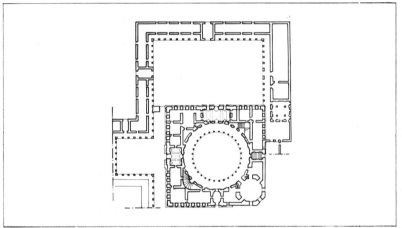

after the hospital was begun, and the attribution to Egas seems more probable. Covarrubias certainly designed another famous building in Toledo, the Alcázar, in 1537. This façade (Plate 505), like the contemporary University at Alcalá de Henares (1537-53) by Rodrigo Gil, shows a regressive use of Italian forms stuck on to a large, simple block for purely decorative purposes.

The court of the Alcázar was different in style from the façade (it was destroyed in the Spanish Civil War), and bore a close resemblance to the two lower storeys of the Cancelleria in Rome. The attribution to Covarrubias is, therefore, not very likely and it is known to have been completed by Francisco de Villalpando, the translator of Serlio and an exponent of a more severely classical style. A similar example of the new severity can be found in another building in Toledo connected with Covarrubias — the Tavera Hospital, built by his patron, Cardinal Tavera, between 1542 and 1579 (Plate 507). In this case, however, it is known that the design was made by the Cardinal's secretary, a priest named Bartolomé de Bustamante, who had travelled in Italy. The court is almost identical with the one formerly in the Alcázar, but the façade shows a much greater feeling for texture, in an Italian (Giulio Romano?) sense, not a Plateresque one, and it is worth noting that the building was begun several years before Vignola's Villa Giulia (cf. Plates 330-36).

Diego de Siloe, like Covarrubias, was a sculptor before turning to architecture and was influenced by the Frenchman Vigarny, but his masterpieces show an almost Bramantesque sense of classical form. In 1528 he made what was described as a 'Roman' design for Granada Cathedral, which he had to defend to Charles V, who found it too classical by contrast with the royal tombs. His splendid staircase in Burgos Cathedral (1519-26), the Escalera Dorada, has been shown to derive from Bramante's project for the Cortile del Belvedere, so it would seem that Siloe had firsthand knowledge of modern Roman architecture.

The first plan of Granada Cathedral (Plate 509) was drawn up by Egas, but the work was taken over by Siloe in 1528, and the great rotunda is his masterpiece. This was designed as a sort of church within a church, for the perpetual adoration of the Blessed Sacrament, and it has been suggested that Siloe modelled his design upon the Church of the Holy Sepulchre in Jerusalem: this may well be so, but the actual interior is reminiscent of the interior of Pavia Cathedral — and there may well be a common factor in Bramante's early projects for St. Peter's, which certainly adapt the Holy Sepulchre type of *martyrium*, while Pavia Cathedral is itself connected with Bramante.

Contemporary with Siloe's cathedral was the unfinished palace for Charles V built inside the Alhambra of Granada (Plates 510-12), and, like the cathedral, it is a good example of Italianate classicism before the Escorial. The palace was designed by a painter, Pedro Machuca, in 1526-27 and worked on until 1568. Machuca had been a painter practising in Italy who returned to Spain in 1520 and he obviously knew the work of Bramante and his school, although he left before the first Mannerist buildings were erected. The most striking feature of the palace is that it consists of a square inserted into the Alhambra, with one corner canted and made into an octagonal oratory, and with four entrances, one in the centre of each side, leading into a great circular court about one hundred feet in diameter (Plate 510). This was built by Luis Machuca after his father's death in 1550, but apparently in accordance with his designs. This means that it must have been designed some years earlier, and the two remarkable features — the two-storey, Doric and Ionic portico enclosing a circle, and the straight entablatures (not arcades) — remind us of Caprarola and Michelangelo's Capitol respectively, but both of these were designed long after Machuca had left Italy. It seems that he is deliberately trying to recreate the ancient circular court which had been projected, but never built, at the Villa Madama, and to do so he uses the correct Doric and Ionic colonnades, again perhaps derived from a Bramantesque prototype — the Palazzo Massimo *cortile* of the 1530s. The façade (Plate 511) is equally surprising if it is to be dated around 1526, for it is a rich variation on the House of Raphael, including one of the earliest uses of rusticated pilasters, and it is hardly less sophisticated than the versions by Sanmicheli, Giulio Romano, or Sansovino, all of which are probably of a later date. This must have been an astonishing building in Spain in the 1520s, as unusual as Inigo Jones's first Palladian designs in the England of James I. Certainly it had no immediate influence, and its true successor was another royal palace, much larger and even more austere by comparison with the extravagances of the Plateresque — El Escorial.

From 1550 the most important patron in Spain was the King, Philip II. He had succeeded to Spain and Naples in 1555, when Charles V retired to Yuste, and he was a connoisseur of painting, as we know from his long relationship with Titian. His Italianate artistic sympathies and his personal character — rigid, devout, and almost morbidly conscientious — would make him out of sympathy with the Plateresque and attracted to the severity of the Vignolan style practised in Rome from the 1550s. Herrera was exactly the architect he required, and he hardly needed to write to him: 'Above all, do not forget what I have told you — simplicity of form, severity in the whole, nobility without arrogance, majesty

513. *Juan de Herrera, Madrid, El Escorial (engraving).*
514. *Madrid, El Escorial, plan of monastery.*
515. *Juan de Herrera, Madrid, El Escorial, façade of church.* ▷

without ostentation.' He was referring to the Escorial, the huge monastery-mausoleum-fortress-palace he built of grey granite in the middle of the countryside thirty miles from Madrid, set against a background of mountains. After the death of Charles V in 1558, it was decided to build a mausoleum and a Jeronymite monastery and church with a royal palace as well, all contained in a vast block, 670 feet by 530 feet, with seventeen internal courts on a grid-iron pattern similar to Filarete's hospital in Milan, which had had so great an influence in Spain. The history of the design is not yet clear: in 1559 Juan Bautista de Toledo, a philosopher, mathematician, and classical scholar, was summoned by the King to return from Naples and prepare a design, the execution of which began in 1563, at the time when Juan de Herrera was appointed his assistant. It is said that Juan Bautista had worked on St. Peter's under Michelangelo, and although this may be an exaggeration, he must have had some experience as an architect in Italy before returning to Spain. He died in 1567 and his design for the great church was sent to Florence for criticism by the members of the Accademia del Disegno, who raised thirty-four points. Juan Bautista was succeeded by an Italian, G.B. Castello of Bergamo, who built the Imperial staircase, and Herrera did not really get a chance to prove himself as an architect until 1572. (He was born about 1530, was twice in Italy in the period 1547-51 and 1551-59, and had been a courtier before his appointment as assistant to Juan Bautista.) He completed the whole gigantic undertaking in 1584 and died in 1597. To complicate matters further, it was decided, about 1572, to obtain designs from all the leading Italian architects — twenty-two of them, including Alessi, Tibaldi, Palladio, and Vincenzo Danti. Vignola was then commissioned to prepare a plan from the results. These are all lost, but it seems that Vignola did not want the commission and Alessi was invited to Spain instead. In fact, however, the design by Herrera was executed between 1574 and 1582, and it shows the strong influence of Vignola and Serlio. Finally, it is known that Philip himself modified and simplified several drawings. The result is often called cold and monotonous, but by comparison with most sixteenth-century Spanish architecture it would be better called grand and simple.

The plan (Plate 514) shows that although it was designed at a late stage, the church was the dominant feature of the whole complex. It recalls the huge baths of the Romans — such as the Baths of Diocletian, as reconstructed by Palladio — rather than the smaller-scale imagination of Filarete. Diocletian's Palace at Split in Jugoslavia has been suggested as a parallel, and this certainly has the same grandeur. The church itself is obviously derived from the projects for St. Peter's, as may be seen from the shape of the great piers,

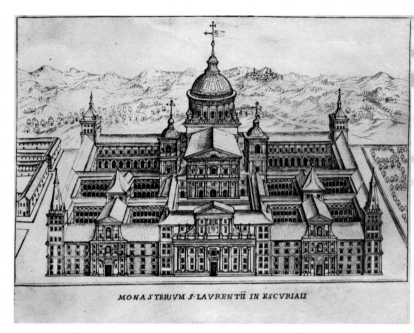

MONASTERIVM S·LAVRENTII IN ESCVRIALI

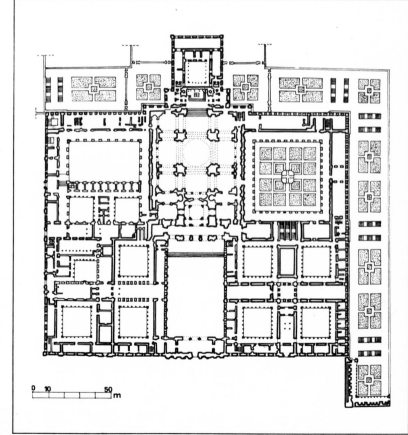

0 10 50 m

and the vestibule between the church proper and the court is reminiscent of Sangallo's engraved design. Here again, however, there are several precedents, for the shape and the outside (Plate 515) are closely reminiscent of Alessi's Santa Maria di Carignano at Genoa (Plate 374), which was itself modelled on St. Peter's. Furthermore, the unusual detail of an aisle running round the perimeter for the exclusive use of the clergy is taken from Tibaldi's San Fedele in Milan (Plate 381).

As in France, the full impact of the classical style was delayed until well into the sixteenth century, but, in the work of Herrera, Spain produced an architect able to stand comparison with his Italian contemporaries such as Tibaldi and Alessi, and this austere style was to continue to exert great influence on official architecture in Spain, even when the exuberance of the Baroque seemed to have swept all before it.

The architectural situation in the Northern countries was, by comparison with France and Spain, somewhat confused. This arose principally from politics — Germany, the Low Countries, and England were all, in varying degrees, convulsed by the Reformation. The attraction of ancient Rome was as great for the Protestant as for the Catholic lands, but it was more difficult to attract Italian artists and also far more difficult for Northerners to travel in Italy. This physical circumstance made life harder for painters, sculptors, or architects than for writers, especially after the invention of printing. The greatest of all the Northern humanists, Erasmus, steeped as he was in the ancient world, nevertheless lived in Gothic surroundings in Holland, in England, and in Switzerland.

The division of the Netherlands from a single area of language and culture into two politically and religiously opposed camps, one of which was dominated by Spain, was reflected in the fragmentation of Germany, where the religious wars devasted the country and dragged on into the seventeenth century. All these factors make it difficult to trace any coherent development of style, and the introduction of Renaissance ideas seems partly fortuitous, as an individual architect comes and goes.

As in France and Spain, there were very early examples of a pure Italian style in Germany and eastern Europe. The most surprising are the Facetted Palace in Moscow and the chapel of 1507 in Esztergom Cathedral by an architect connected with Giuliano da Sangallo. However, there are four buildings of the early sixteenth century, all in the southern parts, which were actually executed by Italian masters or under very strong Italian influence. These are the Fugger Chapel in Augsburg, of 1509-18, the Sigismund Chapel on the Wawel, Cracow, by Bartolommeo Berecci, of 1516-33, the

Residenz at Landshut in Bavaria, begun in 1536, and the Belvedere at Prague, of 1535-60. The chapel in Cracow was built by a Florentine for King Sigismund I, who had married Bona Sforza, which may explain why the chapel is of a Lombard domed type rather than Florentine. The Landshut Residenz was deliberately copied from the Palazzo del Te and was built by a colony of Mantuan masons; the Belvedere at Prague is probably also by Italians, and it has been suggested that some of the details come from Serlio (first published in 1537), so the dependence on Italian models is evident. The Fugger Chapel (Plate 516) is more interesting in that it is clearly very influenced by Venetian ideas, which is hardly surprising in Augsburg and in a chapel built for an internationally-minded family. It can none the less reasonably be called the first building of the Renaissance in Germany, if only because of its function as a training-ground for German artists. Yet when the spectator raises his eyes above cornice level, he finds the traditional German Gothic starvault, and this stylistic coexistence was typical of all the Northern countries for many years to come (cf. the contemporary Chapel of Henry VII, Westminster Abbey: Plate 528).

It was not until the second half of the sixteenth century that a Northern Renaissance style began to emerge. In the year 1550, the first of the German architectural treatises appeared — Hans Blum's *Quinque Columnarum Exacta descriptio atque deliniatio*, which deals with the five Orders. It was followed by his *Ein kunstrych Büch von allerley antiquiteten* (c. 1562) and other works, and in 1565 and 1568 by the Dutchman Vredeman de Vries's *Architectura* and *Artis Perspectivae*, both published in Antwerp. Finally, in 1598, there appeared the nightmarish fantasies of Wendel Dietterlin's *Architectura, von Ausstheilung Symmetria und Proportion der Fünff Seulen*, published in Nuremberg and consisting of 203 engravings, not one of which bears the slightest resemblance to anything Bramante would have recognized (Plate 518). It was very popular, and its 'strapwork' decorations were often adapted (but rarely actually copied) by Dutch, Flemish, and English masons as well as German ones.

The Ottheinrichsbau of the castle at Heidelberg (Plate 517) takes its name from the Elector Ottheinrich (1556-59), who endeavoured to introduce humanist learning and culture as well as ancient architectural forms, here probably derived from Serlio's treatise. The great similarity between German and Netherlandish architecture at this date can be seen in the portico of the Cologne Rathaus (Plate 519), built by Wilhelm Vernucken between 1569 and 1573, which owes a good deal to the great prototype at Antwerp (Plate 525).

Munich, a strongly Catholic city, welcomed the Jesuits in 1559 and had a greater affinity with Rome than many German cities. The Antiquarium, begun as the first museum in Germany by Wilhelm

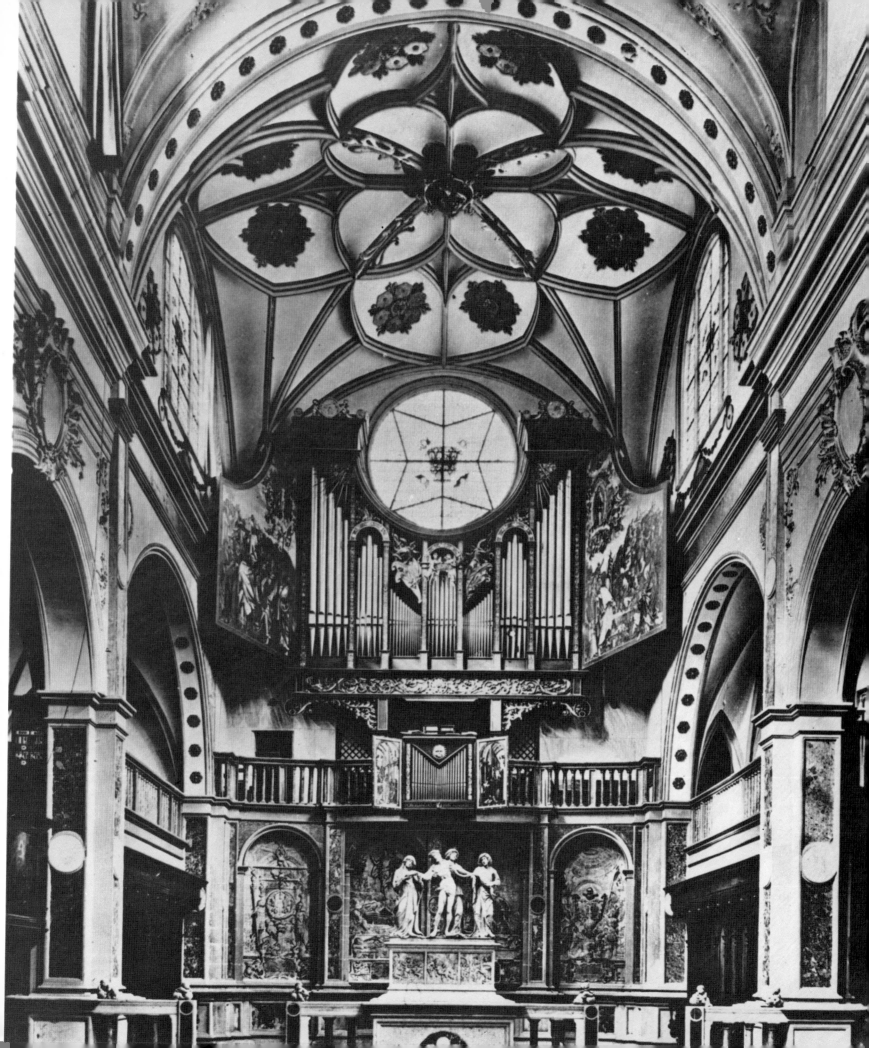

Egckl in 1569 (Plate 520), and the Jesuit church of Saint Michael both take us much nearer to the spirit of Counter-Reformation Rome than any earlier German building. The church was built between 1583 and 1597, the chancel and transept (Plate 522) being added after 1592 by Friedrich Sustris, a Flemish architect working for the patron, Duke William V of Bavaria. It is not known who designed the nave or façade, and it may be that, as frequently happened elsewhere, the Jesuits themselves supplied drawings. This seems less likely in the case of the façade (Plate 521), since it is far less Roman in feeling and combines a very distant reminiscence of Vignola's Gesù with the traditional gable form of a German house. This combination was easily adapted to town halls and grand town houses (e.g. the Pellerhaus, Nuremberg, 1602-7): it reached its culmination in the sober style of Elias Holl (1573-1646), whose masterpiece, the Rathaus at Augsburg, was built between 1615 and 1620 (Plate 530). Holl was an exact counterpart to Inigo Jones in England, for he had also been to Italy at about the same time as Jones, and his simple style belongs to the seventeenth century rather than the sixteenth.

The southern Netherlands had one great example of the High Renaissance style in the Raphael cartoons for the Vatican tapestries which were woven in Brussels, under the supervision of Raphael's assistant — Tommaso Vincidor da Bologna. The court at Brussels and Malines employed foreign artists, and Margaret of Austria, the Regent, made alterations to the palace at Malines in 1517. A few years later, alterations were made to the outer ward of the castle at Breda. Vincidor himself was responsible for the court of Breda Castle in the 1530s (Plate 523), and the extraordinary treatment of the entablature above the ground-floor arcade, or the insertions above the Ionic capitals, show that even an assistant of Raphael was unable to impose a fully Roman style. Yet this is one of the most classical buildings of the period, and the House of the Salmon at Malines, of 1530-34 (Plate 527), or the Greffe at Bruges, also of the 1530s, are more typical. Like Vincidor, Alessandro Pasqualini was a Bolognese, but not a trained architect. He built the tower of the church at Ijsselstein, near Utrecht, in about 1532, which is far more classical than anything else to be seen in the northern Netherlands for many years (Plate 524).

At the beginning of the century, the rise of Antwerp as one of the great ports of the world led to the dominance of Antwerp masters in painting, and the rise of the printing trade there augmented its importance as a centre of learning. The first translation of Serlio was printed in Antwerp, and many other treatises and books of engravings as well. Amsterdam, at this time, lagged behind Ant-

werp, so the most influential of the great town halls of the period
is the one built by Cornelis Floris de Vriendt (1514-1575). He had
been in Rome about 1538, and had produced two books of engravings
in 1556 and 1557, before building the Antwerp Town Hall (Plate 525)
between 1561 and 1566. It seems that several designs were submitted,
including one by an Italian architect, but there is no doubt that the
building is substantially Floris's, however much he may have
learned from the other designs. It is the characteristic building
of the first phase of classicism in Flanders, with its great central
frontispiece like earlier Gothic examples, yet expressed in terms of
the classical Orders, probably taken from a plate in Serlio.
The decoration is comparatively restrained, and the use of a
rusticated basement not only provides a welcome horizontal, but
also introduces the right amount of textural contrast to the very
large windows. The roof, of course, is steeply pitched in the Northern
manner, so that it differs markedly from any Italian building: yet
the whole has a feeling of simplicity and harmony that shows it
to be the result of a genuine search for classical qualities, and for
this reason alone it is wrong to think of it as a Mannerist work,
unless Flemish Mannerism is understood in a different sense from
the style practised by Giulio Romano. Many other town halls in
the Netherlands and Germany were influenced by it, that at The
Hague being as early as 1564.

From about 1580, Dutch architecture began to become independent, and the town halls, public weigh-houses, and market buildings are usually in a classical style, the Haarlem Weigh-House of
1598 (Plate 526) which has been attributed to Lieven de Key being
a particularly good example. Key, the leading architect of the time,
was a Haarlem man whose early work, the Town Hall of Leiden
of 1595, shows affinities with contemporary French and English
(Burghley House; Plate 532) work as well as with Antwerp Town
Hall. Key's later works, such as the Haarlem Meat Market (1602-3),
or the tower of the Nieuwekerk (1612), lead on into the work of his
younger contemporary, the Amsterdamer Hendrik de Keyser, with
whom Dutch architecture enters a Baroque, rather than Renaissance,
phase.

Like Holland or Germany, England was very distant from Italy
and was still further cut off by the Reformation. The brief reign
of Mary Tudor (1553-58), which promised, through her marriage
to Philip II of Spain, to bring England back into the ambit of
Italian civilisation, was too short to achieve anything notable in the
arts, while the reaction under her sister Elizabeth I (1558-1603)
effectively cut off all contact with Europe for most of the second
half of the century. On the other hand, unlike Germany and the

523. *Tommaso Vincidor, Breda Castle, court.*
524. *Alessandro Pasqualini, Ijsselstein, church tower.*

525. *Cornelis Floris de Vriendt, Antwerp, Town Hall.*
526. *Lieven de Key, Haarlem, Weigh-House.*

Low Countries, England was politically stable under the new Tudor dynasty, so that building for comfort rather than defence was possible. The new dynasty encouraged a new aristocracy who, in turn, were enabled to build because they had enriched themselves by the sequestration of Church lands as well as by their active involvement in trade. Architecturally, the result is a vigorous national style, often crude, and almost totally out of contact with the intellectual presuppositions of classical architecture. The details are derived at second or third hand from pattern-books such as those by Vredeman de Vries or Wendel Dietterlin, although Serlio was popular from the beginning and was translated into English (significantly, from the Dutch and not from the Italian original) in 1611.

Just as in Germany (Fugger Chapel) or Poland (Cracow, Royal Tombs), so in England there was from a very early date at least one example of a pure Italian style. The English example is particularly significant because it is a royal tomb — that of Henry VII, founder of the new dynasty — and is a work of an important Florentine sculptor, Pietro Torrigiano; it is in the chapel in Westminster Abbey founded by Henry as another dynastic glorification. The tomb (Plate 528) was made between 1512 and 1518 in England (where, according to Cellini, Torrigiano did not enjoy himself). The chapel was begun in 1503 and finished in 1519 and is the most complete contrast imaginable, since it is the finest flowering of that peculiarly English form of Late Gothic known as Perpendicular. Another example of Perpendicular, perhaps more subtle, is King's College Chapel, Cambridge, where the only recognition of the Italian Renaissance is the decorative carvings on the screen, and they are as late as 1532-36.

As elsewhere in Europe, Italian influence came in by means of decorative details, and it was many years before the structural principles were understood, let alone copied. The Royal Palace of Nonsuch, begun in 1538 for the would-be Renaissance Prince, Henry VIII, was perhaps the first major 'Renaissance' building and arose from Henry's jealousy of Francis I of France. Nonsuch was destroyed long ago, but the few drawings and engravings of it, together with a fireplace said to have come from the palace, all show that it was far more Franco-Flemish than Italian and was probably an encouragement to those who wanted to cover every surface with 'antick' ornament. Before Nonsuch, however, there were at least two important buildings in the same strain: Sutton Place, near Guildford, and Hampton Court Palace. Sutton Place was begun about 1523 by Sir Richard Weston, who had been in France and had attended the Field of the Cloth of Gold, that exercise in vulgar and ostentatious rivalry between Henry VIII and Francis I. The plan, with a central court and great gatehouse, was fairly traditional, but there are two new

528. *Pietro Torrigiano, London, Westminster Abbey, Chapel of Henry VII, Tomb of Henry VII.*
529. *Hardwick Hall, Derbyshire, plan.*
530. *Elias Holl, Augsburg, Rathaus, façade.*
531. *Hampton Court, Wolsey's Closet, detail of ceiling and part of wall.*

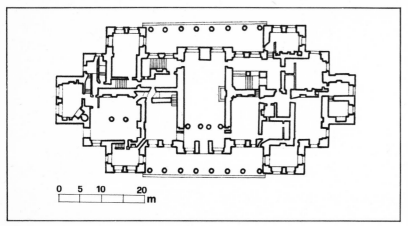

features. The front door was set in the centre of the entrance front for symmetry instead of being offset to suit the arrangement of the Great Hall inside, and there is also a Long Gallery. This latter was certainly derived from Hampton Court, which seems to have been, under Wolsey, the first building to have such a feature.

Hampton Court itself, greatly enlarged in the seventeenth century, was originally the palace of Cardinal Wolsey, who, at the height of his European influence and power, kept a household of five hundred. He began Hampton Court, a few miles from London, in 1514, in the age of Leo X and before anyone had heard of Luther. By 1529, his own power was in disastrous decline and he gave the building to Henry VIII. After his fall, Henry enlarged the palace and work continued on it until 1540. The original Wolsey Palace had a Long Gallery, but the present Great Hall, which is entirely traditional English except for the carved detailing, is Henry's. Wolsey's Closet, a small room with an attempt at an Italian compartmented ceiling (Plate 531), shows how little comprehension there was of contemporary Italian art.

The planning of this large building was based on a series of courts with ranges of buildings round all four sides, exactly like the traditional form of an Oxford or Cambridge college, and indeed Wolsey's other magnificent foundation, Cardinal College (now Christ Church), Oxford, is a good example of the type.

Henry VIII died in 1547, still nominally a Catholic, but since his son, Edward VI, was still a minor, a Regent was appointed. The Lord Protector Somerset was identified with the Protestant party, and, until his fall in 1549, Somerset was responsible for a marked French influence introduced through his own great town palace, Somerset House. This was begun about 1547 and was demolished in the eighteenth century, but its appearance is known from a drawing (Plate 537) and it was one of the most influential houses of the period. Écouen, begun by Bullant only a year or two earlier, was probably the model for Old Somerset House, but the influence of Philibert de l'Orme has also been detected in it.

In 1550 Somerset was succeeded as Lord Protector by the Duke of Northumberland, and he sent John Shute, 'paynter and archytecte', to Italy 'to confer with the doings of the skilful masters in architecture, and also to view such ancient monuments thereof as are yet extant'. This was not only a reversal of Somerset's policy, but it is, as far as we know, the sole instance at the time of an English architect (the word itself was new to the language) with a firsthand knowledge of ancient and modern architecture in Italy. Unfortunately, we know nothing of Shute as a builder, although his Italian studies did result in the first book on architecture in the English language, *The First and Chief Groundes of Architecture*, pub-

lished in 1563, the year of Shute's death, and based predictably on Serlio, although Vignola's treatise on the Orders, published in 1562, is a closer parallel.

Longleat, in Wiltshire, is one of the greatest achievements of Elizabethan architecture (Plate 535), and is a descendant of Old Somerset House. It was built by Sir John Thynne, who had been in charge of building at Old Somerset House and had also been in France, but the mason — and almost certainly the designer — was Robert Smythson (*c.* 1536-1614), one of a family of masons and the major figure in English architecture in the reign of Elizabeth.

The building history of Longleat is complex, but it seems that the present house dates substantially from 1572 (except the interior). The most surprising thing about Longleat, in the context of English architecture of the 1570s and 80s, is the simplicity and restraint of massing and detail. Three of the sides have projecting bays in the centre and at each end, while the fourth entrance front has four major projections and a fifth, smaller one for the front door, which leads into the traditional screens-passage. This means that the Great Hall has been moved from the centre of the house to one side, thus satisfactorily combining the central front door with the traditional entrance into the screens-passage. The first impression of the house is of lightness and delicacy, since the proportion of void to solid is completely different from the fortified type of manor house. The bay-window, a typical English feature, is used as a device to obtain vertical accents so as to form a grid-shape with the strongly emphasized horizontals of the entablatures, which are very correctly treated, though reminiscent of French work in the handling of details.

Smythson was probably also the architect of two other major Elizabethan houses, Hardwick Hall in Derbyshire, and Wollaton, near Nottingham — indeed, Smythson is buried in Wollaton Church and his tomb describes him as '*Gent., Architector and Survayor unto the most worthy house of Wollaton*', a description which can hardly have been possible before then. Hardwick, which is attributed to him, shows the rectilinearity of Longleat carried a stage further (Plate 536), and the plan is also an advance on Longleat, since a much more compact grouping has been obtained, largely by turning the axis of the Great Hall through 90° so that it forms the core of the house, with the front door now opening into the screens-passage which has been ranged with the entrance (Plate 529). Hardwick was built very quickly between 1590 and 1596, so that Longleat and Hardwick between them span a period of some thirty years, during which time the major influences were Flemish and German rather than Italian. The style of Smythson's contemporaries can be seen in houses such as Burghley, near Stamford, built for Elizabeth's

535. *Sir John Thynne, Longleat, Wiltshire, main façade.*
536. *Robert Smythson, Hardwick Hall, Derbyshire, façade.*

minister, Lord Burghley. The house was begun in 1556, but the extravagant court is dated 1585 (Plate 532) and is obviously French-inspired, perhaps from Anet, although the decoration is more Flemish, and was, indeed, partly shipped from Antwerp. It is known that Lord Burghley sent to Paris for copies of French architectural books, and he specifically mentions de l'Orme.

Kirby Hall, Northampton, on the other hand, is more problematic. It was begun in 1570, but the main front, dated 1572 (Plate 533) has a Giant Order of Ionic pilasters, which are not only the earliest in England, but are comparatively early anywhere. It seems certain that John Thorpe, to whom the house was formerly attributed, was only seven when it was begun, and the architect — who may possibly have derived the idea from Saint-Maur-lès-Fossés (Plate 491) — remains unknown.

With the new century, changes came over English architecture. Hatfield House (Plate 534), near London, built for Robert Cecil, Earl of Salisbury, the younger son of Lord Burghley, is both more comfortable and less extravagant than Burghley; more important, the garden front has an Italianate loggia on either side of the central tower. There is a payment of £. 10 in the Hatfield accounts for February 1610, 'for drawinge of some architecture'. The payment was to Inigo Jones, and it is now thought that perhaps this was one of the earliest works of the man 'through whom there is hope that sculpture, modelling, architecture, painting, acting and all that is praise-worthy in the elegant arts of the ancients, may one day find their way across the Alps into our England'. These words were written in 1606, and in less than twenty years they were fully justified: the Banqueting House in Whitehall (Plate 538), the Queen's Chapel at Saint James's Palace, and the Queen's House at Greenwich show, at last, that the lessons of Palladio had been fully learned, and a truly classical style could be practised in England.

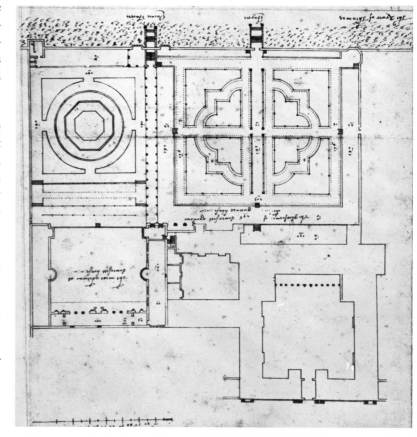

SYNOPTIC TABLES / BIOGRAPHIES / SELECTED BIBLIOGRAPHY /
INDEX / LIST OF PLATES / LIST OF PHOTOGRAPHIC CREDITS

FLORENCE	ROME	NORTHERN ITALY	OTHER ITALIAN CENTRES	EUROPE
1418-46 Florence Cathedral (Santa Maria del Fiore), dome, lantern, apse F. BRUNELLESCHI				
1419 Spedale degli Innocenti F. BRUNELLESCHI				
1421 San Lorenzo, Basilica, Old Sacristy: work begun by F. BRUNELLESCHI				
1429-46 Santa Croce, Pazzi Chapel F. BRUNELLESCHI				
1436 Santo Spirito F. BRUNELLESCHI				
1437-52 San Marco, Monastery, Library: reconstruction by M. MICHELOZZI				
1444-64 Palazzo Medici Riccardi M. MICHELOZZI				
c. 1446-50 Palazzo Rucellai: project by L.B. ALBERTI (realized by B. ROSSELLINO)				
		1450 Tempio Malatestiano, Rimini, interior: transformation begun by M. DE' PASTI		
		1450 Tempio Malatestiano, Rimini L.B. ALBERTI		
	c. 1451-55 St. Peter's: first projects by B. ROSSELLINO	1451-55 Castello Sforzesco, Milan: work by A. FILARETE		
1452 *De re aedificatoria*: L.B. ALBERTI offers version to Pope Nicholas V				

FLORENCE	ROME	NORTHERN ITALY	OTHER ITALIAN CENTRES	EUROPE
	1455 Palazzo Venezia, court: work begun by B. ROSSELLINO			
		1456-65 Ospedale Maggiore, Milan A. FILARETE		
			1459-64 Pienza: replanning of city by B. ROSSELLINO	
		1460 San Sebastiano, Mantua: project by L.B. ALBERTI		
		1461-64 *Trattato di Architettura* A. FILARETE		
		1462 Medici Bank, Milan M. MICHELOZZI	1462-63 Palazzo Piccolomini, Pienza B. ROSSELLINO	
			1468 Palazzo Ducale, Urbino: work begun by L. LAURANA, F. DI GIORGIO	
		1470 Sant'Andrea, Mantua: project by L.B. ALBERTI		
		1470-75 Santa Maria Maggiore, Bergamo, Colleoni Chapel G.A. AMADEO		
		1475 Milan Cathedral: work begun by G.A. AMADEO		
			1478 (before) Rocca di Sassocorvaro F. DI GIORGIO	
1480 Villa Medici, Poggio a Caiano: work begun by G. DA SANGALLO				

FLORENCE	ROME	NORTHERN ITALY	OTHER ITALIAN CENTRES	EUROPE
		1481 Engraving of *Ruins and Figures* D. BRAMANTE		
		1482 Santa Maria presso San Satiro, Milan: work begun by D. BRAMANTE		
			1484 Palazzo del Governo degli Anziani, Ancona F. DI GIORGIO	
			1485 Santa Maria del Calcinaio, near Cortona F. DI GIORGIO	
			1485 Santa Maria delle Carceri, Prato: work begun by G. DA SANGALLO	
			1486 Palazzo Comunale, Jesi F. DI GIORGIO	
				1487-89 Colegio Mayor de Santa Cruz, Valladolid, Spain E. DE EGAS
1488 Palazzo Strozzi B. DA MAIANO		1488 Santa Maria delle Grazie, Milan, apse D. BRAMANTE		
	c. 1489-95 Palazzo della Cancelleria			
1490 Palazzo Gondi: work begun by G. DA SANGALLO				
		1492 Sant'Ambrogio, Milan, Canonica: work begun by D. BRAMANTE		1492-95 Medinaceli Palace, Cogolludo, Guadalajara, Spain L. VÁZQUEZ
			1495 Palazzo della Rovere, Savona G. DA SANGALLO	

FLORENCE	ROME	NORTHERN ITALY	OTHER ITALIAN CENTRES	EUROPE
			1498-1500 Casa Santa, Loreto, dome G. DA SANGALLO	
				1500-4 Bridge of Notre Dame, Paris, France FRA GIOCONDO
	1502 Tempietto of San Pietro in Montorio: work begun by D. BRAMANTE			
	1504 Santa Maria della Pace, cloister D. BRAMANTE			1504-14 Hospital of Santa Cruz, Toledo, Spain E. DE EGAS
	1506 St. Peter's D. BRAMANTE			
			1508 Forte Michelangelo, Civitavecchia A. DA SANGALLO THE YOUNGER	
	1509- c. 1510 Villa Farnesina B. PERUZZI			
	1509 Sant'Eligio degli Orefici: work begun by RAPHAEL, and others			
	1510-15 Palazzo Baldassini A. DA SANGALLO THE YOUNGER			
	1512 Chigi Stables, via della Lungara: project by RAPHAEL			
	1514 St. Peter's: RAPHAEL succeeds D. BRAMANTE			
	1514-15 St. Peter's: work by FRA GIOCONDO			

FLORENCE	ROME	NORTHERN ITALY	OTHER ITALIAN CENTRES	EUROPE
1515 San Lorenzo: competition for façade				
1516-20 San Lorenzo: drawings and projects for façade by MICHELANGELO	c. 1516 Villa Madama: work begun by RAPHAEL			
	1518 San Giovanni dei Fiorentini A. DA SANGALLO THE YOUNGER		1518 San Biagio, Montepulciano A. DA SANGALLO THE ELDER	
	1519 San Giovanni dei Fiorentini: work begun by J. SANSOVINO			
1520-34 San Lorenzo, Medici Chapel MICHELANGELO				
1523-59 Biblioteca Laurenziana MICHELANGELO	1523-24 Palazzo del Banco di Santo Spirito A. DA SANGALLO THE YOUNGER			
		1524-35 Palazzo del Te, Mantua G. ROMANO		
				1527 Alhambra, Royal Palace, Granada, Spain: work begun by P. MACHUCA
				1527 Santa Maria del Campo, near Burgos, Spain D. DE SILOE
				1528 Palais de Fontainebleau, France: new construction begun by G. LE BRETON
				1528-59 Granada Cathedral, Spain D. DE SILOE
		c. 1530 Palazzi Pompei, Canossa, Bevilacqua, Verona M. SANMICHELI		

FLORENCE	ROME	NORTHERN ITALY	OTHER ITALIAN CENTRES	EUROPE
	1532 Palazzo Massimo alle Colonne: reconstruction by B. PERUZZI			
		1533 Palazzo Corner della Ca' Grande, Venice J. SANSOVINO		
		1535 La Zecca, Venice: work begun by J. SANSOVINO		c. 1535 Palais de Fontainebleau, France: work begun by F. PRIMATICCIO
		1537 Libreria Sansoviniana and Loggetta del Campanile di San Marco, Venice: work begun by J. SANSOVINO		
	c. 1538 Piazza del Campidoglio and Capitoline palaces: projects by MICHELANGELO			
	1541 Palazzo Farnese: work begun by A. DA SANGALLO THE YOUNGER			
	1546-49 Palazzo Farnese: work by MICHELANGELO	1546 Porta Palio, Verona: work begun by M. SANMICHELI		c. 1546 Château d'Ancy-le-Franc, France S. SERLIO
	1546-64 St. Peter's: work by MICHELANGELO			1546 Palais du Louvre, Paris, France: work begun by P. LESCOT
				1547-59 Château d'Anet, France P. DE L'ORME
		1548 Lazzaretto, Verona M. SANMICHELI		
		1549 Basilica Palladiana, Vicenza: work begun by A. PALLADIO		

FLORENCE	ROME	NORTHERN ITALY	OTHER ITALIAN CENTRES	EUROPE	
1550 First edition of *Lives* G. VASARI	1550 Villa d'Este, Tivoli: project by P. LIGORIO				
	1550-53 Sant'Andrea in via Flaminia G. VIGNOLA				
	1551-55 Villa Giulia: work directed by G. VIGNOLA	1551 Villa Capra (La Rotonda), Vicenza A. PALLADIO			
		1553 Villa Trissino, Cricoli G. TRISSINO			
		1553-58 Palazzo Marino, Milan G. ALESSI			
1554 Palazzo Vecchio: work begun by G. VASARI		1554 Palazzo Ducale, Venice, Scala d'Oro J. SANSOVINO			
		c. 1557 Palazzo Grimani, Venice M. SANMICHELI		1557 Château de Saint-Germain- en-Laye, France P. DE L'ORME	
			1558-73 Villa Farnese, Caprarola G. VIGNOLA		
1560 Uffizi: work begun by G. VASARI	1560-61 Palazzo Farnese: project by G. VIGNOLA			1560 Château de Chantilly, France, Petit Château: work begun by J. BULLANT	
1560 Palazzo Pitti: completed by B. AMMANATI					
	1561 Santa Maria degli Angeli: work by MICHELANGELO				
	1562 Porta Pia MICHELANGELO				
				1563 El Escorial, Madrid, Spain: work begun by J. DE HERRERA	

FLORENCE	ROME	NORTHERN ITALY	OTHER ITALIAN CENTRES	EUROPE
	1564 Santa Maria Maggiore, Sforza Chapel MICHELANGELO	1564 Collegio Borromeo, Pavia: work begun by P. TIBALDI		1564 Royal Palace, Aranjuez, Spain: project by J. DE HERRERA
	1564 St. Peter's: work begun by G. VIGNOLA			
		1565 San Giorgio Maggiore, Venice A. PALLADIO		
			1566 Villa Lante, Bagnaia G. VIGNOLA	
1567-69 Ponte Santa Trinita B. AMMANATI		1567 Milan Cathedral, Baptistery: work by P. TIBALDI		
1568 Second edition of *Lives* G. VASARI	1568 Il Gesù: project begun by G. VIGNOLA			
		1569 San Fedele, Milan: work begun by P. TIBALDI		
		1571 Il Redentore, Venice A. PALLADIO		1571-85 El Alcázar, Toledo, Spain J. DE HERRERA
1574 Uffizi, Porta delle Suppliche B. BUONTALENTI				
		1579-80 Teatro Olimpico, Vicenza A. PALLADIO		
				1580-88 Wollaton House, Nottinghamshire, England R. SMYTHSON
				1583-98 Casa Lonja, Seville, Spain J. DE HERRERA
	1586-93 St. Peter's, dome: completed by G. DELLA PORTA, D. FONTANA			

FLORENCE	ROME	NORTHERN ITALY	OTHER ITALIAN CENTRES	EUROPE	
		1588 Teatro Olimpico, Sabbioneta V. SCAMOZZI		1591-97 Hardwick Hall, Derbyshire, England R. SMYTHSON	

ALBERTI, LEON BATTISTA

Born c. 1404 in Genoa; died 1472 in Rome. He accompanied his family into exile in Venice, and then to Bologna where he studied law and where they remained until their return to Florence in 1428. After periods spent in Bologna, Ferrara, and Florence, he went to Rome in 1432 and again in 1433 to study buildings and monuments. Lionello d'Este summoned him to Ferrara for the monument to Nicholas I, and thus bonds were formed between them which were to lead to Alberti's commission for the Tempio Malatestiano in Rimini.

In Rome, Alberti became Pope Nicholas V's expert on urban development and on the layout of individual buildings; among these were the reinforcement works in St. Peter's, restoration work in Santo Stefano Rotondo, San Teodoro, and Santa Prassede, and supervision of the new fortifications.

While working on the Tempio Malatestiano he was also occupied in Florence on the Palazzo Rucellai. In 1467, again at the request of Giovanni Rucellai, he designed the Tempietto del Santo Sepolcro in the church of San Pancrazio in Florence. It is not easy to date the work on the façade of Santa Maria Novella, but it was probably begun about 1455.

In 1459 Alberti moved to Mantua where Ludovico Gonzaga entrusted him with the construction of the church of San Sebastiano (the building dates from 1460). Ten years later he designed the church of Sant'Andrea, which was begun in 1472 by Luca Fancelli. About 1470 he also prepared drawings for the chancel of Santissima Annunziata in Florence (executed by Michelozzo from modified designs).

In addition to his architectural projects, Alberti was engaged in theoretical work, which resulted in the publication of several pamphlets and treatises. The most important of these are: *Della Statua*, attributed by some critics to the period after 1464, but more probably a youthful work (perhaps before 1435); *Trattato della Pittura*, finished in Latin in 1435 and in Italian in 1436; and *De re aedificatoria libri X*, drafted by the beginning of 1452, but revised during the following years.

ALESSI, GALEAZZO

Born c. 1512 in Perugia; died 1572 in Perugia. Alessi moved in 1536 to Rome, where he was employed at the court of Cardinal Ascanio Parisani. His most important works are to be found in Genoa, where he went in 1548, probably at the request of Bartolomeo Sauli for whom he built a mansion which has since been destroyed. The Sauli family also commissioned him to build the basilica of Santa Maria di Carignano (1552).

In addition to Villa Cambiaso and Villa Pallavicino della Peschiera, Alessi's name is associated with a series of mansions in Genoa along the Strada Nuova, now via Garibaldi; among them Palazzo Cambiaso (1565), Palazzo Parodi (1567), and Palazzo Cataldi should be mentioned. During this period he often went to Milan and to Perugia, especially in the years after 1560. In Milan, for Tommaso Marino of Genoa, he began Palazzo Marino in 1553, and completed it in 1558. In 1561, he built the church of San Barnaba, and in 1565 he worked on the façade of Santa Maria presso San Celso.

He finally settled in his native city in 1569, where he built the belfry of Santa Maria Nuova, the church of Sant'Angelo della Pace (c. 1545), the Sala del Consiglio and the chapel in the Palazzo dei Priori (1572). The church of Santa Maria del Popolo and, not far from the city, the villa for Cardinal Fulvio della Corgna (1580) were erected according to his plans.

Other buildings in which he took part still remain in Bologna, Brescia, and Piacenza. At Assisi he renovated the interior of the cathedral of San Rufino (1571) and prepared the model for Santa Maria degli Angeli (1568).

AMADEO, GIOVANNI ANTONIO

Born 1447 in Pavia; died 1522 in Pavia. Amadeo worked as an architect and sculptor in Lombardy, mainly in Milan and in his native city. His first known project is the door of the small cloister in the Certosa of Pavia, on which he worked with his brother Protasio in 1466, and in which the young Amadeo showed himself to be a follower of the ancient Campione tradition as well as of the new trends of the Tuscan Renaissance.

From 1470–75 Amadeo built the Colleoni Chapel in Santa Maria Maggiore, Bergamo, with the Tomb of Medea and the monument to Bartolomeo Colleoni. The great simplicity of the chapel's structure contrasts with its ornate sculptural decoration.

In 1475 he worked in Milan Cathedral on the Chapel of San Giuseppe (now destroyed). To this period can also be attributed the church doors, the Old Sacristy, and the monks' lavabo in the Certosa of Pavia (which show the influence of the Mantegazza brothers), and the construction of the three belfries or outside pinnacles. Amadeo made a clay model for the entire façade in 1490, modifying the previous ideas held by Solari and Dolcebuono. He acted as superintendent of the whole project, together with the Mantegazza brothers, Giacomo della Porta, Briosco, and others until 1499, the same year in which work commenced on the dome of Milan Cathedral. In 1481, Amadeo had succeeded Solari as director of construction on the cathedral, collaborating with the most important foreign and Italian architects, among them Bramante and Leonardo.

From 1481–96 he was in charge of work on the Ospedale Maggiore in Milan, which had been begun by Filarete and was to be continued by Solari. He undertook the reinforcement of the Ganda bridge over the Adda between 1492–95, and began the construction of Palazzo Bottigella in Pavia, now greatly altered on the outside but well preserved inside the courtyard. In 1498 Amadeo built the Lanfranco Tomb in the church of the same name in Pavia and also superseded Rocchi as director of work on Pavia Cathedral, which was to be completed in 1502.

AMMANATI, BARTOLOMEO

Born 1511 in Florence; died 1592 in Florence. Throughout his life, especially during the period of his artistic formation as an architect and sculptor, Ammanati travelled a great deal and became acquainted with many notable people of the time. He may have moved to Venice in 1527, for he was working there with Sansovino on the Libreria Sansoviniana. Later, he was to return to Venice after spending several years in Florence and in Urbino.

From 1550 he worked in Rome, in the service of Julius III, where he came into contact with Michelangelo, Vignola, and Vasari. With Vignola, from 1553–55, he collaborated on Villa Giulia (the general plan was by Vasari).

He moved to Florence in 1555 and was commissioned to complete the project by Michelangelo for the Biblioteca Laurenziana (1559). The following year Ammanati was entrusted with the completion and enlargement of Palazzo Pitti, which called for an open courtyard towards the Boboli Gardens. From 1567–69 he was engaged on the construction of Ponte Santa Trinita, while working, at the same time, on the cloister of Santo Spirito. Among Ammanati's buildings in Florence the Grifani, Mandragone, and Giugni palaces should be mentioned.

In Lucca, in addition to the Palazzo della Signoria (begun in 1578) he was also responsible for Palazzo Bernardi-Micheletti.

Upon returning to Rome, Ammanati built a number of mansions and then became associated with the Jesuit Order (for whom he built the church and college of San Giovannino degli Scolopi in Florence).

BENEDETTO DA MAIANO

Born 1442 at Maiano; died 1497 in Florence. Benedetto often worked in collaboration with his brother Giuliano: in Florence, on the Sala dei Gigli in Palazzo Vecchio (1476–81); in San Gimignano, on the Chapel of Santa Fina in the Collegiata (1470–75); in Rome, on the Carafa Chapel in Santa Maria sopra Minerva.

He erected the Tomb of San Savino in Faenza Cathedral, the Tomb of Maria of Aragon in Monte Oliveto in Naples (1484–95), and the Tomb of Filippo Strozzi in Santa Maria Novella in Florence (1491). He also worked on the New Sacristy in Florence Cathedral.

His most important works are the loggia in front of the church of Santa Maria delle Grazie in Arezzo (1490–91), and Palazzo Strozzi in Florence (1488 and after) commissioned by Filippo Strozzi.

BRAMANTE, DONATO

Born c. 1444 at Monte Asdrualdo, near Urbino (now Fermignano); died 1514 in Rome. There is a remarkable lack of biographical information about Bramante, the more striking by comparison with our knowledge of Raphael (who was probably a relation) and Michelangelo, whose life and character are so fully documented. Bramante was certainly very well known in the last years of his life, and both Serlio and Palladio testify to his fame in the late sixteenth century, so there can have been no lack of interest in him. Yet despite his position at the Papal court, and the huge undertakings commissioned by his greatest patron and supporter, Julius II, we have only a few meagre details of his personality, mostly preserved by Vasari, very little mention of him in the documents at present known, and absolutely no facts about the first thirty years of his life. He was, however, supposed to have had a great knowledge of Dante, a convivial temper, and such self-confidence in destroying older buildings to make way for his own, in particular St. Peter's, that he was known as *Maestro Rovinante* or *Guastante*. His personal appearance is known to us from the portrait, traditionally identified as Bramante, in Raphael's fresco of *The School of Athens*.

He was presumably trained in Urbino, where he must have seen the palace under construction, but the first certain record of him is the fresco he painted in 1477, at Bergamo, fragments of which survive. From Sabba Castiglione, who probably knew him in Milan and Rome, we learn that he was a 'cosmographer, poet in the Italian language, and valiant painter, as a disciple of Mantegna, and great perspectivist, as a pupil of Piero della Francesca, and so excellent in architecture...'. The Bergamo fragment as well as frescoes attributed to him and now in the Brera, Milan, confirm his indebtedness to Mantegna and to Piero della Francesca. His activity as a cosmographer is unknown, but he wrote some poetry, like Raphael, though certainly not as good as Michelangelo's, and his love of puns and cryptograms was recorded by contemporaries.

Bramante must have moved to Lombardy to start his architectural career, since he seems to have begun to work for the Sforza court at Vigevano in the late 1470s, at much the same time as his activity at Santa Maria presso San Satiro in Milan. The extraordinary engraving known as *hedifitiis et figuris*, referred to in a document of 1481, shows that his grasp of architectural form was still very uncertain and painterly.

During the 1480s and 1490s he continued to work for Lodovico Sforza and he must have been in constant contact with Leonardo da Vinci, especially in the 1490s when both men were working at Santa Maria delle Grazie. Yet there are no important references to Bramante in Leonardo's numerous manuscripts, and the effect of this collaboration on Bramante's development, though crucial, must be inferred from stylistic analysis. He probably studied Vitruvius at this time, judging from the mention of him by Bramante's pupil Cesare Cesariano in his edition of Vitruvius (Como, 1521). The odd treatment of the tree-columns in the Canonica di Sant'Ambrogio in Milan confirms this.

Although he made drawings for his projects, especially for St. Peter's, only one (the Parchment Plan in the Uffizi) is certainly his, and that is a measured drawing which gives no indication of his calligraphy.

At the fall of the Sforzas in 1499 Bramante left for Rome, where he spent the remainder of his life.

BRUNELLESCHI, FILIPPO

Born 1377 in Florence; died 1446 in Florence. Brunelleschi was the first architect of modern times to be the subject of a comparatively long biography, an anonymous *Life*, written about forty years after his death. Unfortunately, the only extant manuscripts of this *Life* are incomplete, and their style is extremely polemical. The author (whom many believe to have been the humanist Antonio Manetti) regards Brunelleschi as the first man to have revived the ancient style of architecture, and he displays a bitter animosity towards many of Brunelleschi's contemporaries, especially Ghiberti.

Brunelleschi's fame was established by his brilliant solution to the apparently insuperable problem of the dome of Florence Cathedral, but his importance in architectural history depends almost as much upon his evolution of modernized classical forms to meet the needs of his own time. He was trained as a goldsmith and entered the Guild in 1404, but he was already practising sculpture by 1401 when he entered the competition for the Baptistery doors in Florence. Although Ghiberti won the contest, Brunelleschi was consulted in 1404 about the dome of the cathedral.

It is likely that between 1401-4 he went to Rome, probably with his friend Donatello, to study ancient sculpture. The *Life* indicates that Brunelleschi spent considerable time in Rome, but it is difficult to fix the dates or the length of the various stays with any precision. In all probability he visited Rome several times between 1401-17, at least once with Donatello, and perhaps again with him in 1433-34 (when Donatello is known to have been in Rome).

It is certain that he was engaged in repairing a bridge in Pisa in 1415, and for the next twenty years most of his energies went into the dome of Florence Cathedral. The documents of the Opera del Duomo give evidence of Brunelleschi's progress, and records of payments to him, Donatello, and to others prove that models on a considerable scale were constructed before the *operai* finally decided (1420) to appoint three overseers—Brunelleschi, Ghiberti, and a mason—and to start building. The *Life* records Brunelleschi's displeasure at sharing the responsibility with Ghiberti, whom he finally succeeded in having dismissed in 1425; thus all credit for construction should go to Brunelleschi. He completed the dome in August, 1436, and he won the competition for the lantern design held immediately afterwards. Construction of the lantern was begun a few months before Brunelleschi's death in 1446, and it seems to have been executed by his successor, Michelozzo, according to his designs.

While the dome was being built, Brunelleschi was also working on the Spedale degli Innocenti, the Old Sacristy of San Lorenzo and the rebuilding of the church itself, and the Pazzi Chapel in the cloister of Santa Croce—all to become norms for later Tuscan architects.

Soon after the Pazzi Chapel design, about 1430, Brunelleschi probably went to Rome again, for about a year to eighteen months, for his name is recorded in Florentine documents fairly regularly until December, 1432, and then there is a gap until July, 1434. His renewed study of Roman architec-

ture seems to be borne out by the change in style of his works designed after 1434. Santa Maria degli Angeli and Santo Spirito are stylistically more 'Roman'—heavier in feeling—than the Pazzi Chapel, which shows a stylistic change that indicates a partial redesigning of the chapel after his return from Rome.

Brunelleschi's personal character is very clearly revealed through numerous anecdotes in the *Life*, upon which Vasari depended heavily, but to which he added additional examples to show Brunelleschi's sharp, sarcastic, and essentially Tuscan wit.

BULLANT, JEAN II

Born c. 1510/20 at Amiens; died c. 1578 at Écouen. He went to Rome to study sometime during 1540-50, and his activity dates from about 1550-78, probably the year of his death.

Appointed *Contrôleur des Bâtiments du Roi*, he held this post from 1557-59, working in the service of Catherine de' Medici and Henri II. Among Bullant's projects are numerous châteaux, including Fontainebleau, Chambord, La Fèrez (he worked on the bridge and gallery from about 1552-62), Écouen (the famous porticoes were completed before 1560), and Vincennes (he built the chapel between 1574-78).

After 1560, Anne de Montmorency had the Petit Château built at Chantilly from Bullant's designs. For Catherine de' Medici he began the construction, in the Tuileries, of the pavilion for the queen's residence, according to a project by Philibert de l'Orme; this, however, was never completed. Other works by Bullant can only be identified through a few remains: the Hôtel de Soissons in Paris, burial monument of the Montmorency family, and the Valois Chapel at Saint-Denis. There are also other buildings which may be Bullant's, but their attribution is not supported by any evidence; these include the churches of Belloy, Luzarches, and Sarcelles.

Bullant wrote several theoretical works, among them *Reigle générale d'architecture des cinq manières de colonnes* (Rouen, 1564).

BUONTALENTI, BERNARDO

Born 1536 in Florence; died 1603 in Florence. Most of Buontalenti's work as an architect, sculptor, painter, and illuminator was carried out in Florence. He grew up at the Medici court, among the Mannerists working there at that time, and for over sixty years his art was at the service of Cosimo I and his son Francesco, who appointed him superintendent of all civil and military buildings of the state. His first major architectural work was the granducal Villa Pratolino, near Florence, commissioned by Duke Francesco for Bianca Cappello. It was constructed between 1569-75, and demolished at the end of the nineteenth century after various transformations.

In 1574 Buontalenti began the construction of the Casino di San Marco, the town house of Duke Francesco. It was a singular work which combined great simplicity in its structure with imaginative ornamentation in the doors and windows. The following year he was engaged in the restoration and decoration of Villa della Petraia (Florence) and Villa Ridolfi at Marignolle. In 1575 he also drew up designs for the enlargement of Santa Maria Nuova hospital, which was eventually carried out between 1611–18 by his pupil Giulio Parigi.

From 1563–80 he directed work on the Uffizi and, on the upper floor, began the first nucleus of the gallery and constructed the large corridor leading from the gallery to Palazzo Pitti. About 1576 he supervised the construction of the Boboli grotto which was to house Michelangelo's four *Slaves*.

Buontalenti's most notable religious work is the façade of the church of Santa Trinita in Florence. The decoration of the two chapels in Santo Spirito, and various alterations to the church of Santa Maria Maggiore also date from the same period. His projects for the façade of San Lorenzo and for Florence Cathedral were never realized. Construction of the Princes' Chapel in San Lorenzo, begun by Buontalenti, was later completed by Matteo Nigetti.

He also constructed numerous mansions, and in 1593 he began Roberto Strozzi's palace. It was known as Palazzo Nonfinito, and was later finished by Nigetti and Santi di Tito. Palazzo Corsini, subsequently enlarged by Silvani, also dates from these years.

Buontalenti worked on the façade of the church of Santo Stefano dei Cavalieri in Pisa (1596), left incomplete by Vasari, and in 1605, at the request of Ferdinando I, he began the Loggia dei Banchi.

Buontalenti was also a military architect and his most important work is the Fortezza di Belvedere, above Florence, erected (1590) by order of Ferdinando I.

CODUCCI, MAURO

Born c. 1440 at Lenna, in the Brembana Valley; died 1504 in Venice. There is no precise information about his artistic training as an architect and carver, but it is probable that he worked at first in Romagna.

In 1468–69 he was certainly in Venice, where he built and decorated the Camaldolensian church of San Michele in Isola. The Palazzo Corner-Spinelli in Venice is also from those years, but the bell tower of San Pietro di Castello is later, and dates from 1482–90. Upon the death of Gambello in 1483, Coducci was appointed master builder of San Zaccaria, and worked on the construction of the church, which was completed about 1490.

He was elected 'overseer' of San Zanipolo by his fellow-members of the Scuola di San Marco, and he completed the entire construction with a stupendous staircase, later demolished, but along the lines of which he designed the double staircase for the Scuola Grande di San Giovanni Evangelista in 1498. In the years between 1492–97 Coducci began building Santa Maria Formosa and San Giovanni Crisostomo, both of which were left incomplete at his death. In Santa Maria della Carità, the Cappella del Salvatore and the grandiose monument to the

Doge Barbarigo are attributed to him.

In the sphere of civic architecture he is credited with Palazzo Zorzi at Ponte San Severo, and the Clock Tower (in collaboration with Bartolomeo Bon) and Palazzo Vendramin-Calergi (formerly Loredan) in Venice, which was begun about 1500 but was not completed until after his death.

DELLA PORTA, GIACOMO

Born 1533 in Genoa; died 1602 in Rome. There is little information about his artistic activity as an architect and sculptor, centered for the most part in Rome, except for the period between 1565–70 when he was in Genoa working with Scorticone at the Annunziata dei Frati Minori. He was a pupil of Vignola, whom he succeeded in directing the construction of various buildings, among them St. Peter's, Il Gesù, Palazzo Farnese, and those at the Campidoglio.

Della Porta was very active as a church builder, and was involved with the completion of Il Gesù, the design of the façade and round chapels of the Madonna and San Francesco, the façade of San Luigi dei Francesi (1580–84), and with the Madonna dei Monti (1580), Sant'Atanasio dei Greci (1580–83), and San Giuseppe Falegname. He was also engaged in the continuation of work in the church of San Giovanni dei Fiorentini. His major work was as the architect in charge of the fabric of St. Peter's, a project which occupied him from 1573 until his death in 1602, but it is the dome of St. Peter's (which he built under Sixtus V, in collaboration with Domenico Fontana) that, more than any other work, is most often linked with della Porta's name.

His works of civic architecture include Palazzo Maffei (later Marescotti), Palazzo Crescenzi (later Serlupi) in via del Seminario, Palazzo Capizucchi and Palazzo Paluzzi (later Spinola) in Piazza Campitelli. Della Porta also began the construction of Palazzo Muti near the Campidoglio, the Clementine College, and Palazzo Aldobrandini (later Chigi) in Piazza Colonna; he took part in the construction of the Palazzo della Sapienza (specifically, the portico and upper loggia of the courtyard), and the Palazzo Farnese (the upper loggia). The completion of the façade and the staircase of Palazzo Senatorio at the Campidoglio are also his work.

Several buildings outside Rome are also generally attributed to della Porta: the Town Hall of Velletri, the church of Santa Sinforosa at Tivoli, and especially Villa Aldobrandini at Frascati.

In 1575 the *Congregazione sopra le fonti* appointed him 'architect of the fountains of Rome'. To della Porta, in fact, we owe the fountains in Piazza Colonna, Piazza Aracoeli, Piazza delle Tartarughe, and the fountain at the Madonna dei Monti, in addition to many others erected in Rome by the Municipality.

DE L'ORME, PHILIBERT

Born 1510 in Lyons; died 1570 in Paris. After completing his studies in theology, he went to Rome in 1533, and devoted himself with great enthusiasm

to the study of classical antiquity. During his stay, which lasted about three years, de l'Orme was noticed by Marcello Cervini, the future Pope Marcellus II, who obtained a benefice for him at San Martino del Bosco in Calabria.

He returned to France in the suite of Cardinal Jean du Bellay, ambassador of Francis I, and, during a brief period of activity in Lyons, he built a small hôtel in the classical style for Antoine Bullioud. Saint-Maur-lès-Fossés was built for Cardinal du Bellay, and dates from 1541. In 1545 he was named Inspector of Fortresses in Brittany, an appointment which he carried out with scrupulous care, although he made many enemies along the way. After the death of Francis I in 1547, his successor, Henri II, gave de l'Orme the title of *Architecte du Roi*, and entrusted him with the direction of all royal buildings with the exception of the Louvre, which was reserved for Pierre Lescot. For eleven years de l'Orme exercised an artistic dictatorship, directing all work undertaken for the king at the châteaux of Fontainebleau, Saint-Germain-en-Laye, Villers-Cotterêts, Vincennes, Saint-Léger-en-Yvelines, Monceaux, and Madrid.

The Château d'Anet, built in 1547 for Diane de Poitiers, was his best work, but it is now, unfortunately, partly destroyed. During that year he also prepared designs for the Tomb of Francis I and his queen, which was to be erected in the Abbey of Saint-Denis with the help of several sculptors (1557–58). Favours, as well as many religious benefices, were showered upon him by the king, and he organized the ceremonies and celebrations for the consecration of the queen at Saint-Denis and for the entrance of Henri II into Paris. He also built a large pavilion on the grounds of the Hôtel des Tournelles during this time.

In 1559 Henri II died, and de l'Orme fell into disgrace and was replaced by Bullant as superintendent of the royal buildings. Catherine de' Medici forced Diane de Poitiers to sell the Château de Chenonceaux, but de l'Orme's great plans for its enlargement were never carried out. In 1563 the queen mother bought Saint-Maur-lès-Fossés from Cardinal du Bellay's heirs, and de l'Orme was entrusted with the task of enlarging it. The same year work was begun at the Tuileries Palace for Catherine de' Medici.

De l'Orme left two treatises, *Nouvelles Inventions pour bien bastir et à petits frais* (Paris, 1561), and *Premier Tôme de l'Architecture* (Paris, 1567), only the first volume of which was finished. The importance of these theoretical works in France was paramount, for they initiated a technical and didactic literature which was to serve in the instruction of both architects and their patrons.

DOSIO, GIOVANNI ANTONIO

Born 1533 in Florence or at San Gimignano; died 1609 in Rome or Naples. There is documentary evidence, in 1548, of Dosio's presence in Rome, and in 1569 he published a considerable number of drawings entitled *Urbis Romae aedificiorum illustrium quae supersunt reliquiae*.

Prior to 1575 he was active as a sculptor, and

from 1575 onwards he worked as an architect. From 1574–90, except for a few short trips to Rome, Dosio lived in Florence, where he constructed various religious and civic buildings.

In 1586 he took part in the competition sponsored by Grand-Duke Francesco for the façade of Florence Cathedral, but work was never carried out, due to the duke's death. In 1591 Dosio served as architect of the church of the Carthusian Monastery of San Martino, in Naples.

Little is known of the last twenty years of Dosio's life, although it is probable that he was working in Rome. In 1609 there is again evidence of his presence in Naples, and of his death either there or in Rome.

EGAS, ENRIQUE DE

Born c. 1455 perhaps in Toledo; died 1534 in Toledo. Egas was very well known around 1500, and active in many cities, including Toledo, Santiago de Compostela, and Granada. Between 1480–92 he built the Colegio Mayor de Santa Cruz at Valladolid for Cardinal Mendoza. The Hospital of Santa Cruz in Toledo (1504–14), one of the most famous Renaissance monuments in Spain, is also attributed to Egas. He constructed the drum and dome of the Mozarabic Chapel in Toledo Cathedral, and probably also the staircase of San Juan de Los Reyes. Egas may have directed work for a certain period on the Royal Hospital at Santiago de Compostela, erected between 1501–11 in accordance with his designs. He began building Granada Cathedral in 1523, but it was continued after 1528 by Diego de Siloe. His main work in Granada is the Royal Chapel in the cathedral, erected from 1505–7.

FALCONETTO, GIOVANNI MARIA

Born 1468 in Verona; died c. 1535 in Padua. Falconetto was chiefly active in Padua and the surrounding area. In 1524 he worked on the Villa Cornaro (later Benvenuti) at Este, and in Padua on the Odeon and the Loggia Cornaro. He built the San Giovanni (1528) and Savonarola (1530) gates and the gate of the Palazzo del Capitano with the Clock Tower (1532). About 1530 he took part in rebuilding the Monte di Pietà, constructing the upper floor.

In addition to the façade of the church at Codevigo, Falconetto built one of his most interesting and important works near Padua: the Villa dei Vescovi at Luvigliano di Torreglia (1529– c. 1535).

FERRINI, BENEDETTO

Born in Florence (date of birth is uncertain); died 1479 near Bellinzona. Ferrini worked during the second half of the fifteenth century, and in 1456 he entered the service of Francesco Sforza. In 1461 he was in Venice for a consultation regarding the palace for the Sforza dukes of Milan, already begun by Bartolomeo Bon. He collaborated with Filarete

in 1463 on the Castello Sforzesco in Milan, under the name of Benedetto da Firenze. From 1469 onwards he worked on the Certosa at Pavia, on Gadio's recommendation.

A design for a chapel in Milan Cathedral dates from about 1471, as do some fortifications at Savona, Galliate, and Romanengo. Shortly afterwards, however, the Savona arsenal collapsed and Ferrini was considered responsible for the accident; although he managed to escape, his family was imprisoned.

From 1471–75 he built the castles at Abbiategrasso and Vigevano, as well as those at Castiglione, Cremona, Orzinuovi, and Varzi.

His last work was Sassocorvaro Castle, near Bellinzona.

FILARETE, ANTONIO (Antonio Averlino)

Born c. 1400 in Florence; died c. 1470, perhaps in Rome. Filarete's first important project, the bronze doors of the basilica of St. Peter's in Rome, was commissioned by Eugenius IV in 1433, and he worked on them for about twelve years. He was simultaneously engaged on tombs (no longer preserved) in St. Peter's and in the church of San Giovanni in Laterano, Rome. His work as an architect commenced in Milan at the Sforza court; he had taken refuge there after fleeing from Rome (1447), and after short stays in Florence (1448) and Venice (1449) where he probably worked on the palace for the Sforza dukes of Milan. One of the first indications of his activity in the Duchy of Milan was his visit to Cremona in 1454 for 'works to be done for that Commune'. In addition to some layouts, Filarete erected a triumphal arch (of which no trace remains) for Francesco Sforza and Bianca Maria Visconti.

During these years Filarete was working on the Castello Sforzesco (Porta Giovia) and had been appointed engineer for the fabric of Milan Cathedral. He was commissioned to build a large hospital in Milan, and was sent to Florence to study projects for that purpose. He returned with a design which was approved at once and put into action by Francesco Sforza; the first stone was laid in 1456. Filarete directed the work until 1465, when he was replaced by Guiniforte Solari; his only absence was in 1457, to advise on the construction of Bergamo Cathedral.

Filarete's works include the famous *Trattato di Architettura* in twenty-five books, written between 1461–64.

FLORIS DE VRIENDT, CORNELIS II

Born c. 1514 in Antwerp; died 1575 in Antwerp. Architect, sculptor, and pupil of Giambologna, he visited Rome in 1538, and in 1556 and 1557 published two books on engraving. He was the chief exponent of the Antwerp School, and his principal work, the Antwerp Town Hall, was built between 1561–66. In Antwerp he also built the Hanseatic House (1564–68), which was destroyed in a fire 1893, and a house for his brother Franz (1563–64), also subsequently destroyed.

A number of his works of sculpture, for the most part tombs, and such projects as the monumental choir-screen in Tournai Cathedral (1568–75), are also of architectural interest.

FONTANA, DOMENICO

Born 1543 at Melide, Lake Lugano; died 1607 in Naples. At the age of twenty he began as a stucco worker in Rome. About 1570 Cardinal Peretti, the future Pope Sixtus V, took Fontana into his service. His first important work, Villa Montalto on the Esquiline Hill, although no longer in existence, dates from this period.

In these years he may also have worked on the church of San Luigi dei Francesi and the Palazzo della Cancelleria in Rome, where he designed the large door similar to the one by Sangallo. Much more important, however, was the Sistine Chapel in Santa Maria Maggiore. Fontana's main activity, a new layout of the city on which his brother Giovanni collaborated, took place while Sixtus V was Pope (1585–90). In 1585 Fontana began work on the Papal palace at the Quirinale, on the side facing Piazza di Montecavallo, which was to be finished later under Paul V by Mascherino and Maderno.

Fontana's engineering works in Rome include the Acqua Felice, the Borghetto bridge over the Tiber and, between 1586–89, the erection of the large obelisks in Piazza di San Pietro, Piazza Santa Maria Maggiore, Piazza San Giovanni in Laterano, and Piazza Santa Maria del Popolo. During the same period he also built the double staircase of Santa Trinità dei Monti (the façade was completed by della Porta). In 1587 and 1588 Fontana worked on the Palazzo del Laterano, and on the Loggia of the Benedictines on the north side of the basilica of San Giovanni in Laterano, and, together with Giacomo della Porta, built the dome of St. Peter's.

Between 1587–90 Fontana was engaged on the construction of the new Vatican Library, which connects the two galleries facing the Cortile del Belvedere; on the completion of the Vatican loggie; and on a corridor from the Papal palace to the Gregorian Chapel in St. Peter's. During the same years he also began the first two floors of the Papal palace adjacent to the Cortile di San Damaso. The Palazzo Mattei-Massimo-Albani is among the works attributed to Fontana during the Roman period.

Commissioned by Sixtus V, Fontana restored the columns of Trajan and Marcus Aurelius and built a number of aqueducts.

Owing to various intrigues, Fontana was relieved of his post as Papal Architect and forced to leave Rome at the death of Sixtus V. From 1592 he worked in Naples in the service of the Viceroy, Count Mirano, as Royal Architect and chief engineer of the kingdom. Here Count Olivares commissioned him to build the two roads to Chiaia and Santa Lucia, and to adorn them with fountains. He also built Palazzo Carafa della Spina. About 1600 he began his most important work, the Royal Palace, to be completed according to his design in 1730.

FRA GIOCONDO (Giovanni da Verona)

Born c. 1433/35 in Verona; died 1515 in Rome. Information about his activity is only available from 1489, when he was in the Kingdom of Naples in the service of Duke Alfonso di Calabria. It is supposed that he received a humanistic education. In Naples, apart from archaeological study, and his designs and advice for the building of fortifications, he appears to have worked on the Poggioreale Palace—in particular, on the gardens.

He went to France in 1495 in Charles VIII's suite and resided at Amboise where he may have worked on the château. From 1500-4 he designed and worked on the Bridge of Notre-Dame in Paris. At Blois, he planned an aqueduct to supply water to the gardens.

Fra Giocondo was recalled to Venice in 1506 where he was engaged on defence and irrigation projects. He improved the Brentone Canal for the downflow of the Brenta; he was involved with the defences of Monselice (Vicenza) and Padua and with the reinforcement of Treviso and Cremona. From 1503-8 he drew up projects for the stone bridge in Verona, which was built in 1520, after his death. In 1513 a fire destroyed the Ponte di Rialto and part of the surrounding area in Venice. Fra Giocondo submitted reconstruction projects for the district and the bridge, but to his disappointment they were rejected and he withdrew to Rome where Julius II arranged for him to assist Raphael as architect and superintendent of the fabric of St. Peter's. He remained active from 1514 until his death in June 1515.

Fra Giocondo's intense humanist and philological activity, and his numerous designs and writings (*De architectura et mathematicarum disciplinarum usu*), are also important facets of his contribution to architecture.

FRANCESCO DI GIORGIO

Born 1439 in Siena; died 1501 in Fighille. He is first recorded in 1464, working in Siena as a sculptor; later he worked as a painter. He occasionally received engineering commissions, and between 1469-70 he was engaged on the Siena fountains and on other waterworks.

In 1477, together with his pupil Cozzarelli, he entered the service of Federigo da Montefeltro, and was awarded his first architectural commission. Before 1478 he was working on the Rocca di Sassocorvaro for Count Ottavio Ubaldini, Federigo's treasurer.

At Urbino, he was commissioned to complete the Palazzo Ducale. He worked on the reconstruction of the cathedral, and he perhaps built San Bernardino, although the attribution is doubtful, and the date should be changed to between 1482-91. But his untiring activity was directed above all to fortresses, fortifications, and military works, and his involvement with the Montefeltro family and their wars (1478) enriched his experience as a military architect. During these years he began planning the fortresses for Duke Federigo, described by Francesco himself in his *Trattato di architettura, ingegneria e arte militare*: Cagli (destroyed in 1502), Sassofeltrio, Tavoleto, Serra Abbondio, Montavio (still almost intact), and Mondolfo.

Between 1482-89 he intensified his work at the Urbino court, from which he made short journeys to Gubbio, Cortona (to work on Santa Maria del Calcinaio, commissioned in 1484), Siena, Ancona (where in 1484 he worked on the Palazzo del Governo degli Anziani, following his own design), Jesi (where he designed the Palazzo Comunale in 1486), and Maremma (1487). In 1489, yielding to the pressure of his fellow citizens, he returned to Siena. Shortly after, he became official architect of the Sienese Republic, and was appointed architect of the cathedral, where he worked between 1497-99. He was also engaged on the design for the Sacristy of the Carmine church. Towards 1490 he was in demand everywhere as consultant architect and engineer, and he made more frequent and longer journeys to Gubbio, to Milan, where he advised on the tiburio of the cathedral, to Bracciano, to Urbino, and to Naples.

In 1494 he returned to Naples and took part in the defence against the French. After a short stay at Urbino in 1499 he returned to Siena for good and retired to Fighille, where he died two years later.

GIULIO ROMANO (Giulio Pippi)

Born 1492 (according to Vasari) or 1499 (according to others) in Rome; died 1546 in Mantua. He entered Raphael's workshop while still very young and executed numerous paintings; his hand can be recognized in many of Raphael's later works. In 1515 he was working in the Sala dell'Incendio in the Vatican, in the Farnesina, and in 1516-19 he was entrusted by Raphael with the supervision of the decoration of the Vatican Loggie.

Raphael's death in 1520 launched a period of good fortune for Giulio Romano, especially as an architect. He had already collaborated on the construction of a villa for Cardinal Giulio de' Medici, now Villa Madama. His first important works, Palazzo Maccarani (now Brazzà), and Villa Lante on the Janiculum, date from 1520-24.

In 1524 he moved to the court of Mantua at the invitation of Duke Federigo II Gonzaga. Under his artistic direction Mantua was largely rebuilt and protected from flooding by the river Mincio. His first ducal commission, the Palazzo del Te, was begun about 1526 and completed towards 1534. The building and decoration of the Palazzo della Paleologa also took place in these years and was done to celebrate the arrival in Mantua of Margherita del Monferrato; the Palazzo di Marmirolo is from the same period. Both were highly praised by contemporaries, but are now destroyed. In Mantua he also worked on the Cortile della Mostra of the Palazzo Ducale, on the transformation of Polirene Abbey in San Benedetto Po (1539-42), and on the old Mantua Cathedral commissioned by Cardinal Ercole Gonzaga.

In 1545 he was working in Bologna on the façade of San Petronio, together with Cristofero Lombardo. After Duke Federigo's death Paul III recalled Giulio to Rome in 1546 to entrust him with the design of the fabric of St. Peter's, but before leaving for Rome he fell ill and died in the same year.

HERRERA, JUAN DE

Born c. 1530 at Mobellan (Santander); died 1597 in Madrid. He visited Italy, Germany, and the Low Countries, returned to Spain in 1551, and went on a second trip to Italy in 1553. On Charles V's death he entered the service of Philip II. His most important work, which occupied him for nearly all of his life, was the Escorial monastery. The general project had been drawn up by Juan Bautista de Toledo in 1562.

Shortly before work was begun (1563) Herrera had been appointed assistant to Juan Bautista, whom he succeeded as supervisor of building in 1567. In 1575 he laid the first stone for the erection of the church, on which he lavished the utmost care and which was finished in 1582. Two years later the monastery was also completed.

Among Herrera's other important works are the designs for El Alcázar in Toledo (1571-85) and the Aranjuez Palace (designs dated 1564). One of his most perfect buildings is the Seville Loggia, the building of which (1589-98) was entrusted to Juan Minjares.

Herrera's illness in 1584 caused him to cease activity as an architect, although he continued to supply designs (Valladolid Cathedral) and to devote himself above all to engineering works and town planning.

HOLL, ELIAS

Born 1573 in Augsburg; died 1646 in Augsburg. Before beginning his real activity as an architect, Holl travelled considerably, and of particular importance was the period he spent in Venice (1600) and in northern Italy. He was in Vienna in 1601-2, and returned to Augsburg, where he was appointed municipal architect (1602). About 1630 this position was rescinded and he spent the last years of his life in poverty.

The Rathaus (1615-20) was his principal work in Augsburg, although there are numerous public and private buildings in which he had a hand. Among them are the Bäcker-Zunfthaus (1602), the rebuilding of the Zeughaus (1602-7), the Willibaldsburg at Eichstätt (1609-19) and, again at Augsburg, the Barfüsser-Brücke and the Weber Kaufhaus (1611), Saint Anne's School (1613), and the Heiliggeist Spital, built between 1623-31.

KEY, LIEVEN DE

Born c. 1560 in Ghent; died 1627 in Haarlem. From 1580-91 he was in London, but he returned to Haarlem where he was appointed master stonecutter and master mason of the city, and it is here that he left the majority of his works. The Weigh-House, built in 1598, may be his. The old Haarlem Meat Market, erected in 1602-3, is his masterpiece. In 1612, the bell tower of the new church was built by van Campen, and from 1620–30 the long wing at the Town Hall on the Zijlstraat was built to his design. Apart from the west tower of the church of Saint Anna at the Oudemannenhuis, the other works are located at Leyden: the Town Hall (1595–97), the project for the Gemeenlandhuis van Rhijnland (1596–98), and the grammar school in the Lokhorststraat (1599).

LAURANA, LUCIANO

Born c. 1420/25 in Zara; died 1479 in Pesaro. Laurana was in Mantua in 1465, while Alberti was directing work on San Sebastiano. He was invited to Pesaro by Alessandro Sforza and during a short stay perhaps supplied some designs for the ducal palace in that city. Laurana probably prepared drawings and plans for the Urbino palace from 1466, but was not appointed chief architect of the Urbino fabric by Federigo da Montefeltro until two years later. He directed work on the palace until about the middle of 1472, when he went to Naples in the service of the Aragonese, as 'master of artillery'.

Laurana connected two existing buildings, the Palazzetto della Jole and the so-called Castellare, laid out the courtyards, and erected the west ('Torricini') façade, and he probably designed and partially completed the interior, the throne room, the Guard, Angel, and Audience rooms, and the hanging garden and main staircase of the Palazzo Ducale, before he left Urbino. Francesco di Giorgio succeeded him as director of works.

In 1476 Laurana was working on the fortress at Pesaro, the foundations of which had been laid two years earlier and which he was to complete in 1479. He died the same year, after supplying the designs for the Senigallia bridge.

LE BRETON, GILLES

Le Breton's main activity was carried out between 1526–58. He was a member of a family of architects, and together with his father he worked at the Château de Chambord. Appointed *Maître général des oeuvres de maçonnerie du Roi* in 1527, he devoted himself almost solely to the Palais de Fontainebleau. In 1528 he began construction of the new buildings on the entrance court, the Cour Ovale, the Porte Dorée (1528–35), two blocks between the Porte Dorée and the ancient *donjon*, the Pavillon de Messieurs les Enfants, the chapel (1540–50), and the rebuilding of the main staircase (1540).

LESCOT, PIERRE

Born 1510/15 in Paris; died 1578 in Paris. Lescot was a contemporary of de l'Orme, and a number of his works and even his reputation are linked with the name of the sculptor Goujon. With him Lescot carried out his first documented work, the ambo in the church of Saint-Germain-l'Auxerrois (1539–44), fragments of which are now in the Louvre. The collaboration with Goujon extended to the Hôtel Carnavalet (1545–50), later altered and completed

by François Mansart in 1635 (now the Musée Historique de la Ville de Paris), the Fountain of the Innocents (1547–49), and the rebuilding of the Louvre. In 1546 Lescot was asked to superintend reconstruction of the old Louvre, but this commission, confirmed under Henri II (1547–59), was rescinded at the latter's death. From then onwards we have no further news of him. His work at the Louvre consists solely of the south-west wing of the Cour Carrée.

Outside Paris, Lescot built the Abbey of Clermont at Laval, planned the château and church of Fleury-en-Brie, and a château at Vallery, of which only the ruins remain. He visited Rome in 1556.

LIGORIO, PIRRO

Born 1513/14 in Naples; died 1583 in Ferrara. Ligorio, architect, painter, writer, topographer, and antiquarian, was a member of a noble family. Early in his life he moved to Rome where, at first, he devoted himself solely to painting. In 1550 Ippolito II d'Este, who had become Governor of Todi, commissioned him to build the Villa d'Este in Tivoli; the projects were carried out by G.A. Galvani (1550–72).

Appointed *fabricae palatinae* in 1555, he entered the service of Paul IV in 1558, for whom he erected a loggia in the Vatican (1558–61). While assisting Michelangelo with the fabric of St. Peter's, he was also engaged on the Belvedere Theatre (now destroyed), Palazzo Torres-Lancellotti in Piazza Navona (1560), and Pius IV's Palazzino on via Flaminia. At Michelangelo's death (1564) he succeeded to the post of architect of the fabric of St. Peter's, together with Vignola.

As a result of charges brought against him by the sculptor Giacomo della Porta, he was imprisoned in 1565. In 1568, after requesting the protection of Alfonso II d'Este, he settled in Ferrara, where he was made an honorary citizen in 1580, and where he died three years later.

Of his works in Ferrara mention should be made of Alfonso d'Este's library (1571) and the design for Ariosto's tomb (1573). His booklet on the antiquities of Rome, published in 1553, is still famous.

MACHUCA, PEDRO

Born perhaps in Toledo; died 1550 at Granada. Machuca studied in Florence with Giuliano da Sangallo (c. 1516). The only evidence of his work as an architect (Machuca was first a painter) is the Casa Real Nueva in Granada, begun in 1527 for Charles V; the work was continued, from 1558, by his son Luís.

MICHELANGELO (Michelangelo Buonarroti)

Born 1475 in Caprese; died 1564 in Rome. We are unusually well informed on the life of the greatest artist of the sixteenth century, since he was the first artist about whom two biographies were written in his own lifetime, and a third very shortly

after his death. These were by Vasari (1550), Condivi (1553), and Vasari in his second edition (1568); the *Life* by Condivi is virtually an autobiography, since it was written under Michelangelo's supervision. In addition to these full narrative accounts of his works there are numerous original documents, including drawings, models, and a large number of his letters. Unfortunately, the letters are less informative than might be expected, as is apparent in the Anglo-Saxon understatement of the letter to his father, written from Rome in October 1512, and referring to the completion of the Sistine Chapel ceiling: 'I have finished the chapel I have been painting; the Pope is very well satisfied.'

Because of the wealth of documentation there are few attributional problems, but there are many problems—especially with his architecture—in determining the degree of his participation in various works; it is difficult to distinguish between his plans and how they were realized—whether by him or by his assistants and successors. Several works —such as the façade of San Lorenzo in Florence, which occupied him from 1515/6–20—were never executed at all, and his intentions have to be reconstructed from the wooden model in the Casa Buonarroti and from drawings and documents. Other works—such as the dome of St. Peter's— were executed by others after his death, so that his intentions have again to be reconstructed. In instances such as these it is also necessary to estimate the extent to which Michelangelo would himself have modified his design, as we know him to have done in other cases.

His earliest architectural works come comparatively late in his career, when he was about forty. The initial project was the chapel for Leo X in Castel Sant'Angelo, but his first important works were all connected with the Medici church of San Lorenzo in Florence. He began, in 1514, with the façade designs already mentioned, and continued, after abandoning the façade, with the New Sacristy, or Medici mortuary chapel, and finally with the Biblioteca Laurenziana. In these works, as his contemporaries quickly realized, he attempted to create an entirely new style of architecture in which sculpture was an integral element rather than mere surface decoration. He established this style before he left Florence for Rome in 1534, although the buildings themselves were unfinished, and were only partially completed by others at a much later date. In Rome, where he lived from 1534 until his death thirty years later, Michelangelo was at first too busy with the *Last Judgement* and other commissions to practise architecture. Only from 1546 until his death was he considerably preoccupied with it, in particular with the construction of St. Peter's.

The works from this period—the replanning of the Capitol, the completion of the Palazzo Farnese, the Porta Pia, the Sforza Chapel in Santa Maria Maggiore, the transformation of the Baths of Diocletian into Santa Maria degli Angeli, the projects for San Giovanni dei Fiorentini, as well as St. Peter's itself—all reveal a new approach to classical antiquity and a refusal to be bound by the Vitruvian rules which obsessed so many of his contemporaries (Sangallo) and juniors (Vignola). In these very late works Michelangelo penetrated to the heart of

Roman architectural grandeur, as Bramante had done, but in terms of a more 'modern' sensibility, so that much of his influence was exerted upon the artists of the Baroque rather than upon his immediate successors.

MICHELOZZI, MICHELOZZO DI BARTOLOMEO

Born 1396 in Florence; died 1472 in Florence. Sculptor, architect, and bronze founder, from 1420 Michelozzo worked with Ghiberti on the *St. Matthew* at Orsanmichele, and on the first doors of the Florence Baptistery. From 1423–28 he collaborated on several important works with Donatello: the monument to the Antipope Giovanni XXIII in the Baptistery, the Brancacci Tomb in Naples, and the Aragazzi Tomb at Montepulciano, for which Donatello did most of the sculpture and Michelozzo the architecture. The most important work done in conjunction with Donatello was, however, the exterior pulpit of Prato Cathedral, built in 1434–38 from a model dating from 1428.

After his still partly Gothic façade of Sant'Agostino in Montepulciano, he began to follow Brunelleschi's style, as is apparent in the church and monastery of San Marco in Florence (1437–51). In 1433–34 he was in Venice with Cosimo de' Medici, working on the library of San Giorgio Maggiore, later destroyed in the fire of 1614.

Still following Brunelleschi's style, he created new forms for the Novitiate Chapel in Santa Croce, Florence (c. 1445), for the vaulted tabernacle of San Miniato al Monte (1447–48), and for Villa Cafaggiolo and Villa Careggi, both in Florence (1451–59). On the death of Brunelleschi, Michelozzo was appointed supervisor of Florence Cathedral (1446–57), and the construction was carried out scrupulously in accordance with Brunelleschi's designs.

From 1444–64 he worked at Palazzo Medici Riccardi, and in 1444–45 on the porch, cloister, and dome of Santissima Annunziata, Florence. Milanese examples of Michelozzo's art are the Portinari Chapel of Sant'Eustorgio and the Medici Bank, dating from 1462, of which only the door, ornamented by Lombard sculptors, remains (now in the Castello Sforzesco). Palazzo dei Rettori at Ragusa is also by Michelozzo.

PALLADIO, ANDREA (Andrea di Pietro)

Born 1508 in Padua; died 1580 in Vicenza. He began life as a stone mason, and about 1536 his talents were recognized by Trissino, the author of *L'Italia liberata dai Goti*, who encouraged Andrea to study mathematics, music, and Vitruvius, and who gave him the name of Palladio. In 1545 they went to Rome together, beginning for Palladio a series of visits to the antiquities which stretched over many years and resulted in the production of two guidebooks to Rome (both published in 1554) as well as a large number of drawings. Many of these, now in the Royal Institute of British Architects in London, have exerted an incalculable influence on British architecture.

Palladio's architectural career began with one of his most important commissions, the recasing of the Basilica at Vicenza, begun in 1549. At the same time, the villa built by Trissino for himself inspired Palladio to reconstruct the ancient villa, as described by Pliny and other writers, and to give it a definitive form. He was fortunate in that the economic circumstances of the mid-sixteenth century led many noble Venetian families to withdraw their capital from the Levant and to invest in land in the Terra Firma. The classical type of villa was ideally suited to their needs.

From 1550 onwards he was also commissioned to build a series of splendid palaces in Vicenza. He worked comparatively little outside Vicenza and its immediate neighbourhood, but the only important churches designed by him were in Venice. Two of them, San Giorgio Maggiore (begun 1566) and Il Redentore (begun 1576), are among his greatest masterpieces.

Palladio was also important as a theorist and archaeologist. In addition to his two Roman guidebooks, he produced the illustrations for an edition of Vitruvius published in 1556 by his friend and patron Daniele Barbaro, Patriarch of Aquileia. Most important of all, however, was Palladio's own treatise *I Quattro Libri dell' Architettura*, published in 1570.

PERUZZI, BALDASSARE

Born 1481 in Siena; died 1536 in Rome. In the first part of his life he worked mainly as a painter until, in 1503, he became one of Bramante's assistants at the Vatican in Rome. He came into contact with Agostino Chigi, who commissioned him to build the Villa Farnesina (1505). The exterior and part of the interior decoration is also Peruzzi's. Between 1515–18 he worked at Carpi, where he designed the project and model for the new cathedral, the project for the façade of the old cathedral, and where he collaborated on the central nave of San Niccolò. At Todi, he assisted in building Santa Maria della Consolazione, and in Rome he took part in the competition for San Giovanni dei Fiorentini.

From 1520–27 he was architect of the fabric of St. Peter's together with Antonio da Sangallo the Younger; he resumed this assignment again in 1531, keeping it until the end of his life.

In 1521–22 he drew up designs for a façade and dome for San Petronio in Bologna, for the portal of San Michele in Bosco (1522), and for the reconstruction of Palazzo Lambertini. Peruzzi returned to Bologna in 1530 and left the design for the Ghislardi Chapel in San Domenico.

He re-established himself in Rome, and made only occasional journeys to attend to some work in his native city. Before the Sack of Rome he made designs for the layout of the garden of Cardinal Trivulzio's villa at Salone, near Tivoli, and for the restoration of the Lateran Baptistery. Returning to Siena in 1527, he was appointed city architect in charge of the fabric of the cathedral and he remained there until 1528, working on the fortifications. After years of travelling between Rome and Tuscany, he settled permanently in Rome where in the last two years of his life he worked

on the Theatre of Marcellus for the Savelli family, restored and continued the Cortile del Belvedere in the Vatican, and rebuilt Palazzo Massimo alle Colonne, which was begun in 1532.

PRIMATICCIO, FRANCESCO

Born 1504 in Bologna; died 1570 in Paris. He worked principally at Fontainebleau, especially after his return in 1541 from a journey to Italy. He had moved to Francis I's court after leaving Mantua and the studio of Giulio Romano, with whom he collaborated (1525–31) on the Palazzo del Te.

At Fontainebleau he worked mostly on interior decorations and stuccoes: in the king's and queen's apartments, and in the Ulysses Gallery. The baptistery portal (1561) and the wing of the Aile de la Belle Cheminée (1568) are also by Primaticcio.

He left little other architectural work except some designs: for the Guise Tomb in the Saint-Laurent Chapel of the castle of Joinville-en-Vallaye, for the Tomb of Henri II, and for the Valois Chapel at Saint-Denis.

RAPHAEL (Raffaello Sanzio)

Born 1483 in Urbino; died 1520 in Rome. Nothing is known of Raphael's architectural works before 1508. In 1509, a papal bull authorized the building of Sant'Eligio degli Orefici. Bramante's name has been proposed for its construction, although the church is often included among Raphael's works, as is Villa Madama, begun in 1516 at the request of Cardinal Giulio de' Medici. However, the villa should be attributed to a group of his collaborators rather than to Raphael alone.

Raphael's contact with the Chigi family resulted in designs for the stables on the via della Lungara (1512) and for the Chigi Chapel in Santa Maria del Popolo. In 1514 Bramante designated Raphael to be his successor as director of the fabric of St. Peter's, and in August, together with Fra Giocondo and Giuliano da Sangallo, he was entrusted with this task. During this period the central plan for St. Peter's was transformed into a basilican plan, a change probably due to Raphael. When Leo X became Pope, interest shifted from the fabric of St. Peter's to the Vatican palaces; continuing the work of Bramante, Raphael completed the second floor of the loggie in the Cortile di San Damaso (1517–19).

While the attribution of Palazzo Vidoni-Caffarelli to Raphael is still uncertain and disputed, the ascription of Palazzo Branconio dell'Aquila to Raphael is certain. The origin of the design for Palazzo Pandolfini in Florence, built by Giovanni Francesco da Sangallo, supposedly from Raphael's plans, remains doubtful.

Raphael took part in the competitions for the façade of San Lorenzo in Florence and for the church of San Giovanni dei Fiorentini in Rome. In 1518, together with Antonio da Sangallo, he prepared a plan which was never carried out for a square to be situated where Piazza del Popolo is today.

ROSSELLINO, BERNARDO

Born 1409 in Settignano; died 1464 in Florence. His first documented work is the completion of the façade of the Misericordia church in Arezzo, dating from 1433–35. The superstructure of the Palazzo della Fraternità dei Laici in Arezzo dates from 1433, as does the ciborium (subsequently lost) of Sante Flora e Lucilla, also in Arezzo. From 1435–41, he worked at the Badia in Florence, where a fragment of a tabernacle survives in the Chiostro degli Aranci. The monument to Leonardo Bruni in Santa Croce in Florence, carried out together with his brother Antonio, dates from 1444–51. The influence of Donatello and Brunelleschi is evident in the doors of the Sala del Concistoro in the Palazzo Pubblico, Siena, and in the ciborium in Sant'Egidio, Florence, as well as in the tombs of Orlando de' Medici (Santissima Annunziata, Florence), Neri Capponi (Santo Spirito, Florence), Giovanni Chellini (San Domenico, San Miniato al Tedesco), and in the Tomb of the Beata Villana (Santa Maria Novella, Florence). He also collaborated with Alberti on the construction of the Palazzo Rucellai.

Although he was summoned to Rome by Pope Nicholas V, and entrusted with a series of projects, only the restoration of Santo Stefano Rotondo can be identified for certain as Rossellino's work. Between 1447–55 he was commissioned to rebuild the basilica of St. Peter's. He presented a design in the form of a Latin cross, but only a choir behind the apse of the old basilica was begun. Even though work was broken off in 1455 and was resumed in 1505 the construction was later demolished.

Rossellino was also involved in transforming the ancient town of Corsignano into the modern Pienza, where the planning of the Piazza del Duomo and the Palazzo Piccolomini (1462–65) are of particular interest. The design for the Palazzo Piccolomini in Siena was carried out from 1469 by Pietro Paolo, son of Porrina da Casale, and dates from the same year.

In the last years of his life he undertook work of minor importance for Santissima Annunziata, Florence, and for the lantern of the dome of Florence Cathedral.

SANGALLO THE ELDER, ANTONIO DA

Born c. 1453 in Florence; died 1534 in Florence. He was assiduous in his work as an engineer and military architect, but his artistic personality was surpassed by his nephew Antonio and his brother Giuliano, and he became completely independent only at the latter's death.

His most famous work is the church of San Biagio at Montepulciano, built between 1518–45. Although there is little documentary evidence, numerous other buildings show his hand or are directly inspired by his style, among them the Contucci, Cercini, del Pecora, and Tarugi palaces.

While working on San Biagio, he erected the del Monte palace (now the Town Hall) at Monte San Savino for the future Pope Julius III. At Arezzo he added the side aisles to Santissima Annunziata (1521) and also transformed Sant'Agostino, in Colle Val d'Elsa (1521). In Florence he worked at the Palazzo Vecchio from 1496.

A large part of his activity consisted of military work: the fortress at Civitacastellana (from 1494), fortifications at Poggibonsi and Nepi, and the old fortress at Leghorn (from 1515).

SANGALLO THE YOUNGER, ANTONIO DA

Born 1483 in Florence; died 1546 in Rome. He began his architectural career under the guidance of his uncles Giuliano and Antonio the Elder, and moved while still young (1503) to Rome, where he remained nearly all his life. In Rome he collaborated with Raphael, and in 1520 succeeded him as supervisor of the fabric of St. Peter's, for which he made numerous designs and a famous wooden model (1539–46).

Among his first Roman buildings are the lower part of Santa Maria di Loreto at Trajan's Forum (from 1507), Palazzo Baldassini (1510–15), the designs and work on San Giovanni dei Fiorentini (from 1518), the interior of Santa Maria di Monserrato (1518), and restoration work and the chapel of Cardinal Alborense in San Giacomo degli Spagnoli. The Farnese family commissioned the Palazzo Farnese in 1517 and Antonio radically altered the design later, but did not live to complete it.

The following year at Orvieto he built the ingenious well of San Patrizio and left a design for Palazzo Pucci. In the meantime he had built the façade of the Mint in Rome, now the Palazzo del Banco di Santo Spirito (1523–24), and he worked on the façade and interior of Santo Spirito in Sassia (1538–44). The Sala Regia and the Cappella Paolina in the Vatican engaged him in the last years of his life.

Among the engineering works that occupied Antonio the Younger throughout his career are the castle at Capodimonte; completion of the Forte Michelangelo at Civitavecchia (before 1513); the Fortress of Caprarola (1515), later transformed into a villa by Vignola; the Fortezza da Basso in Florence (1534–37); the Porta Santo Spirito in Rome (from 1537); the Ancona Fortress (1537); and the fortifications at Castro and Nepi.

SANGALLO, GIULIANO DA

Born c. 1445 (year of birth is uncertain) in Florence; died 1516 in Florence. Giuliano was the son of Francesco Giamberti, founder of the Sangallo family. He was in Rome in 1465, where he devoted himself above all to the study of ancient monuments, as is evidenced by the book of designs kept in the Vatican Library (Cod. Lat. Barberino 4484) and the collection at the Municipal Library in Siena. During his stay in Rome he was engaged on the loggia of Palazzo Venezia (between 1469–74).

He is documented after 1479 in Florence, although works carried out before that date can be attributed to him: Palazzetto Cocchi in Piazza Santa Croce, and the palace which at that time belonged to Bartolomeo Scala and is now included in the Gherardesca Palace in the Borgo Pinti.

From 1479 he worked on the convent of Santa Maria Maddalena dei Pazzi; the following year Lorenzo the Magnificent commissioned the Villa Medici at Poggio a Caiano. In 1485 he was commissioned to build Santa Maria delle Carceri at Prato. He was elected master builder of Florence Cathedral in 1488, but refused the nomination, perhaps because he was involved in other tasks. That year, he presented a model of a palace to the King of Naples, and was working on the San Gallo church in Florence (destroyed in 1529). The following year he was engaged on the Sacristy in Santo Spirito, received payment for a model of Palazzo Strozzi, and prepared designs for the Palazzo Gondi, begun in 1490.

Giuliano did not neglect military architecture, a field of particular importance for his brother Antonio and his nephew Antonio the Younger. About 1480 he supervised the fortifications of Colle Val d'Elsa, before 1488 he directed the fortification works of Poggio Imperiale at Poggibonsi, in 1500 he constructed the fort at Borgo Sansepolcro, and in 1502 the fort at Arezzo and the small one at Nettuno.

His first stay in Rome had brought him into contact with Cardinal Giuliano della Rovere, whom he followed into exile in France. At Savona, he worked on the della Rovere Palace (1495) which was later altered although the façade of three superposed Orders remains intact. At Lyons, in 1496, he submitted the model for a palace for the King of France.

He was back in Italy in 1499, at Loreto, for the contract to construct the dome of the cathedral, but the decline of the Medici family decreased the possibilities for work. In 1500 he went to Florence, Rome, Sansepolcro, and again to Florence in 1503, to work on the project for the Palazzo Gondi there.

When his old protector Giuliano della Rovere was elected Pope Julius II he went to Rome, hoping to obtain important commissions, but the presence of new colossal artistic personalities kept him on the fringe. He did prepare designs for the loggia of the papal musicians and for New St. Peter's, and was on the move between Rome, Bologna, Florence, and Pisa. His hopes were raised again by the pontifical election of Leo X, son of Lorenzo the Magnificent, and he prepared a design for the Papal palace to be erected in Piazza Navona (1513). In 1514 he was nominated master mason of the fabric of St. Peter's where he probably worked as a subordinate, with Bramante, Raphael, and Fra Giocondo.

His last works are the numerous drawings carried out for the competition for the façade of San Lorenzo in Florence, which was held in 1515.

SANMICHELI, MICHELE

Born 1484 in Verona; died 1559 in Verona. When only sixteen, he went to Rome where his artistic personality was formed, probably in the circle of Bramante and Giuliano da Sangallo. The information available about Sanmicheli is full of gaps, and the dating of his works is not always easy. It is known that before 1527 he worked at Orvieto and at Montefiascone where, prior to 1519, he built the cathedral.

In 1509 he became master mason of the fabric of Orvieto Cathedral and built the tympanum and other parts of the façade, and the altar of the Magi (1514–c.1527). He also worked in the Petrucci Chapel of San Domenico (1516) and at Palazzo Petrucci, in Orvieto. Sanmicheli's activity as an architect and military engineer began when Clement VII sent him and Giuliano da Sangallo to inspect the forts in Emilia and Romagna. Later (1530–31), at Francesco II Sforza's request, he inspected the fortresses of Lombardy (the fortifications of Legnago date from these years).

He fled from the Sack of Rome (1527), returned to Verona, and entered the service of the Venetian Republic. Sanmicheli's three Veronese buildings date from the 1530s: the Pompei, Canossa (begun c. 1533 and still in construction in 1537), and Bevilacqua palaces. In San Bernardino, Verona, he erected the Cappella Pellegrini (dating from c.1526–27 and still unfinished in 1557); between 1534–41 he finished the choir-screen of Verona Cathedral. At the time he was transforming the ancient walls of Verona into a chain of fortifications for the Republic, and was engaged in specific reinforcement work in the city: the Barberigo ramparts (1531), the doors of the Palazzo del Podestà (1553) and of the Capitano (1530–31), the Porta Nuova (1533–40; altered during the mid-nineteenth century), the Porta San Zeno (1541), the Porta Palio (begun 1546 and still unfinished in 1557). Appointed engineer in the service of the state for the lagoon and the fortifications in 1535, he began a series of long inspection trips to Dalmatia and the eastern part of the Venetian Republic: Zara, Sebenico, Corfu, and Cyprus. He built the Forte Sant'Andrea di Lido (1543–49), and the fortifications at Orzinuovi, Padua, and Peschiera. In 1548, in the neighbourhood of Verona, he began the Lazzaretto hospital, finished the lower part of the Santa Maria in Organo façade, and erected the dome of San Giorgio in Braida. In the year of his death the church of the Madonna di Campagna was begun (1559–61), according to his plan. Between 1540–50 he designed Villa Soranza.

In Venice he worked on the Palazzo Cornaro-Mocenigo at San Polo and began the Palazzo Grimani (design from 1559). In the last year of his life he prepared the designs for Palazzo Roncale in Rovigo.

SANSOVINO, ANDREA (Andrea Contucci)

Born 1460 in Monte San Savino; died 1529 in Monte San Savino. Documentary evidence about his architectural work is scanty, but it is likely that during his artistic formation he came into contact with Giuliano da Sangallo.

In 1513 Leo X nominated him master mason of the fabric of Loreto Cathedral, and of the sculptural work for the decoration of the Casa Santa. Part of this title was rescinded in 1520, and he then served only as superintendent of sculptural work.

In 1519 he prepared drawings for the cortile of the Town Hall at Jesi, which was carried out by Giovanni di Gabriele from Como. At Monte San Savino he was engaged primarily on the cortile of the Sant'Agostino convent (design from 1523) and on the loggia of the market.

SANSOVINO, JACOPO (Jacopo Tatti)

Born 1486 in Florence; died 1570 in Venice. He was launched on his artistic career by his father, who entrusted him to Andrea Contucci (Sansovino). About 1506 he went to Rome for the first time. He remained there for several years, devoted himself to the study of antiquities, and became famous through his first sculptures. Returning to Florence in 1511, he took part in the competition for the façade of San Lorenzo, but his design was rejected. Back in Rome about 1516 he attempted his first architectural works, probably the reconstruction of Palazzo Lante (1518); the same year he began to build Palazzo Gaddi. He had won the competition for San Giovanni dei Fiorentini with a design made in 1514, and he also provided designs and suggestions for the rebuilding of San Marcello (1519).

Between 1521–23 he visited Venice for the first time and, during a short stay, he was consulted about restoration of the domes of San Marco. After the Sack of Rome he fled to Venice and became chief architect there. In 1529 he succeeded Bartolomeo Bon, assuming the position of *Capomaestro* of San Marco, and completed the Procuratie Vecchie. While reorganizing the centre of Venice he worked on three buildings for which he gained fame: La Zecca, or the Mint (commissioned in 1535), the Libreria Sansoviniana (the library was planned in 1537 and quickly resumed in 1545 after the vault had collapsed), and the Loggetta at the foot of the campanile (1537–40).

The official commissions for the Republic did not impede his work as a sculptor, or his acceptance of other commissions. In 1532 he prepared designs for San Francesco della Vigna (1534) and he studied the rebuilding of the little church of San Geminiano (which was to occupy him until the last decade of his life). He also worked at San Martino, San Giuliano, and San Fantino, all in Venice.

Among his important civil works are the Palazzo Corner della Ca' Grande (begun in 1533 and still not finished in 1556), the Palazzo Dolfin and the Scala d'Oro in the Ducal palace (designed in 1554). Sansovino also left architectural works on the mainland, including the Villa Garzoni at Pontecasale near Padua, designed c. 1540.

SCAMOZZI, VINCENZO

Born 1552 in Vicenza; died 1616 in Venice. Scamozzi's artistic training was completed in the Vicenza milieu, and he was an assiduous and attentive reader of Vitruvius and Palladio. In 1572 he settled in Venice, but he went to Rome in 1578, 1585, and in 1598, and travelled widely in Poland, France, and Germany, becoming famous all over Europe. In 1604 he was summoned to Salzburg to design the new Bishop's Palace and the cathedral (1607).

Among his principal works executed in Italy are the church and convent of San Gaetano at Padua (1581–86, 1591) and Palazzo Trissino on the Corso at Vicenza (1592). He supervised construction of the Procuratie Nuove in Venice and presided over the work from 1583–93. In 1588 he erected the Teatro Olimpico in Sabbioneta, and in 1593 he submitted the design for an ideal city founded at Palmanova, supervising the gates of the city (1603–5) and the cathedral (1615–37) with particular care.

In 1615 he published his treatise in Venice, entitled *Dell'Idea dell'Architettura universale*.

SERLIO, SEBASTIANO

Born 1475 in Bologna; died 1554 in Fontainebleau. More famous for his theoretical work than for his practical results, he began, in 1537, to publish his books on architecture which were issued separately and in irregular succession.

In 1541 Francis I summoned him to France and entrusted him with the direction of work at Fontainebleau, where Serlio designed *Le Grand Ferrare* (of which only a gate remains). His main work in France is the Château d'Ancy-le-Franc in Burgundy, designed about 1546. On the death of Francis I he moved to Lyons where he supervised the plan of the town.

In Venice, where he went to live after the Sack of Rome, he worked on Palazzo Zeno (1531) and at San Francesco della Vigna (1533). In 1539 he made a design for a wooden theatre in Vicenza, and also left a design for the Town Hall in Rimini, which was subsequently built in 1562 by Ludovico Carducci.

SILOE, DIEGO DE

Born c. 1495 in Burgos; died 1563 in Granada. Son of the sculptor and architect Gil de Siloe, he worked in Italy, specifically in Naples, as an assistant to Bartolomé Ordonez. His early career began at Burgos where he built the Golden Staircase (1519–26) and various tombs and altars in the cathedral. At Santa Maria del Campo, near Burgos, together with Juan de Solas, he built a church with a towered façade (1527). He collaborated with Juan de Alava on the façade, courtyard, and church of the Archbishop's College at Salamanca.

In 1528 he moved to Granada where he executed his main work; in the same year he began to work on the cathedral (1528–59), the foundations of which had already been laid years before. Between 1528–43 he completed the church of San Girolamo.

He left designs for the cathedrals of Málaga and Cadiz (1549), and in addition to numerous plans for country churches near Granada, he built San Salvador at Ubenda (1536) and San Gabriel (begun in 1552) at Loja.

SMYTHSON, ROBERT

Born 1536; died c. 1614 at Wollaton. Smythson was the descendant of a family of English masons. One of his first works was Longleat House (Wiltshire), which had been begun in 1554 by John Thynne. Smythson took over the supervision after it had been partly destroyed by a fire in 1567. Between 1580–88 he built Wollaton House (Nottinghamshire), one of the most important buildings of the Elizabethan period. Between 1568 and his death he designed Worksop Manor (Nottinghamshire), built for George Talbot, and erected (1590–96) Hardwick Hall (Derbyshire) for the Countess of Shrewsbury.

TIBALDI, PELLEGRINO

Born 1527 in Puria di Valsolda; died 1596 in Milan. He was taken to Bologna by his father while still very young, and he is known to have been in Rome in 1549, when he worked on the Tomb of Paul III. Those works attributed to his early years include the Ferretti Palace, the rebuilding of the Loggia dei Mercanti in Ancona, and the Poggi Chapel in San Giacomo Maggiore, Bologna.

Tibaldi's output as a painter was considerable. From Rome he moved once more to Bologna, then to Loreto and to Ancona. In 1564 he was in Pavia, where he laid the first stone of the Collegio Borromeo (the façade was tampered with later).

He was nominated architect of the city of Milan and of the cathedral, and in 1566 he prepared the design for the cortile of the Canonica degli Ordinari of the cathedral (carried out from 1527–1604) and also designed the Baptistery (c. 1567). Another important Milanese work is the church of San Fedele (1569), later continued by Martino Bassi and Ricchino. After a short stay in Bologna, Tibaldi remained in Milan almost without interruption from 1570–81 and from 1583–87, and was extremely active as designer and consultant at San Sebastiano (1577). San Carlo al Lazzaro (1576–92) is also ascribed to him. Drawings for enlarging the Ospedale Maggiore in Lodi, designs for the Marian sanctuary at Caravaggio (1571), and those for Rho (1584) are attributed to Tibaldi as well.

In 1583 he provided drawings for the façade of the Santuario della Madonna dei Miracoli at Saronno, while the bell tower of Monza Cathedral, Palazzo Galli at Gravedona (1583), Palazzo Natta at Como, and the church of Santi Martiri in Turin were built according to his designs.

Perhaps because of the intrigues and the hostility which had arisen around and against him, Tibaldi left Milan for the court of Philip II in Spain where he worked on the Escorial. In 1596 he returned to Milan and died there the same year.

VASARI, GIORGIO

Born 1511 in Arezzo; died 1574 in Florence. When he was thirteen years old, Vasari was taken to Florence where he joined the Medici court. He was to remain closely connected with the Medici all his life, and when they were compelled to leave Florence in 1527 he left too. First he worked in the service of Ippolito in Rome (1531), then for Ottaviano (from 1532), and finally for Duke Cosimo, with whom he kept in contact after 1555

until the end of his life.

Vasari's first architectural work, preserved at Arezzo, includes one of his own houses and the drawings for the base of the organ and for the choir of the cathedral (1535–47). In 1550 in Rome he entered the service of Julius III, for whom he constructed a villa. After work on the Villa Giulia in Rome, he produced models and drawings for Santa Maria Nuova at Cortona (1554), collaborated on the Madonna dell'Umiltà at Pistoia, and commenced work at the Palazzo Vecchio in Florence. One of his wooden models of the transformation work dates from 1555.

In 1560 he began work on the Uffizi (which was to be completed in 1580 after his death). In 1562 he presented the first model for the Palazzo dei Cavalieri in Pisa, on which he had been working since 1558. In Arezzo he worked on the transformation of the Pieve (1560–64), on the reconstruction of the cathedral (from 1564), and in 1573 he began the Loggie Vasariane. He returned to Florence to work on alterations at Santa Croce and at Santa Maria Novella (1565–71).

However, the name of Vasari is associated with the famous *Lives*, first published in Florence in 1550, rather than with any other work. In 1568 Vasari supervised a second edition of the '*Vite*...', newly enlarged and with the addition of Lives of living and dead artists, from the year 1550 up to 1567.'

VÁZQUEZ, LORENZO

Born in Segovia (years of birth and death are uncertain). Active 1487; died early sixteenth century. Vázquez was a Spanish architect whose Medinaceli Palace (1492–95) at Cogolludo, near Guadalajara, is among his best known works. Another, the Colegio Mayor de Santa Cruz at Valladolid may be slightly earlier.

The greater part of his work is at Guadalajara: the Mendoza Palace (he designed a whole group of buildings for various members of the Mendoza family); the courtyards of the houses for the Avalos families and those for the Instituto de Segunda Enseñanza; Plaza Mayor; and the work in Santa Maria de la Fuente. Near Guadalajara, at Mondejar, before 1508, he erected the church in the San Antonio monastery. At Calamorra he was engaged on work for the castle.

VIGNOLA, GIACOMO DA (Giacomo Barozzi)

Born 1507 at Vignola; died 1573 in Rome. Vignola was trained in Bologna as a painter and perspective designer. Although the leading Bolognese perspectivist was Sebastiano Serlio, it is not known whether Vignola had any close contact with Serlio before he visited Rome, or even perhaps France (where he went in 1541, the same year as Serlio).

In Rome, Vignola worked on a projected edition of Vitruvius which was never completed, but Vignola benefited by his employment as a draughtsman of the antiquities of Rome. His own treatise on the Orders, published in Rome about 1562,

probably grew out of his experiences in the 1530s. At the same time he worked under both Antonio da Sangallo the Younger and Peruzzi, and the styles of both men exerted a considerable formative influence on his own: Sangallo's use of rustication is particularly noticeable in such early works as the Palazzo Bocchi, Bologna, and even in the main entrance of Villa Giulia.

In 1540 Vignola was working for Primaticcio, whom he accompanied to France in 1541 to work for Francis I at Paris and Fontainebleau. He stayed only a short time and was back in Bologna by 1543. After Sangallo's death in 1546 Vignola inherited his lucrative connection with the Farnese family, and two of his masterpieces—Il Gesù and the villa at Caprarola—were built for them. His other main works in the 1550s were Villa Giulia and Sant'Andrea in via Flaminia, Rome, both for Julius III. These works brought him into contact with Vasari, Ammanati, and the aged Michelangelo himself, whom he succeeded as *Capomaestro* of St. Peter's.

Vignola died in Rome in 1573, and is buried in the Pantheon.

VINCIDOR, TOMMASO

Born in Bologna (year of birth is uncertain); died c. 1536 perhaps at Breda. Vincidor was a painter and architect whose name is linked with Breda Castle, which was rebuilt after 1530 in imitation of a Florentine palace. He went to Flanders to supervise the making of tapestries designed by his master, Raphael, for the Sistine Chapel. These tapestries influenced the 'grotesque' style of decoration which became popular in France, as at the Château de Blois, in the first half of the sixteenth century.

VITOZZI, ASCANIO

Born 1539 in Orvieto; died 1615 in Turin. Vitozzi was descended from the Baschi gentry and passed the first years of his life at Orvieto. Embarking on a military career, he took part in the Battle of Lepanto (1571), in the capture of Tunis (with Prospero Colonna), and in the conquest of Portugal (1580) while, at the same time, devoting himself to the art of building fortifications. During Gregory XIII's pontificate he was in Rome where he carried out embankment works on the Tiber and the draining of the Chiane marshes.

He was called to Turin in 1584 where he remained almost uninterruptedly in the service of Carlo Emanuele I, and was considerably active as a civil and military architect. To Vitozzi we owe the plans for the churches of Monte dei Cappuccini, Santissima Trinità, Spirito Santo, and Corpus Domini, subsequently completed by Carlo di Castellamonte. The hermitage of the Camaldolesi on the Turinese hillside, and the Vicoforte Sanctuary near Mondovì—essential parts of which (such as the dome) were resumed and completed by Francesco Gallo in the eighteenth century—are by Vitozzi as well. He also produced several town plans, greatly desired by Carlo Emanuele I, such as those for Piazza Castello and for the Strada Nuova.

BIBLIOGRAPHY OF SOURCES

FOWLER, L., and BAER, E., *The Fowler Architectural Collection of the Johns Hopkins University*, Baltimore, 1961.

SCHLOSSER, J., *La Letteratura artistica*, Florence, 1964.

SOURCES

ALBERTI, L.B., *De re aedificatoria*, Florence, 1485; It. ed., Florence, 1550; modern ed. (Latin and It.), Milan, 1966; (Eng. trans., *Ten Books on Architecture*, by J. Leoni, ed. by J. Rykwert, London, 1955).

BULLANT, J., *Reigle générale d'architecture des cinq manières de colonnes*, Rouen, 1564 (ed. Salomon de Brosse, 1619).

CONDIVI, A., *Vita di Michelangelo*, Rome, 1553; (Eng. trans., *The Life of Michelangelo Buonarroti*, by H.P. Horne, Boston, 1904).

DE L'ORME, P., *Premier Tôme de l'Architecture*, Paris, 1567; (facsimile ed., London, 1967).

DE L'ORME, P., *Nouvelles Inventions pour bien bastir et à petits frais*, Paris, 1561.

DIETTERLIN, W., *Architectura, von Ausstheilung Symmetria und Proportion der Fünff Seulen*, Nuremberg, 1593; (facsimile ed., New York, 1968).

DU CERCEAU, J., *Les plus excellents Bastiments de France...*, 2 vols., Paris, 1576 and 1579; (facsimile ed., Paris, 1868).

DUPÉRAC, E., *I vestigi dell'Antichità di Roma, raccolti e ritratti in perspectiva con ogni diligentia...*, Rome, 1575 and other eds.

FALDA, G.B., *Nuovi disegni dell'architettura e piante dei palazzi di Roma*, Rome, 1675.

FERRERIO, P., *Palazzi di Roma dei più celebri architetti*, Rome, 1655.

FILARETE, A., *Trattato di Architettura*, [1461-64]; (Eng. trans., *Treatise on Architecture*, trans. and ed. by J.R. Spencer, 2 vols., New Haven, 1965).

FRANCESCO DI GIORGIO, *Trattato di architettura, ingegneria e arte militare*, ed. by C. Maltese, Milan, 1967.

LEONARDO DA VINCI, *The Literary Works of Leonardo da Vinci*, ed. by J.P. Richter, 2 vols., 3rd ed., London, 1970.

PALLADIO, A., *I Quattro Libri dell'Architettura*, Venice, 1570; facsimile ed., Milan, 1945; (several Eng. trans., including *The Four Books of Architecture*, by I. Ware, intro. by A.K. Placzek, New York, 1965).

PIUS II (AENEAS SILVIUS PICCOLOMINI), *Memoirs of a Renaissance Pope...*, trans. by F. Gragg, ed. by L. Gabel, New York, 1959.

SCAMOZZI, V., *Dell'Idea dell'Architettura universale*, Venice, 2 vols., 1615; (facsimile ed., London, 1964).

SERLIO, S., *Regole generali di Architettura*, Venice, 1537 et seq. (ed. by G. Scamozzi, Venice, 1584 and 1619); Book VI first pub. in facsimile, Milan, 1966.

SHUTE, J., *The First and Chief Groundes of Architecture*, London, 1563; (facsimile ed., London, 1964).

VASARI, G., *Le Vite de' Più Eccellenti Architetti, Pittori, et Scultori...*, Florence, 1550; 2nd enlarged ed., Florence, 1568; (Eng. trans., *Lives...*, by G. du C. De Vere, 10 vols., London, 1912-15); the most important modern ed. is that by R. Bettarini and P. Barocchi, Florence, 1966-, in the course of publication, containing the texts of 1550 and 1568.

VIGNOLA, J. BAROZZI DA, *Regola delli Cinque Ordini d'Architettura*, Rome, 1562.

Vita Anonima di Brunellesco (attrib. to A. Manetti; ms. c. 1480; Eng. trans., *The Life of Brunelleschi*, by C. Enggass, with introd. by H. Saalman, University Park, Pa., 1970).

MODERN WORKS

ACKERMANN, J.S., *The Architecture of Michelangelo*, 2 vols., New York, 1961-64.

ACKERMANN, J.S., *Palladio*, Harmondsworth, 1966.

ANDERSON, W.J., and STRATTON, A., *The Architecture of the Renaissance in Italy*, 5th ed., London, 1927.

Ars Hispaniae. Historia Universal del Arte Hispánico, 19 vols., Madrid, 1947-66.

ARGAN, G.C., *Brunelleschi*, Milan, 1955.

BARONI, C., *L'architettura lombarda dal Bramante al Richini*, Milan, 1941.

BARONI, C., *Bramante*, Bergamo, 1944.

BATTISTI, E., *L'antirinascimento*, Milan, 1962.

BAUM, J., *Baukunst und dekorative Plastik der Frührenaissance in Italien*, Stuttgart, 1920.

BENEVOLO, L., *Storia dell'architettura del Rinascimento*, 2 vols., Bari, 1968.

BERTOLOTTI, A., *Artisti lombardi a Roma nei secoli XV, XVI, XVII*, Milan, 1881.

BERTOTTI SCAMOZZI, O., *Le fabbriche e i disegni di Andrea Palladio e le terme romane figurate dal medesimo*, 2nd ed., 4 vols., Naples, 1872-73.

BEVAN, B., *History of Spanish Architecture*, London, 1938.

BLUNT, A., *Artistic Theory in Italy, 1450-1600*, Oxford, 1956.

BLUNT, A., *Art and Architecture in France, 1500-1700*, Harmondsworth, 1957.

BLUNT, A., *Philibert de l'Orme*, London, 1958.

BONELLI, R., *Da Bramante a Michelangelo*, Venice, 1960.

BOTTARI, G.G., and TICOZZI, S., *Raccolta di lettere sulla pittura, scultura ed architettura scritte dai più celebri personaggi dei secoli XV, XVI e XVII*, Milan, 1822-25.

BRIGANTI, G., *Il manierismo e P. Tibaldi*, Rome, 1945.

BRIGANTI, G., *La maniera italiana*, Rome, 1961; (Eng. trans., *Italian Mannerism*, by M. Kunzle, Leipzig, 1962).

BRUSCHI, A., *Bramante architetto*, Bari, 1969.

CAMÓN AZNAR, J., *La arquitectura plateresca*, Madrid, 1945.

CARLI, E., *Pienza, la città di Pio II*, Rome, 1966.

CASSINA, F., *Le fabbriche più cospicue di Milano*, 2 vols., Milan, 1840.

CENDALI, L., *Giuliano e Benedetto da Maiano*, Florence, 1926.

CHASTEL, A., *Art et Humanisme à Florence au temps de Laurent le Magnifique*, Paris, 1959.

CHASTEL, A., *The Age of Humanism: Europe, 1480-1530*, trans. by K.M. Delavenay and E.M. Gwyer, New York, 1964.

CHASTEL, A., *The Studios and Styles of the Renaissance, 1460-1500*, London, 1965.

CHASTEL, A., *The Crisis of the Renaissance, 1520-1600*, trans. by Peter Price, Geneva, 1968.

DIMIER, L., *Le Primatice*, Paris, 1928.

Dizionario Enciclopedico di architettura e urbanistica, ed. by P. Portoghesi, 6 vols., Rome, 1968-69.

Encyclopedia of World Art, 15 vols., New York, 1959-68.

FLETCHER, B., *A History of Architecture on the Comparative Method*, 17th ed., London, 1961.

FOLNESICS, H., *Brunelleschi*, Vienna, 1915.

FORSSMAN, E., *Palladios Lehrgebäude*, Stockholm, 1963.

FÖRSTER, O.H., *Bramante*, Vienna, 1956.

FOSSI, M., *B. Ammanati architetto*, Naples, 1967.

FREY, D., *Michelangelo-Studien*, Vienna, 1920.

GEBELIN, F., *Les châteaux de la Renaissance*, Paris, 1927.

GENGARO, M.L., *L.B. Alberti*, Milan, 1939.

GEYMÜLLER, H., *Raffaello Sanzio studiato come architetto*, Milan, 1884.

GIOVANNONI, G., *Saggi sulla architettura del Rinascimento*, 2nd ed., Milan, 1935.

GIOVANNONI, G., *Antonio da Sangallo il Giovane*, 2 vols., Rome, 1959.

GIROUARD, M., *Robert Smythson and the Architecture of the Elizabethan Era*, London, 1966.

GOLZIO, V., and ZANDER, G., *L'arte in Roma nel secolo XV*, Bologna, 1968.

GREENWOOD, W.E., *The Villa Madama, Rome*, London, 1928.

HARTT, F., *Giulio Romano*, 2 vols., New Haven, 1958.

HAUPT, A., ed., *Renaissance Palaces of Northern Italy and Tuscany*, 3 vols., London, 1931.

HAUTECOEUR, L., *Histoire de l'architecture classique en France*, 7 vols., Paris, 1943-57.

HERSEY, G., *Alfonso II and the Artistic Renewal of Naples*, New Haven, 1969.

HEYDENREICH, L., *Leonardo da Vinci*, 2 vols., London, 1954.

HIEBER, H., *Elias Holl*, Munich, 1923.

HOFFMANN, T., *Raffael in seiner Bedeutung als Architekt*, Zittau-Leipzig, 1908-11.

KREFT, H., and SOENKE, J., *Die Weserrenaissance*, Hameln, 1964.

KUBLER, G., and SORIA, M., *Art and Architecture in Spain and Portugal and their American Dominions*, Harmondsworth, 1959.

LANGENSKIÖLD, E., *Michele Sanmicheli*, Uppsala, 1938, (in Eng.).

LAZZARONI, M., and MUÑOZ, A., *Filarete*, Rome, 1908.

LETAROUILLY, P.M., *Édifices de Rome moderne*, 4 vols., Paris, 1868-74.

LOTZ, W., 'Die ovalen Kirchenräume des Cinquecento', *Römisches Jahrbuch für Kunstgeschichte*, VII, 1955, pp. 7-99.

LOWRY, B., *Renaissance Architecture*, New York, 1963.

LUPORINI, E., *Brunelleschi*, Milan, 1964.

MAGNUSON, T., *Studies in Roman Quattrocento Architecture*, Stockholm, 1958.

MALAGUZZI-VALERI, F., *G.A. Amadeo*, Bergamo, 1904.

MARCHINI, G., *Giuliano da Sangallo*, Florence, 1942.

MARIACHER, G., *Jacopo Sansovino*, Milan, 1962.

MORISANI, O., *Michelozzo architetto*, Turin, 1951.

MURRAY, P., *The Architecture of the Italian Renaissance*, 2nd ed., London, 1969.

NEURDENBURG, E., *Hendrick de Keyser*, Amsterdam, 1934.

NICOLINI, F., *L'arte napoletana del Rinascimento*, Naples, 1925.

PAATZ, W., and E., *Die Kirchen von Florenz*, 6 vols., Frankfort, 1940-54.

PACCAGNINI, G., *Il Palazzo del Te di Mantova*, Milan, 1957.

PANE, R., *L'architettura del Rinascimento a Napoli*, Naples, 1937.

PANE, R., *Andrea Palladio*, 2nd ed., Turin, 1961.

PAOLETTI, P., *L'architettura e la scultura del Rinascimento a Venezia*, 2 vols., Venice, 1893-97.

PAPINI, R., *Francesco di Giorgio architetto*, 2 vols., Florence, 1946.

PEDRETTI, C., *A Chronology of Leonardo's Architectural Studies after 1500*, Geneva, 1962.

PEVSNER, N., *An Outline of European Architecture*, 6th (Jubilee) ed., Harmondsworth, 1960.

PICA, A., *Il Gruppo monumentale di S. Maria delle Grazie in Milano*, Rome, 1937.

RICCI, C., *L'architettura del Cinquecento in Italia*, Turin, 1923.

RONZANI, F., and LUCIOLLI, G., *Le fabbriche civili, ecclesiastiche e militari di M. Sanmicheli*, Turin, 1862.

ROTONDI, P., *Il Palazzo Ducale di Urbino*, 2 vols., Urbino, 1951; (Eng. trans., London, 1969).

RUIZ DE ARCANTE, A., *Juan de Herrera*, Madrid, 1936.

Michele Sanmicheli, exhibition catalogue, Verona, 1960.

SANPAOLESI, P., *Brunelleschi*, Milan, 1962.

SANTINELLO, G., *L.B. Alberti*, Florence, 1962.

SEPE, G., *Rilievi e studi dei monumenti antichi nel Rinascimento*, Naples, 1939.

SHEARMAN, J., *Mannerism*, Harmondsworth, 1967.

SOERGE, G., *Untersuchungen über den theoretischen Architekturentwurf von 1450-1550 in Italien*, Cologne, 1957.

STEGMANN, C., and GEYMÜLLER, H., *Die Architektur der Renaissance...*, Munich, 1885-1908; *Architecture of the Renaissance in Tuscany*, abridged ed., 2 vols., New York, [1924].

SUMMERSON, J., *Architecture in Britain, 1530-1830*, 4th ed., Harmondsworth, 1963.

TAFURI, M., *L'architettura del Manierismo nel Cinquecento Europeo*, Rome, 1966.

TAFURI, M., *Jacopo Sansovino e l'architettura del '500 a Venezia*, Padua, 1969.

TOLNAY, C. DE, *Michelangelo*, 5 vols., Princeton, 1943-60.

TOMEI, P., *L'architettura a Roma nel Quattrocento*, Rome, 1942.

TORSELLI, G., *Palazzi di Roma*, Milan, 1965.

URBAN, G., 'Die Kirchenbaukunst des Quattrocento in Rom', *Römisches Jahrbuch für Kunstgeschichte*, IX-X, 1961-62, pp. 74-287.

VENTURI, A., *Storia dell'arte italiana*, 25 vols., Milan, 1901-40.

VIALE, V., *Gotico e Rinascimento in Piemonte*, Turin, 1939.

WALCHER-CASOTTI, M., *Il Vignola*, 2 vols., Trieste, 1960.

WILLICH, H., *Giacomo Barozzi da Vignola*, Strasbourg, 1906.

WILLICH, H., and ZUCKER, P., *Die Baukunst der Renaissance in Italien, bis zum Tode Michelangelos*, 2 vols., Potsdam, 1914-29.

WITTKOWER, R., *Architectural Principles in the Age of Humanism*, 3rd ed., London, 1962.

WÖLFFLIN, H., *Renaissance und Barock*, Munich, 1889; (Eng. trans., *Renaissance and Baroque*, by K. Simon, Ithaca, N.Y., 1966).

ZEVI, B., *Michelangelo architetto*, ed. by P. Portoghesi, Turin, 1964.

ZÜRCHER, R., *Stilprobleme der italienischen Baukunst des Cinquecento*, Basel, 1947.

LIST OF PLATES

396

LIST OF PHOTOGRAPHIC CREDITS

NOTE: *Photographs by Pepi Merisio. All those supplied by other sources are gratefully acknowledged below. The numbers listed refer to the plates.*

A.C.L., Brussels: 525, 527

Alinari, Florence: 13, 14, 70, 79, 113, 118, 134, 212, 236, 296, 297, 298, 299, 325, 326, 354, 358, 359, 361, 363, 364, 376, 377, 436

Anelli, Sergio, Electa Editrice, Milan: 11, 17, 18, 49, 121, 157, 192, 194, 195, 200, 215, 238, 239, 243, 245, 247, 300, 304, 305, 313, 314, 316, 319, 328, 337, 338, 347, 348, 352, 367, 368, 387, 395, 410, 412, 432, 435, 440, 441, 446, 447, 449, 465, 466, 472, 490, 491, 513

Balestrini, Bruno, Electa Editrice, Milan: 100, 484, 485, 489

Bazzecchi, Ivo, Florence: 6, 7

Biblioteca Ambrosiana, Milan: 183, 188

Biblioteca del Escorial, Madrid: 9, 10

Bibliothèque Nationale, Paris: 185, 186, 187, 189

Bighini, Otello, Madrid: 501, 502, 507, 508, 511

Birelli, Diego, Mestre: 386, 388, 391, 393, 396, 397, 398, 399, 400, 401, 403, 404, 405, 406, 407, 413, 414, 415, 416

British Museum, London: 170, 201

Bruno, Giuseppe, Mestre: 69, 71, 72, 73, 75, 76, 82, 83, 84, 85, 103, 109, 112, 119, 120, 168, 272, 273, 274, 275, 276, 277, 279, 280, 281, 282, 283, 284, 285, 286, 287, 389, 408, 409, 411, 419, 420, 421, 422, 423, 424, 427, 429, 430, 433, 434, 437, 438, 439, 442, 443, 444, 450, 451, 452, 453, 454, 455, 456, 458, 459, 460, 461, 462, 467, 468, 469, 470

Cameraphoto, Venice: 65

Ciganovic, Josip, Rome: 506

Courtauld Institute of Art, London (British Crown Copyright Reserved): 232, 234, 278, 534

Deutscher Kunstverlag Bavaria, Gauting (West Germany): 516, 517, 519, 521

Electa Editrice, Milan: 87, 88, 99, 104, 110, 111

Esparcieux, Claude, Fontainebleau: 486, 487, 488

Foto Chiolini, Pavia: 167, 378, 379

Foto Mas, Barcelona: 503, 504, 512, 515

Foto Oscar Savio, Rome: 208

Gabinetto Fotografico Nazionale, Rome: 216, 259

Gabinetto Fotografico Soprintendenza alle Gallerie, Florence: 133, 197, 202, 203, 204, 214, 233, 237, 288, 302, 303, 323

Keetman, Jan, Bavaria Verlag, Gauting (West Germany): 522

Keetman, Peter, Bavaria Verlag, Gauting (West Germany): 520

Kleinhempel, Ralph, Hamburg: 306

Ministry of Public Building and Works, London (British Crown Copyright Reserved): 533

Monti, Eugenio, Rome: 260.

Monti, Paolo, Milan: 102, 105, 106, 108, 372

National Monuments Record, London (British Crown Copyright Reserved): 532, 534

Pagani, Bruno, Saronno: 384, 385

Photo Courteville Louis, *Réalités*, Paris: 474

Photo M. Des Jardins, *Réalités*, Paris: 498

Photo Vincent, Fréal, Paris: 476, 478

Photographie Bulloz, Paris: 473, 475, 497

Photographie Giraudon, Paris: 479, 481, 482, 496, 499

Rijksdienst voor de Monumentenzorg, The Hague: 523, 524, 526

Royal Institute of British Architects, London: 244, 431, 445, 537

Sheridan, Ronald, London: 528, 531, 535, 536, 538

Soprintendenza ai Monumenti, Florence: 5

Staatliche Museen, Berlin: 74

Steinkopf, Walter, Berlin: 1, 209, 210, 211, 213

Teylers Museum, Haarlem: 310

Vatican Museums, Rome: 226, 235

Verroust, Jacques, Neuilly: 492, 493, 500

Victoria and Albert Museum, London: 144

Windstosser, Ludwig, Bavaria Verlag, Gauting (West Germany): 530

By gracious permission of Her Majesty Queen Elizabeth II: 184

Courtesy of Professor Otello Caprara, Bologna: 34

Courtesy of Paul Mellon Collection, Upperville, Virginia: 205